MICHIGAN TRA

Raymond J. Malace

MICHIGAN
TRAVEL✦SMART®

SECOND EDITION

Stephen Jones

John Muir Publications
Santa Fe, New Mexico

John Muir Publications, P.O. Box 613, Santa Fe, New Mexico 87504

Printed in the United States of America
Second edition. First printing April 1999.

ISSN: 1522-1717
ISBN: 1-56261-472-X

Editors: Peg Goldstein, Chris Hayhurst
Graphics Editor: Heather Pool
Production: Rebecca Cook
Design: Marie J.T. Vigil
Cover Design: Janine Lehmann
Typesetting: Kathy Sparkes
Map Style Development: American Custom Maps—Jemez Springs, NM USA
Map Illustration: Kathy Sparkes, Laura Perfetti
Printing: Publishers Press
Front cover photos: Inset—© Andre Jenny/Unicorn Stock Photos
                    (Michigan State Capitol)
                    Large—© 1994 Jim Schwabel/New England Stock Photo
                    (Sleeping Bear Dunes National Lakeshore)
Back cover photo: © Michael Shedlock/New England Stock Photo
                    (Empire Bluff at Sleeping Bear Dunes National Lakeshore)

Distributed to the book trade by
Publishers Group West
Berkeley, California

MICHIGAN TRAVEL·SMART: A GUIDE THAT GUIDES

Most guidebooks are basically directories, providing information but very little help in making choices—you have to guess how to make the most of your time and money. *Michigan Travel·Smart* is different: By highlighting the very best of the state and offering various planning features, it acts like a personal tour guide rather than a directory.

TAKE THE STRESS OUT OF TRAVEL

Sometimes traveling causes more stress than it relieves. Sorting through information, figuring out the best routes, determining what to see and where to eat and stay, scheduling each day in order to get the most out of your time—all of this can make a vacation feel daunting rather than fun. Relax. We've done a lot of the legwork for you. This book will help you plan a trip that suits you—whatever your time frame, budget, and interests.

SEE THE BEST OF THE STATE

Author Stephen Jones has lived in Michigan all his life. He has hand-picked every listing in this book, and he gives you an insider's perspective on what makes each one worthwhile. So while you will find many of the big tourist attractions listed here, you'll also find lots of smaller, lesser known treasures, such as the Hands-On Museum in Ann Arbor and the National Ski Hall of Fame and Museum in Ishpeming. And each sight is thoroughly described so you'll know what's most—and sometimes least—interesting about it.

In selecting the restaurants and accommodations for this book, the author sought out unusual spots with local flavor. While in some areas of the state chains are unavoidable, wherever possible the author directs you to one-of-a-kind places. We also know that you want a range of options: One day you may crave steak or seafood, while the next day you would be just as happy (as would your wallet) with a chili dog. Most of the restaurants and accommodations listed here are moderately priced, but the author also includes budget and splurge options, depending on the destination.

CREATE THE TRIP YOU WANT

We all have different travel styles. Some people like spontaneous weekend jaunts, while others plan longer, more leisurely trips. You may want to cover as much ground as possible, no matter how much time you have. Or maybe you prefer to focus your trip on one part of the state or on some special interest, such as history, nature, or art. We've taken these differences into account.

Though the individual chapters stand on their own, they are organized in a geographically logical sequence, so that you could conceivably fly into Detroit, drive chapter by chapter to each destination in the book, and end up close to where you started. Of course, you don't have to follow that sequence, but it's there if you want a complete picture of the state.

Each destination chapter offers ways of prioritizing when time is limited: In the Perfect Day section, the author suggests what to do if you have only one day to spend in the area. Also, every Sightseeing Highlight is rated, from one to four stars: ★★★★—or "must see"—sights first, followed by ★★★ sights, then ★★ sights, and finally ★—or "see if you have spare time"—sights. At the end of each sight listing is a time recommendation in parentheses. User-friendly maps help you locate the sights, restaurants, and lodging of your choice.

And if you're in it for the ride, so to speak, you'll want to check out the Scenic Routes described at the end of several chapters. They take you through some of the most scenic parts of the state.

In addition to these special features, the appendix has other useful travel tools:

- The Mileage Chart and Planning Map help you determine your own route and calculate travel time.
- The Special Interest Tours show you how to design your trip around any of six favorite interests.
- The Calendar of Events provides an at-a-glance view of when and where major events occur throughout the state.
- The Resource Guide tells you where to go for more information about national and state parks, individual cities and counties, local bed-and-breakfasts, and more.

HAPPY TRAVELS

With this book in hand, you have many reliable recommendations and travel tools at your fingertips. Use it to make the most of your trip. And have a great time!

WHY VISIT MICHIGAN?

Michigan is a study in contrasts. It is simultaneously a major urban center and a land of forest wilderness. It is an industrial dynamo and part of America's agricultural heartland. Michigan's auto industry put America on wheels, but depending on the season, other modes of transportation—boats or snowmobiles—are nearly as popular. It is a land of bustling cities and tiny villages. It is high-speed and accessible, yet relaxing and remote. Michigan exudes cultural sophistication but annually stages a husband-calling contest and pig races at the state fair. Then there is the biggest contrast of all—between land and water. The Great Lakes give Michigan its physical shape and are largely responsible for the state's unique character and personality.

For the visitor, all this means a wealth of things to do and adventures to enjoy. Fans of the arts will find concerts, galleries, theaters, and museums in profusion. Avid shoppers will discover exclusive, high-fashion stores, vast factory-outlet malls, and small-town antique shops. Family vacationers can explore Michigan's famous collection of state parks, plumb the depths of an old copper mine, ride a paddlewheel riverboat, or visit a variety of amusement parks. Nature lovers will find an amazing array of wildlife and endless opportunities to observe the state's great natural beauty. And if all you crave is a few hours of lazy sunshine on a lakeshore somewhere, you'll find it in Michigan.

You don't have to love the outdoors to make a trip to Michigan worthwhile—ample entertainment and excitement can be found indoors in the state's cities. But if you really want to know Michigan, if you want to capture the spirit of the state, you will do it outside. The soul of Michigan pulses in the open air. You can hear it in the throbbing drone of the Great Lakes freighters that slide past Belle Isle Park on the Detroit River. You can smell it in the grandeur of the virgin timber at Hartwick Pines. You can feel it in the hot August sand of the Sleeping Bear Dunes National Lakeshore. And you can see it in the pastel Lake Superior sunset over Isle Royale.

When you visit Michigan, be sure to enjoy the museums and the restaurants and the shops and the theaters. But be sure to seek out the deer and elk and Canada goose, the Kirtland's warbler, the ring-necked pheasant, the raccoon, and the moose as well. Walk among the pine, oak, and maple, the hemlock and dogwood. Sail the lakes; canoe the rivers. Take a morning drive past farms and woodlots. Spend an afternoon fishing. Sit by a campfire under the evening stars. Let Michigan's great natural beauty seep into you. That beauty is a souvenir you'll never lose.

HISTORY

Little is known about the earliest inhabitants of Michigan—where they came from or when they arrived—but the best evidence so far indicates that people were living in what is now the Flint area by around 9000 B.C. That was about two thousand years after the end of the most recent great ice age, after the vast glaciers that once covered Michigan and much of northern North America in ice packs thousands of feet thick had begun to recede. Scientists believe those early residents were hunters who fed themselves by killing large animals, such as mastodons and caribou.

As the climate around the Great Lakes became warmer, other people moved into the heavily forested region, surviving by hunting animals much more similar to the wildlife found in the region today and by taking fish from the lakes. By around 100 B.C., agricultural skills had begun to appear, brought from the Hopewell Indian culture farther south, and Michigan peoples were growing corn, squash, and beans.

When the French began exploring the upper Great Lakes in the early 1600s, they identified nine Native American tribes in the region. These tribes fell into three broad groups—the Hurons, the Ottawa, and the Ojibwa (or Chippewa). The heritage of these peoples continues today, not just in the Native Americans whose reservations are spread across the Upper Peninsula and parts of the Lower Peninsula, but in the names of many towns and locations in the state. The name *Michigan* is derived from an Indian phrase that meant "big lake."

Other place names, such as Kalamazoo, Washtenaw, Ontonagon, Muskegon, Tecumseh, Pontiac, and Mackinac, also were handed down from Native American languages.

For two hundred years, the French and the British, and eventually the United States, struggled for control of the rich lands of the Great Lakes region. Fur was the area's first big commercial product, but by the early 1800s, as settlements grew and game thinned out, Michigan's great pine forests became an even more valuable commodity. Timber produced the state's first big economic boom as the virgin forests were almost entirely clear-cut. You can still see many of the fine old Victorian homes built with lumber profits in towns like Muskegon, Ludington, and Rogers City along the Lake Michigan and Lake Huron shores. Lumber spawned furniture and paper production. The discovery of iron and copper in the Upper Peninsula sparked the development of mines. Other manufacturers began to build businesses making food products, chemicals, and pharmaceuticals, and company names like Kellogg, Dow, and Upjohn became familiar across the country.

It was in the first decade of the twentieth century that the Ford Motor Company and General Motors were established. With mass automobile production, Detroit began putting America on wheels. By the 1940s, when consumer automobile production was switched to wartime weapons production, the name Detroit had become synonymous with industry and organized labor. Despite competitive inroads by foreign manufacturers and a general decline in the size of labor unions, Detroit continues to be the heart of the U.S. auto industry and a key base of organized labor.

CULTURES

Culturally, Michigan is a hodgepodge. Although a few traits are common throughout the state (a love of ice fishing and deer hunting; the near-religious conviction that speed-limit signs are merely casual suggestions), you will find tremendous variety among Michigan's people.

Because of the state's long and proud industrial history, Michigan's blue-collar heritage comes as no surprise. It is an important element of the southern cities, particularly in the southeastern region around Detroit. But changes in the auto industry—its growing emphasis on advanced engineering and high technology—and the presence of several world-class research universities have sparked a recent surge in Michigan's professional classes. Outside the major cities, though, much of the state lives a small-town life, with the prevailing local industries—agriculture, tourism, mining—strongly influencing the cultural outlook.

Ethnic variety is another great spice in the stew of Michigan culture. As you would expect in a large urban area like Detroit, many nationalities are represented among the population. Polish culture, especially in such communities as Hamtramck and Sterling Heights, is very strongly represented, as are Italian, Greek, Irish, and other European cultures. But the state also has a very large African American population, large numbers of Mexican Americans, and one of the largest Arab communities outside the Middle East. With this ethnic diversity comes variety in language, religion, and even cuisine. And while the variety is greatest in the heavily populated urban areas, the state's diverse heritage can also be seen elsewhere. For example, the Dutch Reformed influence can be seen in southwestern Michigan, and the Finnish influence can be seen in the mining regions of the Upper Peninsula.

For all its diversity, the state's greatest cultural distinction lies between residents of its two great peninsulas. A single, five-mile band of steel and concrete ties the Upper and Lower Peninsulas together, and at times that bridge seems a none-too-secure link. While much of the antagonism between Yoopers (folks from the Upper Peninsula, or U.P.) and Trolls (those who live "under" the bridge) is playful, a real tension does exist. The Lower Peninsula is dominated by the heavily populated, industrial, urbanized south. The Upper Peninsula glories in its exquisite natural setting and sparse population, which make getting away from it all a very easy thing to do. Many in the Upper Peninsula resent the political and economic power of downstate Michigan, and many people downstate do not really appreciate the U.P. way of life, admiring the laid-back pace and outdoorsy style but not the delicate balance between openness and social reserve. Still, the two peninsulas get along tolerably well, and a certain level of familial bickering is to be expected.

THE ARTS

Southern Michigan is a paradise for art lovers. Major concert venues in metropolitan Detroit and a huge variety of bars and clubs offer live music performances of any style you could want. Jazz is especially popular, with several notable clubs in Detroit and Ann Arbor offering regular appearances by widely known artists. And the annual Montreux-Detroit Jazz Festival draws an international crowd on Labor Day weekend.

Top performers in rock and roll, pop, country, folk, and blues also make regular appearances in the southern part of the state. The Ark in Ann Arbor is one of the country's most respected folk-music clubs. And when Michigan Opera Theater—a highly regarded regional company—christened its new home, the Detroit Opera House, in 1996, Luciano Pavarotti sang at the gala opening.

Detroit is also home to at least two world-class arts organizations: the Detroit Institute of Arts (DIA) and the Detroit Symphony Orchestra (DSO). The DIA's collection includes virtually every era of Western art, from the Mesopotamian to the present, as well as excellent selections of African and Asian art. The DSO, which makes its home at Orchestra Hall, is acclaimed for its many recordings and international concert tour.

Each summer the Ann Arbor Street Art Fairs attracts artists and art lovers from across the country to the outdoor booths that fill many of the city's streets. Throughout the year thriving galleries can be found all over the metropolitan Detroit area, in downtown Detroit's Harmonie Park, as well as in such suburban locales as Royal Oak, Birmingham, Bloomfield Hills, and Ann Arbor. The resort areas around Traverse City, Petoskey, and Mackinac Island are also great places to find intriguing and affordable works by outstanding local and regional artists, including Native American artists. Saugatuck, a small resort town along the Lake Michigan shore in the southwestern corner of the state, originally became famous as a summer retreat for Chicago artists, and galleries remain plentiful there.

While the DIA is undeniably the state's foremost art museum, there are several other small but excellent art museums around the state, in cities such as Kalamazoo, Traverse City, Muskegon, and Flint. One special gallery at Grand Valley State University near Bay City is devoted to the works of noted sculptor Marshall Fredericks.

For admirers of the theatrical arts, Detroit is home to a booming theater district that features homegrown and national professional touring companies. Theater departments at the state's larger public universities also produce and host superb theatrical productions. Just south of Traverse City, the Interlochen Center for the Arts puts on an annual summer festival that is nationally famous and includes concerts, recitals, musicals, operas, dance performances, dramatic productions, and art shows.

CUISINE

In the urban areas of southeastern Michigan, fine dining is one of the larger participatory sports. Metro Detroit contains an astonishing array of ethnic eateries—Polish, Italian, Chinese, Japanese, Korean, Ethiopian, Indian, Thai, German, Greek, Belgian, Cajun, Cuban, French, Hungarian, Irish, Jewish, Lebanese, Mexican, Russian, Scottish, Spanish, Vietnamese, and more. Even within these categories, there is often great variety. In the single block of Detroit's Monroe Street that is known as Greektown, for example, there are more than a half dozen Greek restaurants, each with its own particular flavor.

Seafood restaurants also are very popular—no surprise for a state with rich and bountiful water resources. You will find them in the Detroit area and all along the Great Lakes shores, especially in the more heavily traveled tourist areas. Many offer fairly generic fish menus, seeking only to capitalize on the nautical milieu. Others, however, specialize in local whitefish or trout and do it very well.

Despite the diversity, middle-American cuisine predominates, increasingly so as you move away from the larger urban areas. You will find some excellent and elegant restaurants in such major tourist areas as Traverse City, Petoskey, and Mackinac Island; elsewhere, however, do not expect to find great bastions of culinary imagination. For the most part, Michigan is a meat-and-potatoes kind of place. Just how much so shows in that Upper Peninsula taste treat, the pasty (a hearty pie consisting of meat, vegetables, and potatoes wrapped in a pastry shell).

FLORA AND FAUNA

Michigan is rich in plant and animal life—a gift of the abundant water, fertile soil, and temperate climate that characterize the state. Wildlife-watching opportunities are everywhere, even in major cities. In my yard in Detroit, I have seen possums, squirrels, and other small mammals, as well as many species of migratory birds. And Michigan's deer population has gotten so large that it is becoming fairly common to see deer in heavily populated suburbs not far from Detroit, especially in lightly wooded areas along the freeways—so be careful when driving at night.

The state's huge network of public parks offers an astonishingly broad selection of natural habitats for plant and wildlife viewing. Most of the state parks have nature trails, and many have nature centers with displays or programs that describe the state's natural attributes and native species—both plant and animal.

In southern Michigan you will find many open fields, with lakes and rivers and relatively small expanses of forest dominated by deciduous trees—oak, maple, hickory, chestnut, walnut, and the like. Farther north, especially north of Clare, you see more birch, and the forest balance begins to shift toward pine, spruce, and cedar. The Upper Peninsula is heavily forested, although the eastern portion has its share of open farmland.

Michigan is a great place to watch birds, especially waterfowl. The Great Lakes and the state's thousands of inland lakes provide year-round residences for ducks, geese, and other waterbirds, as well as a migratory way station for many other species. Michigan is the only place to see nesting Kirtland's warblers; and at the Seney National Wildlife Refuge in the central Upper Peninsula, you can spot bald eagles, sandhill cranes, ospreys, and trumpeter swans. Other excellent bird-watching spots are the Kellogg Bird Sanctuary near Battle Creek and the Bay City State Recreation Area.

For a real wildlife treat, visit Isle Royale National Park in Lake Superior. You will encounter moose along the trails and in the campground, as well as foxes, beavers, hares, otters, mink, and muskrat. A few wolves live on the island (and a few in the western U.P.), but you are much more likely to hear them than see them, and even hearing them is rare.

THE LAY OF THE LAND

On the state seal of Michigan is a Latin inscription that means "If you seek a beautiful peninsula, look around you." It is a succinct description of what you will find in Michigan: peninsulas and water. The Great Lakes are unquestionably the state's main geographic feature. The four Great Lakes that border Michigan—Erie, Huron, Michigan, and Superior—give its peninsulas their unique shapes and endow them with more miles of freshwater coastline than any other state.

Water also helps define the Upper and Lower Peninsulas within their shorelines. Michigan has more than 11,000 inland lakes, not to mention dozens of significant rivers and many more streams flowing through its interior. When you are in Michigan, you are never more than about six miles from some body of water. The superb water resources are one of the state's prime attractions—for swimming, boating, and fishing in summer, and as a key source of the annual snowfalls that bring thousands of skiers, snowmobilers, and ice fishers in the winter.

Each peninsula has its own geographical personality, or rather, personality range. The Lower Peninsula begins in the southeast with an intensely urban and industrial region around Detroit. As you move north and west, urban communities such as Ann Arbor, Flint, Lansing, and Grand Rapids are increasingly interspersed with small-town agricultural areas. Although southern Michigan has some lovely hilly areas, until you get north of Clare, in the middle of the "Mitten," the land is relatively flat. From there north to the Straits of Mackinac, you climb into forested highlands, where there are no large cities, industrial operations are limited, and life tends to revolve around seasonal activities: camping and tourism in the summer, color tours in the early to mid-fall, deer hunting in November, and snow sports during the winter.

The east end of the Upper Peninsula has a touristy flavor; it may be hard for some to distinguish it from the northern Lower Peninsula. But visitors will find a more remote, austere, deep-woodsy atmosphere as they move west in the

U.P., where forest products and mining industries still predominate. The U.P. attracts a lot of people to its campgrounds, lakes, streams, and forests, but it is seldom as crowded as the northern Lower Peninsula. It is more remote; you won't find the pricey, country-club style resorts that abound in the Grand Traverse and Little Traverse Bay areas. The Upper Peninsula is beautiful, not fashionable, thank you very much.

OUTDOOR ACTIVITIES

I have yet to hear of the outdoor activity that cannot be pursued, played, engaged in, or simply enjoyed somewhere in Michigan. I'm sure that someone will now notify me of a thrilling new sport—say, Australian-rules wallaby hang-gliding—that is nowhere to be found in the Great Lakes State. To which I say, wait a week.

Michiganders love the outdoors. Their attitude seems to be that no activity is so enjoyable or refined that it cannot be improved by moving it outdoors. Royal Oak became one of the Detroit area's hottest nightspots by turning every available square inch of sidewalk space into open-air cafés. Downtown Detroit's Hart Plaza has been hosting world-famous performers at outdoor jazz and country music festivals for years. Outdoor art exhibits turn Ann Arbor streets into alfresco galleries for a week each July. There's even a nine-screen drive-in theater in Dearborn.

Dyed-in-the-wool urban dwellers who seldom leave Detroit, Ann Arbor, or Lansing flock in droves to city parks and boat basins. Detroit's Belle Isle Park is aswarm with fishers, swimmers, bikers, joggers, golfers, and boat-race enthusiasts in the warm-weather months. Lake St. Clair churns with the wakes of thousands of Detroit and suburban boaters in summer; and in winter, villages of makeshift ice-fishing shanties festoon the lake's frozen shoreline. It is no coincidence that the state's longest-running local television show, lasting nearly four decades, was called *Michigan Outdoors*.

Much outdoor activity is focused on the water. Because the state's vast waterways are so popular, Michigan has more registered watercraft than any other state. Sailing is very popular, and Mackinac Island is the finish line for two major sailboat races each summer—one from Port Huron and the other from Chicago. The Gold Cup hydroplane races also draw hundreds of thousands of spectators to the Detroit River near Belle Isle each summer. Fishing is big both in the Great Lakes and on inland waters. Each November one of the world's largest informal armies—nearly 750,000 strong—takes over the state's fields and forests for the firearms deer-hunting season.

Michigan is famous for its abundant and well-maintained state parks, which offer a wide range of outdoor activities such as swimming, boating, camping, hiking, and picnicking. Many of the parks are open year-round, with great opportunities for skiing—especially cross-country—and snowmobiling in winter. Downhill skiing is also popular, although less widely available. Obviously, Michigan lacks the dramatic mountain runs of Colorado and Wyoming, but appealing ski resorts can be found in a number of areas, especially in the northwestern Lower Peninsula.

A boom in golf-course development, particularly the construction of championship-quality courses in the Traverse City–Petoskey–Gaylord area, has also made Michigan a growing summer vacation destination for avid golfers. Suburban Detroit also boasts professional-caliber courses.

PLANNING YOUR TRIP

Before you set out on your trip, you'll need to do some planning. Use this chapter in conjunction with the tools in the appendix to answer some basic questions. First of all, when are you going? You may already have specific dates in mind; if not, various factors will probably influence your timing. Either way, you'll want to know about local events, the weather, and other seasonal considerations. This chapter discusses all of that, while the Calendar of Events in the appendix provides a month-by-month view of major area events.

How much should you expect to spend on your trip? This chapter addresses various regional factors you'll want to consider in estimating your travel expenses. How will you get around? Check out the section on local transportation. If you decide to travel by car, the Planning Map and Mileage Chart in the appendix can help you figure out exact routes and driving times, while the Special Interest Tours provide several focused itineraries. The chapter concludes with some reading recommendations, both fiction and nonfiction, to give you various perspectives on the state. If you want specific information about individual cities or counties, use the Resource Guide in the appendix.

HOW MUCH WILL IT COST?
What you spend will depend on what kind of vacation you're planning and how you plan to travel. If you intend to visit southeastern Michigan and stay

primarily in hotels, you are going to spend considerably more than if you plan a camping trip in the northern part of the state. A golf vacation will likely be more costly than a fishing trip. That said, Michigan is not generally an expensive place to travel. Luxurious restaurants and accommodations are available, but in most places you should be able to get a good meal in a nice restaurant for $7 to $12 per person and a room for two in the $55 to $75 range. If you are willing to go with one of the budget motel chains or try a smaller, one-of-a-kind motel, you can bring the room price down.

Keep in mind that lodging is generally most expensive in the downtown districts of the state's major cities and in the popular resort areas of the northwestern Lower Peninsula, from Traverse City north to Charlevoix, Gaylord, Petoskey, Harbor Springs, and Mackinac Island. Also remember that motel rates in northern Michigan vary considerably with the time of year, and midsummer is the peak tourist season. I have tried to include a range of price levels for both accommodations and restaurants.

Many visitors take the most economical—and often the most beautiful— approach by bringing along their camper, RV, or tent and staying at one or more of the many public campgrounds in the state. Public campground fees usually range from $6 to $15 a night plus park admission of $4 per vehicle. State parks generally have excellent facilities, with water and electricity hookups in most of the larger campgrounds. Private campgrounds often provide extra facilities such as swimming pools instead of beaches, and special activities like game rooms and miniature golf. But they also cost considerably more.

CLIMATE

Michigan's climate is temperate, but within that broad classification, variation can be considerable—not just season-to-season, but sometimes hour-to-hour. Temperature changes of 20 degrees within a few hours, though not exactly common, are not unheard of.

In southern Michigan, summers tend toward the hot and sticky. Temperatures can be above 85 or 90 degrees for days at a time, with humidity levels that make it more uncomfortable than you might expect. Winter temperatures are normally in the 20s and 30s, although it is not unusual to see a January day in the upper 40s or a string of days below zero. Snow is a regular winter hazard, though the Detroit area has seen some recent winters with hardly any snow.

As you move northward in the state, average temperatures drop in both summer and winter, and annual snowfall increases. The Upper Peninsula has the most consistently cold weather in the state during the winter and much of the heaviest snowfall. Houghton, in the center of the U.P.'s Keweenaw Peninsula, routinely gets more snow than anywhere else in the state because of the steady accumulation of lake-effect snow, caused by the proximity of Lake Superior. But portions of the northern Lower Peninsula along the Lake Michigan shore—particularly from Traverse City north—get a lot of lake-effect snow, too. Summers in the U.P. tend to be sunny and mild; evenings frequently get cool enough for a sweater.

Spring and fall are beautiful seasons in Michigan, although spring weather can be especially inconsistent, dashing from balmy to shivery cold very quickly. Mid-May through mid-June is the peak spring season in most of the state, with flowers in full bloom. Fall weather tends to be a bit steadier and more consistent. The best time for viewing the changing leaves in the Lower Peninsula is mid-September through the end of October.

WHEN TO GO

If you like the outdoors, there is no bad time to visit Michigan. July and August are the warmest months, but you won't mind the snow and cold of January if skiing or snowmobiling is your idea fun. Michigan is geared toward year-round recreation, so the right time to go really depends on your choice of activities.

For warm-weather fans, July and August is the peak summer season with the best weather for camping, boating, and swimming. You'll also find motel prices at their highest levels, especially in the northern resort areas. To avoid peak prices and crowds, try mid- to late June. The weather is usually good then, although lake swimming is not at its best until the hotter late-summer weeks.

Just after Labor Day is another good time to travel—after the summer rates drop but before all the summer attractions close for the season. Of course, family travel at that time may be out of the question because of school conflicts, but those same school conflicts mean the tourist crowds will be considerably thinned.

The best time to avoid is March and early April. Snow is mostly gone, except in the Upper Peninsula, so opportunities for winter sports are just about over, and the weather doesn't warm up enough to make touring really comfortable—even in the southern parts of the state—until mid-April.

TRANSPORTATION

A couple of cities—most notably Ann Arbor and Lansing—have good bus systems, and Amtrak offers trains on a route along the southern tier of the state between Detroit and Chicago. But other than that, don't plan on traveling by public transportation. The state's dearth of mass transit isn't all that surprising when you consider the importance of the auto industry in Michigan.

The vast majority of traveling in the state is done by car, and the highway system is intended to promote that. Winter freezes take their toll on the state's roads in the form of potholes, and the state has only recently accelerated renovation of freeways after years of neglect. But the highway system is good for getting around. I-94 is a main east-west route along the southern tier of the state, while I-75 in the east, U.S. 127 in the center, and U.S. 31 in the west funnel traffic north to the state's camping and resort areas.

In the Upper Peninsula, U.S. 2 crosses the state from St. Ignace to Ironwood by way of Escanaba along the southern tier, while Highway 28 follows an east-west route from Sault Ste. Marie through Marquette and on to Ironwood. Both are two-lane undivided highways for most of their lengths, but traffic generally moves quickly.

Detroit Metropolitan Airport is the largest airport in the state and serves as a major hub for Northwest Airlines. Most of the state's larger cities also have airports with at least commuter links to Metro.

CAMPING, LODGING, AND DINING

Camping is a way of life—or at least a way of travel—for large numbers of Michiganders and visitors alike. Michigan has long had a marvelous system of state parks with clean, comfortable campgrounds that cover the entire state. Even in areas where a good variety of hotels and motels exists (most of the Lower Peninsula and the major cities of the Upper Peninsula), the attractiveness of Michigan's parks often makes camping a first choice for accommodations. And there is no denying the economic advantages, since a campsite in a state park usually costs $16 or less per night. You won't find good motel rooms for less than twice that cost, and most places with comparably scenic settings will charge at least four to six times as much.

But for those who prefer to absorb natural beauty in less intense doses, decent motel accommodations are plentiful just about everywhere. Except for the Thumb, the Lower Peninsula south of Clare has an abundant supply of motel rooms, with all of the widely known national chains as well as many good, small local establishments. North of Clare the supply is sparser, with the well-known chains concentrating on the major tourist towns, such as Traverse City, Petoskey, Gaylord, and Mackinaw City.

In the Upper Peninsula you will find fewer of the familiar chain motels and almost none of the luxury chains. The U.P. still has a lot of small local motels, many of which are quite comfortable and generally less expensive.

Michigan has a variety of excellent restaurants. Like the state's accommodations, they are concentrated in the southern half of the Lower Peninsula but are by no means limited to that region. The northwestern Lower Peninsula has many good restaurants and several great ones, and there are some excellent establishments in Sault Ste. Marie and Marquette in the Upper Peninsula, too.

RECOMMENDED READING

Reading is very popular in Michigan, perhaps because it can easily be done outdoors. Not only does the state offer many wonderful beaches and parks with relaxing settings for the recreational reader, but the large number and widespread distribution of public universities and private colleges means that access to specialized texts for the serious reader is exceptionally good.

Ann Arbor, home of the University of Michigan, is famous for its bookstores for both new and used books. And it was the birthplace of the original Borders Bookstore, a longtime local institution and now a well-known national chain. John King Books in Detroit has about 1 million used books in its inventory, making it one of the country's largest used bookstores. It is a wonderful place to spend a few hours.

When it comes to discussions of Michigan authors and books about the state, the first name that usually arises is Ernest Hemingway. Although he actually was from the Chicago area, he spent his first 18 summers at his family's cottage on Walloon Lake near Petoskey, and northern Michigan appears prominently in some of his early fiction, most notably his Nick Adams stories and his satirical novella, *The Torrents of Spring*. One of Hemingway's best short stories to involve Michigan is "The Big Two-Hearted River." The tale follows a World War I veteran on a fishing trip into the Upper Peninsula backcountry near Seney.

You get a much different picture of Michigan in the work of detective writer Elmore Leonard. Leonard's work ranges far beyond the borders of this or any state, but some of his best writing is suffused with the gritty atmosphere of Detroit. Few writers know the city as well as Leonard, and none has captured its essence so thoroughly. He just flat-out writes good stuff. Check out *City Primeval* for a good introduction to Leonard's work.

Another outstanding contemporary Michigan writer is Jim Harrison. He's best known for his fiction—*Legends of the Fall*—but he's also an excellent poet. Harrison, too, ventures far afield from Michigan in his writing, but his work always has a power, a natural presence that I associate—rightly or wrongly—with northern Michigan. Other poets whose work has been strongly influenced by life in Michigan include Robert Hayden, Dudley Randall, and Phillip Levine.

For an interesting story with the flavor of the Upper Peninsula, pick up a copy of Robert Traver's novel *Anatomy of a Murder*. For that matter, take a look at the Otto Preminger movie made from the book and starring James Stewart. Much of the movie was shot on location in Marquette County. Traver, whose real name was John Voelker, was able to draw on some unusual insights for his murder-mystery tale. Voelker had been a county prosecutor in the U.P. and eventually served on the state Supreme Court. But even more than law, he loved fishing, as you can tell by picking up a copy of his book *Trout Madness*.

For a historical perspective on the state, start with *Michigan: A History of the Wolverine State*, by Willis F. Dunbar and George S. May. It is long but thorough and recent. Another good history is *Michigan: A Bicentennial History*, by Bruce Catton. Catton is most noted for his chronicles of the Civil War, but he was from the northwestern Lower Peninsula, and in this book he trained his considerable historical skills on his home state. One problem with many state histories is that they give short shrift to the Native American cultures that were long-established in the Great Lakes region when the first Europeans arrived. *Rites of Conquest: The History and Culture of Michigan's Native Americans*, by Charles E. Cleland, gives thorough attention to the state's Indian heritage.

If you are looking for a more contemporary cultural take on the state, try *The Reckoning*, by David Halberstam, which takes an in-depth look at the auto industry, Michigan's dominant economic culture; or *Letters from the Leelanau*, by Kathleen Stocking, an eloquent and evocative series of essays that illuminate the spirit of northern Michigan.

And finally, for some help in nature-watching, pick up some guides to the region's birds, mammals, trees, and wildflowers. The Peterson guides are good, but most of the larger bookstores in southern Michigan, and nearly every bookstore elsewhere in the state, have healthy supplies of nature books from which to choose.

1
DETROIT

Detroit has certainly taken its share of flak over the years. Dubbed the nation's Murder Capital in the late 1970s (since surpassed by Miami and Washington, D.C., among others), and notorious for its Devil's Night arson sprees of the 1980s and early 1990s, Detroit has a reputation as a dangerous, gritty, rust-belt eyesore. There's enough truth to that to make the image hard to shake, and as in any big city, visitors should exercise caution while exploring Detroit, especially at night. However, the city has slowly been lifted by a current of economic and cultural development that will startle and impress the visitor who only knows Detroit by reputation.

A thriving theater district has erupted on the north edge of downtown. Construction has begun on two new major-league sports stadiums—the first scheduled to open in spring 2000—adjacent to the theater district. New hotels and office buildings have sprouted up downtown. Armies of citizen volunteers and a get-tough policy by city officials have pretty much squelched the Devil's Night nonsense. And the new housing market is booming.

Sparked by the theater district, Greektown, a few downtown clubs, and the anticipation of gambling casinos in 1999, nightlife in the city is hot again. An array of excellent restaurants makes Detroit a diner's delight. And longstanding gems like the Detroit Institute of Arts, Detroit Symphony Orchestra Hall, and the Museum of African American History offer visitors cultural attractions that rival those of most other major American cities.

DETROIT

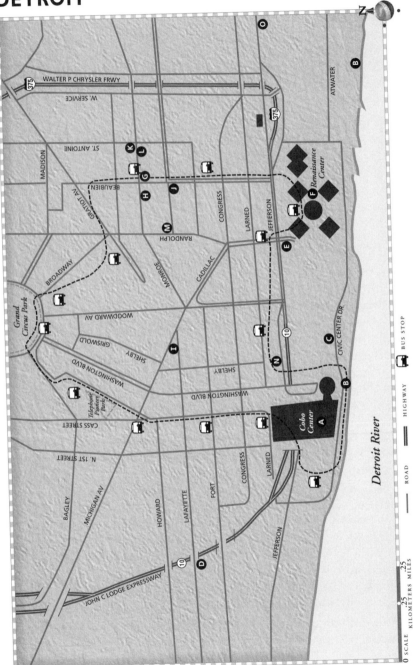

Detroit River

SCALE
0   25
KILOMETERS   MILES
0   25

ROAD   HIGHWAY   BUS STOP

A PERFECT DAY IN DETROIT

The Detroit Institute of Arts does not open until 11, so start the day with an early-morning drive/walk around Belle Isle. The island park is beautiful in its own right, but it also offers superb views of downtown Detroit and Windsor, Canada. A small herd of deer roams freely on the island, and you will not find a more advantageous place from which to watch Great Lakes' freighters chug by.

Spend the late morning and afternoon museum hopping—perhaps a stop at the Dossin Great Lakes Museum on Belle Isle, and then a couple of hours at the DIA, followed by a visit to the Museum of African American History and a finger-snapping pilgrimage to the Motown Historical Museum.

For dinner, check out the *saganaki* (flaming cheese appetizer) in any of the Greektown restaurants; or soak up the view from The Summit, the rotating restaurant at the top of the Renaissance Center. After dinner, pick a show in the Theater District.

DETROIT SIGHTSEEING HIGHLIGHTS

★★★★ BELLE ISLE PARK

One of Detroit's special treasures, this 985-acre island park is the focus of lots of activity. In June it hosts the Detroit Grand Prix auto race, and it is a major spectator spot for the Gold Cup powerboat races on the Detroit River. There are many wooded paths and drives in the park, and a 5.5-mile road circles the island. It is a popular recreation place for picnicking, bicycling, jogging, golf, tennis, fishing, and swimming. Athletic facilities include a running track, and there is a giant slide and a big wooden playscape for children.

SIGHTS

- **A** Cobo Center and Joe Louis Arena
- **B** Diamond Jack's River Tours
- **C** Hart Plaza
- **D** John King Books
- **E** Old Mariner's Church
- **F** Renaissance Center

FOOD

- **G** Blue Nile
- **H** Fishbone's Rhythm Kitchen Cafe
- **I** Lafayette Coney Island
- **J** Loco Bar & Grill
- **K** New Hellas Cafe
- **L** Pegasus Taverna
- **F** The Summit

LODGING

- **M** Atheneum Suite Hotel and Conference Center
- **N** Crowne Plaza Pontchartrain Hotel
- **P** Marriott Hotel
- **O** Shorecrest Motor Inn

Note: Items with the same letter are located in the same place.

Details: Accessible via the MacArthur Bridge at E. Jefferson Ave. and E. Grand Blvd. (1–3 hours)

★★★★ CHARLES H. WRIGHT MUSEUM OF AFRICAN AMERICAN HISTORY
315 E. Warren Avenue, 313/494-5800

A world-class institution, this museum in a dazzling new building at Warren Avenue and Brush Street examines the experiences and culture of African Americans through art and artifacts. It is, in fact, the largest museum devoted to African American history and culture in the United States. Exhibits explore the African roots of African American culture and examine the troubling history of the slave trade. One of the most dramatic and moving displays is a life-size replica of a slave ship. Other exhibits tell the story of the Underground Railroad, which helped runaway slaves from southern states reach freedom in the North. Detroit was an important stop for many escaped slaves, especially after the Fugitive Slave Law forced them to flee all the way to Canada to ensure their freedom. The Detroit River crossing was one of the most common routes. More recent history is examined through exhibits on the Great Migration of the early 1900s, which brought thousands of southern African Americans to Detroit and other northern cities to find jobs in growing industrial operations. In addition to its permanent exhibits, the museum hosts numerous special exhibitions, events, and lectures.

Details: Tue–Sun 9:30–5. $5 adults, $3 age 12 and under. (2 hours)

★★★★ DETROIT INSTITUTE OF ARTS
5200 Woodward Avenue, 313/833-7900

The crown jewel of Detroit's cultural institutions is the DIA, whose galleries contain a world-class selection of art, from ancient to modern. Standout specialty areas include pre-Columbian Native American art, African art, and seventeenth-century Dutch and Flemish paintings. The collections include such masters as Rembrandt, Breughel, Renoir, Picasso, Matisse, Whistler, Miro, Gauguin, Henry Moore, and van Gogh. But the most famous piece is the astonishingly powerful *Detroit Industry* mural, which consumes all four walls of the museum's central courtyard. This masterpiece by Mexican artist Diego Rivera depicts, celebrates, and critiques Detroit's industrial heart.

Details: Wed–Fri 11–4, Sat–Sun 11–5. Tours Wed–Sat at 1 and Sun at 1 and 2:30. Recommended donation $4 adults, $1 children and

*students with identification. Separate admission fees for special exhibitions.
(2–4 hours)*

★★★★ **DETROIT SCIENCE CENTER**
5020 John R Street, 313/577-8400
One of the city's more interesting offerings is the Science Center, a
hands-on museum for kids of all ages. Exhibits include interactive displays on rocks and minerals, laser light, solar energy, and holograms.
IMAX films are shown in a special theater with a screen more than 66
feet tall.
Details: Mon–Fri 10–2, Sat–Sun 11–5. *$3 adults, $2 ages 4–12
and over 60; additional $4 for IMAX theater. (2 hours)*

★★★★ **MOTOWN HISTORICAL MUSEUM**
2648 W. Grand Boulevard, 313/875-2264
A musical style that became world-famous as the Motown Sound was
born in an old brick home that now houses the Motown Historical
Museum. Motown Records founder Berry Gordy established a music
empire that launched such stars as Smokey Robinson, Diana Ross and
the Supremes, Marvin Gaye, and Stevie Wonder. The museum's renovated galleries include musical instruments, photos, costumes, and
other memorabilia from the early Motown days. An original recording
studio and control room are on display.
Details: Tue–Sat 10–5, Sun–Mon noon–5. *$6 adults, $5 over age
55, $4 ages 13–18, $3 under 13. (30 minutes)*

★★★★ **RENAISSANCE CENTER**
Jefferson Avenue and Brush Street, 313/568-5600
The signature piece of the Detroit skyline, the RenCen is undergo-
ing significant change. Built in 1977 at the direction of Henry Ford II,
it has long been a focus of architectural controversy. It was intended
by Ford, and is seen by some, as a symbol of the city's rebirth. The
project was launched in the wake of Detroit's traumatic 1967 riot,
and was completed 10 years later. Fans see modern grace in the center's five circular glass towers (the 72-story center tower houses the
Marriott Hotel while the other towers are devoted to office space;
street-level areas house dozens of shops and restaurants). But crit-
ics have long derided the center for the confusing maze of shops on
its retail levels, its lack of a well-defined entrance, and, most of all,
for the gigantic concrete berms along Jefferson Avenue, which give

the center a forbidding presence at street level. The berms house RenCen's air-conditioning equipment, but they resemble nothing so much as an enormous freeway median strip.

In a dramatic development in 1996, Ford's competitor, General Motors, purchased the center and began moving in its world headquarters. The switch has generated a lot of talk about aesthetic changes—like doing away with the concrete berms and creating a new entrance on Jefferson Avenue. That may take a while to accomplish, but the center is still worth visiting for its collection of shops and restaurants, for the view from its rotating 72nd-floor restaurant, or just for a close-up look at the unusual building.

Details: *1 hour.*

★★★ BELLE ISLE ZOO
Belle Isle, 313/852-4084
The zoo on Belle Isle covers 13 acres and features an elevated walkway for unusual views of animals in natural settings. It is much smaller than the main Detroit Zoo in Royal Oak, but that can make a visit less wearing, especially for small children. The zoo houses plenty of interesting animals—lions, tigers, and maned wolves and spectacled bears from South America, and numerous varieties of spiders.

Details: *May–Oct daily 10–5. $3 adults, $2 ages 62 and over, $1 ages 2–12. (1 hour)*

★★★ CHILDREN'S MUSEUM
67 E. Kirby Avenue, 313/873-8100
Established in 1917 and operated by the Detroit Public Schools, this is the third-oldest children's museum in the United States. Its permanent exhibits include a huge assortment of antique and contemporary toys; large doll and teddy bear collections; cultural artifacts such as clothing, arts and crafts, wood carvings, and other items from all over the world; and many natural history specimens, such as shells and stuffed animals. Just as interesting, however, are the Saturday programs and workshops designed for children ages 4 to 12. Many of the programs and workshops are free, though some charge a fee of $2 or so per child. The programs are a blend of educational and fun activities, such as making Snoopy puppets at a birthday party for the *Peanuts* comic-strip characters or using creative dramatics to bring circus characters to life.

Details: *Oct–May Mon–Fri 1–4, Sat 9–4; June–Sept Mon–Fri 1–4. Admission is free. (1 hour)*

Travel Michigan

★★★ COBO CENTER AND JOE LOUIS ARENA
Intersection of Jefferson Avenue and Washington Boulevard, 313/877-8111

This huge collection of vast exhibition halls and meeting rooms is the focus of the city's convention business. Each year, the North American International Auto Show brings enormous crowds to Cobo to see the latest offerings—and a lot of future dreams—from U.S. and foreign automakers. Other big exhibitions focus on boats and camping equipment, a Festival of Trees at Christmastime, and home and garden ideas in the spring. Cobo Arena hosts concerts and other events, and was the scene of the infamous clubbing of figure skater Nancy Kerrigan during the national figure-skating championships. Next door, Joe Louis Arena, 313/983-6606, is the home of the Detroit Red Wings hockey team and the host of many ice shows and other events. It was also the site of the 1980 Republican National Convention, which nominated Ronald Reagan.

Details: 30 minutes

★★★ DETROIT HISTORICAL MUSEUM
5401 Woodward Avenue, 313/833-1805

The historical museum illustrates how life has changed for Detroiters

GREATER DETROIT

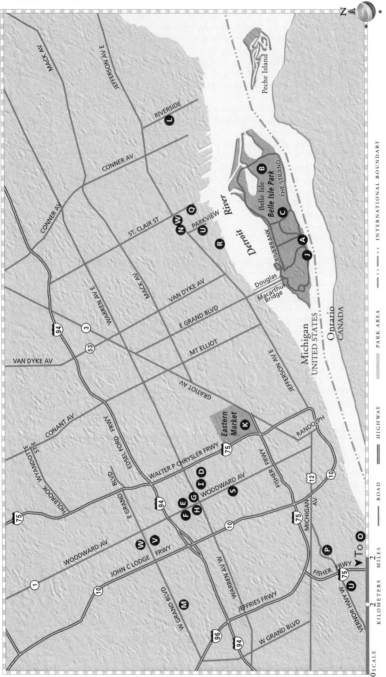

since the city's founding in 1701. Exhibits include reconstructions of early street scenes and period automobiles. Of special interest are the Gallery of Historical Costumes and the Toy Gallery.

Details: Wed–Fri 9:30–5, Sat–Sun 10–5. $3 adults, $1.50 seniors and ages 12–18; free on Wed. (1 hour)

★★★ DETROIT PUBLIC LIBRARY
Woodward and Kirby Avenues, 313/833-1000

The main branch of the library is directly across from the Arts Institute. The white-marble, Italian Renaissance structure has numerous beautiful murals and Pewabic tiles inside. The Burton Historical Collection, the National Automotive History Collection, and the rare book room are all worth a visit.

Details: Tue and Thu–Sat 9:30–5:30, Wed 1–9. (1 hour)

★★★ DIAMOND JACK'S RIVER TOURS
313/843-7676

Diamond Jack's offers two-hour narrated excursions on the Detroit River that explore the history of one of America's busiest waterways. The tour begins at Hart Plaza, heads upriver around Belle Isle, then turns back downriver along the Canadian shore to the Ambassador Bridge and historic Fort Wayne before returning to

---

SIGHTS

- Ⓐ Belle Isle Aquarium
- Ⓑ Belle Isle Park
- Ⓒ Belle Isle Zoo
- Ⓓ Charles H. Wright Museum of African–American History
- Ⓔ Children's Museum
- Ⓕ Detroit Historical Museum
- Ⓖ Detroit Institute of Arts
- Ⓗ Detroit Public Library
- Ⓘ Detroit Science Center

SIGHTS (continued)

- Ⓙ Dossin Great Lakes Museum
- Ⓚ Eastern Market
- Ⓛ Fisher Mansion
- Ⓜ Motown Historical Museum
- Ⓝ Pewabic Pottery
- Ⓠ Whitcomb Conservatory

FOOD

- Ⓞ Harvey Lo's Yummy House
- Ⓟ Mexican Village

FOOD (continued)

- Ⓠ Sinbad's
- Ⓡ Rattlesnake Club
- Ⓢ The Whitney
- Ⓣ Xochimilco

LODGING

- Ⓤ Blanche House Inn
- Ⓥ Hotel St. Regis
- Ⓦ River Place

Note: Items with the same letter are located in the same place.

Hart Plaza. Along the way, you'll hear a running commentary that describes the founding of Detroit by Antoine de Mothe Cadillac 300 years ago; the history of Gar Wood and speedboat racing that is still held annually on the river; and tales of Prohibition-era bootleggers who smuggled booze across the river from Canada into the United States.

Details: *Boats leave from Hart Plaza and the St. Aubin Park Marina. Summer Tue–Sun 2, 4, and 6; Sept Fri–Sun same hours. $12 adults, $11 seniors, $9 ages 6–16. (2 hours)*

★★★ DOSSIN GREAT LAKES MUSEUM
Belle Isle, 313/852-4051

Among the special attractions on Belle Isle is the Dossin Museum, which illustrates the history of shipping on the Great Lakes. The Gothic Room contains huge hand-carved oak arches and other decorations from the smoking lounge of a Great Lakes steamer that was built in 1912. The museum also features a working pilothouse.

Details: *Wed–Sun 10–5. $2 adults, $1 seniors and ages 12–18. (1 hour)*

★★★ EASTERN MARKET
North of Gratiot Avenue at Russell Street

The Eastern Market has been the place to go for flowers, vegetables, and produce in Detroit since the 1890s. Saturday mornings are especially busy, as thousands of people jam the shops and open-air stalls to do some shopping or just soak up the colorful atmosphere. The market is surrounded by warehouses and importers and is located about a mile from downtown.

Details: *Mon–Fri 5–5, Sat 7–5. (1–2 hours)*

★★★ FISHER MANSION
383 Lenox Avenue, 313/331-6740

One of four mansions of the early auto-industry barons that is open to the public, the Fisher Mansion was built in 1927 on a canal that connects to the Detroit River. The building features elaborate examples of fine stone and wood craftsmanship as well as gold-leaf ceiling and molding details.

Details: *Tours Fri–Sun 12:30, 2, 3:30, and 6. $6 adults, $5 students and age 60 and over, $4 children age 12 and under. (1 hour)*

★★★ HART PLAZA
Woodward and Jefferson Avenues at the Detroit River
This riverfront plaza serves as a venue for a variety of summer entertainment activities. The spectacular annual Freedom Festival fireworks (sponsored cooperatively by Detroit and Windsor, Canada) take place here in late June. Throughout the summer the weekend Ethnic Festivals fill the plaza with a variety of foods, crafts, arts, music, and cultures. And each Labor Day weekend, the Montreux-Detroit Jazz Festival draws thousands of jazz lovers to the city.
Details: 30 minutes.

★★★ JOHN KING BOOKS
901 W. Lafayette Boulevard, 313/961-0622
This is a terrific place to spend an hour—or the better part of a day—browsing through the seemingly endless stacks of used books. King's, in an old glove factory on the west side of downtown, has four floors of display space and an estimated 1 million volumes, making it one of the nation's largest used bookstores.
Details: Mon–Sat 9:30–5:30. (1–2 hours)

★★ BELLE ISLE AQUARIUM
Belle Isle, 313/852-4141
Built in 1904, the aquarium on Belle Isle is one of the oldest public facilities of its kind in the country. Exhibits include more than 100 species of freshwater fish from Asia, South America, and Africa, as well as from the Great Lakes.
Details: Daily 10–5. $2 age 13 and over, $1 ages 2–12. (30 minutes)

★★ OLD MARINER'S CHURCH
170 E. Jefferson Avenue, 313/259-2206
Just west of the RenCen, this church was originally built on Woodward Avenue in 1849. It was moved to its current location in 1955. The stone church is Gothic Revival in design, and the interior blends Christian symbols with nautical designs.
Details: Guided tours available by request. (30 minutes–1 hour)

★★ PEWABIC POTTERY
10125 E. Jefferson Avenue, 313/822-0954
This unique institution is a combination studio, workshop, gallery, and

DETROIT REGION

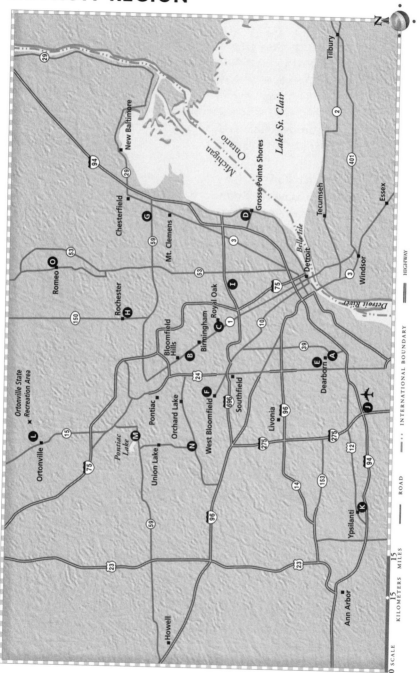

museum, displaying and celebrating the unusual ceramic style known as Pewabic. Historic work by founder Mary Chase Perry Stratton is on display, and contemporary works are available for sale.
Details: *Mon–Sat 10–6. Admission is free. (1 hour)*

★★ **WHITCOMB CONSERVATORY**
Belle Isle, 313/852-4065
This conservatory on Belle Isle stands out visually because of its 85-foot glass dome. Builders assembled the conservatory from parts of an exhibit at the 1904 World's Fair in St. Louis. Botanical displays inside are dominated by a selection of giant palms. Nearby are displays of cacti, tropical plants, ferns, and a large orchid collection. The conservatory also presents a variety of seasonal floral displays. Outside are formal gardens and a fountain featuring a striking bronze sculpture of a gazelle by Marshall Fredericks.
Details: *Daily 10–5. $2 age 13 and over, $1 seniors and ages 2–12. (30 minutes)*

GREATER DETROIT SIGHTSEEING HIGHLIGHTS
★★★★ **DETROIT ZOOLOGICAL PARK**
Woodward Avenue at 10 Mile Road, Royal Oak, 248/398-0900

SIGHTS
- Ⓐ Automotive Hall of Fame
- Ⓑ Cranbrook Educational Community
- Ⓒ Detroit Zoological Park
- Ⓓ Edsel & Eleanor Ford House
- Ⓔ Fair Lane Manor
- Ⓐ Greenfield Village and Henry Ford Museum
- Ⓕ Holocaust Memorial Center
- Ⓖ Lionel Trains Inc. Visitor Center
- Ⓗ Meadowbrook Hall

FOOD
- Ⓘ Loui's Pizza

LODGING
- Ⓙ Budgetel Inn—Metro Airport
- Ⓙ Hilton Suites—Detroit Metro Airport
- Ⓐ Dearborn Bed–and–Breakfast
- Ⓐ Dearborn Inn
- Ⓔ Hyatt Regency Dearborn
- Ⓐ Red Roof Inn–Dearborn

CAMPING
- Ⓚ Detroit–Greenfield KOA Resort Kamp
- Ⓛ Ortonville State Recreation Area
- Ⓜ Pontiac Lake State Recreation Area
- Ⓝ Proud Lake State Recreation Area
- Ⓞ Woodland Waters Campground

Note: Items with the same letter are located in the same place.

At the junction of I-696 and Woodward Avenue in Royal Oak, you'll find one of the biggest and best zoos in the United States. Exhibits in the 125-acre park are large and without bars and are organized by continent. One of the most outstanding is the Great Apes of Harambee exhibit, dedicated in 1989 and one of the biggest and best of its kind in the country. In addition to chimpanzees and gorillas, the exhibit includes mandrills and baboons. Other popular exhibits include the Wildlife Interpretive Gallery, the Wilson Aviary with 30 species of exotic birds in a tropical landscape, a coral reef aquarium, and a butterfly-hummingbird garden. The Holden Museum of Living Reptiles is home to a broad range of lizards, snakes, crocodiles, and other reptiles. The penguinarium enables visitors to get close to four different species of penguins as they swim about in a triangular tank. The zoo also has a great assortment of bears, elephants, lions, giraffes, antelopes, and other large mammals. Food concessions are available at various locations throughout the park, and an excellent gift and souvenir shop sits at the park entrance. To reduce walking (it's a big park), from May through September you can ride a free miniature train from the park entrance to the interior.

Details: Apr–Oct daily 10–5, Nov–Mar daily 10–4. $6 adults, $4 over age 61, $3 ages 2–12. (4 hours)

★★★★ GREENFIELD VILLAGE AND HENRY FORD MUSEUM
Village Road and Oakwood Boulevard, Dearborn
313/271-1620

This is an unusual historical collection of autos, inventions, and architecture, created by the captain of industry who once said that history is mostly bunk. The entrance to the museum on this 93-acre site is a replica of Independence Hall in Philadelphia. Inside are acres of displays that trace the development of American industry and technology, and the impact of the automobile on American life. From the museum you step outside into Greenfield Village, an eclectic collection of buildings from all parts of the country, including a one-room Puritan house, Thomas Edison's laboratory from Menlo Park, New Jersey, and a courthouse where Abraham Lincoln once practiced law.

Details: Daily 9–5. Village buildings closed Jan–Mar. Museum or village admission: $12.50 adults, $11.50 over age 62, $6.25 ages 5–12. Combination admission, good for two consecutive days: $22 adults, $11 ages 5–12. (half–full day)

★★★★ HOLOCAUST MEMORIAL CENTER
6602 W. Maple Road, West Bloomfield Township
248/661-0840
The center is a haunting memorial to the 6 million Jews massacred by Hitler's Nazi forces during World War II. When it opened in 1984, it was the nation's first museum dedicated to the Holocaust, and it continues to illuminate the sad, dark truths about that genocide through extraordinarily well-designed displays of film, historical artifacts, photos, and artwork.
Details: *Sept–May Sun–Thu 10–3:30, Fri 9–12:30. Admission is free. (2 hours)*

★★★ AUTOMOTIVE HALL OF FAME
21400 Oakwood Boulevard, Detroit, 313/240-4000
It is fitting that the Automotive Hall of Fame has moved from Midland to a sparkling new home in Dearborn, adjacent to the Henry Ford Museum. The new facility features memorabilia and interactive displays honoring people—inventors, designers, entrepreneurs, and even labor leaders—who have made important contributions to the U.S. auto industry.
Details: *Tue–Sun 10–5. $6 adults, $5.50 age 62 and over, $3 ages 5–12. (1 hour)*

★★★ CRANBROOK EDUCATIONAL COMMUNITY
1221 N. Woodward Avenue, Bloomfield Hills,
248/645-3000
Just off of Woodward Avenue in suburban Bloomfield Hills is a lovely, wooded 315-acre campus that includes four schools, gardens, an art museum, a science center, and a manor house that offer a variety of public programs on the arts and sciences. The Cranbrook Academy of Arts Museum, 248/645-3323, presents changing exhibits of contemporary art as well as works by faculty and students. The Cranbrook Institute of Science, 248/645-3200, is a museum of natural history and other sciences and includes displays of Native American artifacts and rocks and minerals, as well as a planetarium, an observatory, and a nature center.
Details: *Art museum: Tue–Sat 11–5. $5 adults, $3 age 65 and over and students with identification. Institute of Science: Mon–Thu 10–5, Fri–Sat 10–10, Sun noon–5. $7 adults, $4 age 60 and over and ages 3–17. (2 hours)*

★★★ EDSEL AND ELEANOR FORD HOUSE
Lake Shore Drive between Vernier and Nine Mile Roads, Grosse Pointe Shores, 313/884-4222

Edsel Ford (Henry Ford's only son and the father of Henry Ford II) and his wife, Eleanor, were tremendously influential, not only in the auto industry but also as great patrons of the arts. It was Edsel Ford who was responsible for commissioning the breathtaking Diego Rivera murals that are the most famous treasures of the Detroit Institute of Arts. Their 60-room mansion, home to a marvelous collection of art, was designed in the Cotswold style, and a cozy little playhouse out back was designed by renowned architect Albert Kahn.

Details: Apr–Dec Tue–Sat 10–4, Sun noon–4; Jan–May Tue–Sun noon–4. $6 adults, $5 age 60 and over, $4 age 12 and under. (2 hours)

★★★ FAIR LANE MANOR
University of Michigan–Dearborn, 313/593-5590

On the campus of the University of Michigan-Dearborn, off Evergreen just north of U.S. 12, is the elegant estate of auto magnate Henry Ford. It was here that Ford entertained such influential figures as Thomas Edison, President Herbert Hoover, and Charles Lindbergh.

Details: Tours Apr–Dec daily 10, 11, 1, 2, and 3; Jan–May Mon–Fri 1, Sun 1–4:30. $7 adults, $6 age 62 and over and ages 5–12. (2 hours)

★★★ MEADOWBROOK HALL
Oakland University, Rochester, 248/370-3140

On the campus of Oakland University in suburban Rochester is this opulent 100-room Tudor-style mansion that once belonged to the Dodge family, another great auto-industry name. The mansion hosts a classic car show each June and is decorated in grand fashion for the Christmas holidays.

Details: Off Adams Rd. just south of Walton Rd. Tours July–Aug Mon–Fri 10:30, noon, 1:30, and 3, Sat–Sun 1:30, 2:15, and 3; Sept–June Mon–Sat 1:30, Sun 1:30, 2:15, and 3. $8 adults, $6 age 62 and over, $4 ages 5–12. (2 hours)

★★ LIONEL TRAINS INC. VISITORS CENTER
Chesterfield Township, 810/949-4100

The center is a dream come true for toy train enthusiasts. A wide range of models are on display, and after a 10-minute video, visitors can check out an interactive display with 1,000 feet of model train track and as many as 10 trains running at the same time.

Details: Near Mt. Clemens, about 20 miles northeast of Detroit along I-94. Tours are free, but reservations are required. (1 hour)

FITNESS AND RECREATION

The suburban areas around Detroit are blessed with a number of great scenic places to get out for some exercise. Among the most popular are the **Stoney Creek Metropark**, off 26 Mile Road about a half-mile west of Mound Road near Romeo; **Metropolitan Beach Metropark**, at the eastern end of Metropolitan Parkway near Mount Clemens; and **Lower Huron Metropark**, off Savage Road near Bemis Road outside of Belleville. But in the city, without question, the best place to go is **Belle Isle**. The island park in the Detroit River has miles of roads and sidewalks that are excellent for walking, jogging, or bicycling, and there is a running track on the south side of the island. The park has a small golf course, fishing piers, a children's playscape, and a giant slide. When you get worn out you can sit down at a picnic table and watch the freighters and sailboats float by, or gaze at the downtown Detroit skyline a couple of miles away.

FOOD

No matter what kind of food you favor, you will not lack for options in Detroit. The city and surrounding suburban areas have hundreds of very good—and many excellent—restaurants and cafés, covering nearly every ethnic cuisine you can imagine and any dining atmosphere you might desire, from loud and brassy pizza joints to exquisitely elegant restaurants. Two of the city's most popular eating destinations are **Greektown**, on the eastern edge of the downtown area, and **Mexicantown**, a small, busy district within Detroit's large Hispanic community on the near southwest side.

Greektown used to be basically one block of Monroe Street just west of I-375 and about a block north of Lafayette Boulevard. Its borders have been sprawling slowly outward for several years, and now the area offers much more than just Greek food—though that is still the district's bread and butter. The most venerable of the Greek restaurants is the **New Hellas Cafe**, 583 Monroe St., 313/961-5544, where you can select from a variety of superbly prepared traditional dishes. Try moussaka, roast lamb, or *saganaki*, an especially tasty flaming *kasserei* cheese spread over bread. No trip to

Greektown is complete without the shout of "Opa!" as the waiter ignites the cheese. (Be very careful if you hear the table behind you ask for a double order.) Across the street is the **Pegasus Taverna**, 558 Monroe St., 313/964-6800, which is larger, a bit more touristy, and offers more non-Greek options.

One particularly unusual non-Greek ethnic restaurant in Greektown is The **Blue Nile**, 508 Monroe St., 313/964-6699, which specializes in Ethiopian cuisine such as meat and vegetable stews wrapped in bread that resembles pancakes. About a block away is **Fishbone's Rhythm Kitchen Cafe**, 400 Monroe St., 313/965-4600. The menu is New Orleans style, with Cajun-Creole dishes like etouffee, jambalaya, and bronzed redfish. If you're into Tex-Mex cooking, try the **Loco Bar & Grill**, 454 E. Lafayette Blvd., 313/965-3737, which serves meals in a cowboy atmosphere.

Two of the best restaurants in Mexicantown are **Xochimilco** and the **Mexican Village**. Xochimilco, 3409 Bagley, 313/843-0179, has a reputation for good and filling Mexican dishes, such as quesadillas, tacos, enchiladas, and chimichangas. The Mexican Village, 2600 Bagley, 313/237-0333, one of the oldest Mexican restaurants in Detroit, also has an excellent reputation.

For elegant meals there are a number of outstanding options. **The Whitney**, 4421 Woodward Ave., 313/832-5700, is the most impressive, situated in an 1890 stone mansion built by lumber baron David Whitney. The menu is American fare, extremely well prepared in a graceful atmosphere accentuated by antique furnishings.

If you'd prefer a more modern atmosphere with your fine cuisine, try the **Rattlesnake Club**, 300 River Pl., 313/567-4400. Here you will find a contemporary American menu and a lovely dining room on the Detroit River. Dinner is $30 to $50. If romantic views are what you crave, your choice should be **The Summit**, the revolving restaurant at the top of the 70-story Marriott Hotel in the downtown Renaissance Center, 313/568-8600. The food here (emphasis on steak and seafood) doesn't match the others', but none has a view that compares, especially on a clear night. Dinners are $30 to $50.

A good place for inexpensive surf-and-turf dinners or sandwiches is **Sinbad's**, 100 St. Clair St., 313/822-7817. This place is especially popular among the boating crowd—or anyone who just enjoys being by the river—and dinners average less than $15.

If Chinese food is your favorite form of gastronomical adventure, you'll want to pay a visit to Windsor, across the river in Canada. **Harvey Lo's Yummy House**, 1144 Wyandotte St. E., 519/252-1034, serves the tangiest, strongest hot-and-sour soup you're likely ever to find. The rest of the menu is great, too, and the favorable monetary exchange rate makes an average $15 dinner especially economical.

One of the longest-running arguments in Detroit is over who serves the area's best pizza. My vote goes to **Loui's Pizza**, 23141 Dequindre Rd., 248/547-1711, just north of Nine Mile Road in suburban Hazel Park. Loui helped build the reputations of a couple of other well-known local pizza bars before he opened his own place. Be sure to try the antipasto salad, too. Dinner is about $10.

No culinary tour of Detroit would be complete without a pilgrimage to the **Lafayette Coney Island**, 118 W. Lafayette Blvd., 313/964-8198. For nearly 70 years this unpretentious little downtown lunch counter has been serving some of the greatest chili dogs anywhere. A meal is well under $10, and you've got no excuse for not getting there—it's open 24 hours.

LODGING

You will find all sorts of hotels, motels, and inns throughout the Detroit area; every national chain has at least one facility within an easy drive of downtown. In general, the downtown hotels are more expensive and convenient, while the less-expensive lodgings are more widely distributed in suburban areas. Where you look for a room will depend on where in the metropolitan area your trip will be focused, but three of the largest concentrations of rooms are downtown, in suburban Dearborn, and in Romulus, near Detroit Metropolitan Airport. Each is easily accessible from I-94, the region's main east-west artery; and each is convenient to a major north-south route: I-75 downtown, the Southfield Freeway in Dearborn, and I-275 near the airport.

Downtown, the unquestioned giant is the **Marriott Hotel**, the centerpiece of the riverfront Renaissance Center, 313/568-8000. Marriott took over the hotel from Westin in late 1998. The change was engineered by General Motors, which bought the center in 1996 as a new home for its world headquarters and has since undertaken a multimillion-dollar renovation. The hotel has 1,400 rooms in its 70-story tower, with a revolving restaurant at the top, a heated indoor pool, saunas, a whirlpool, and a health club. Many of the rooms overlook the Detroit River. Rates are $175 to $210 a night.

Another downtown stalwart, though it has changed ownership a couple of times in recent years, is the **Crowne Plaza Pontchartrain Hotel**, 2 Washington Blvd., 313/965-0200. The Pontchartrain is directly across the street from Cobo Center, which makes it especially convenient for business and convention visitors. The 25-story hotel has 416 rooms and charges $149 to $169 a night.

An elegant newcomer to the downtown hotel scene is the **Atheneum Suite Hotel and Conference Center**, 1000 Brush Ave., 313/962-2323. The 10-story Atheneum, with 174 rooms and suites, is on the edge of Greektown, one of the city's best and most popular restaurant districts. Rooms range from $125 to $250 a night. North of downtown, in the New Center Area, is the **Hotel St. Regis**, 3071 W. Grand Blvd., 313/873-3000, an elegant 221-room hotel with an Old World look. The hotel is very near the Fisher Theater and is close to three major freeways. Rates are $79 to $115.

A mile or so east from downtown, along Jefferson Avenue, is the **River Place**, 1000 River Pl., 313/259-9500. This hotel, situated on the banks of the Detroit River, offers 108 rooms, a marvelous view of the river and the Canadian shore, a heated indoor pool, a wading pool, saunas, whirlpools, a health club, tennis courts, and a croquet court. Rooms go for $99 to $159 a night. Also on the east side is **Blanche House Inn**, 506 Parkview, 313/822-7090, a bed-and-breakfast in the historic Berry Subdivision. The inn, which has a smoke-free policy, is in an eight-bedroom 1905 Colonial Revival house. Rates range from $65 to $120 a room. The inn also offers good celebrity-watching: The Manoogian Mansion, the mayor's home, is just down the street.

For a more economical hotel close to downtown, you might try the **Shorecrest Motor Inn**, 1316 E. Jefferson Ave., 313/568-3000. With 54 rooms within walking distance of Renaissance Center, the Shorecrest charges $52 to $84 a night.

In Dearborn, one of the largest and busiest hotels is the **Hyatt Regency Dearborn**, 313/593-1234. It's located along the service drive of the Fairlane Town Center Mall, north of Michigan Avenue between the Southfield Freeway and Evergreen Road. The hotel has 771 rooms with an impressively high and open lobby atrium, and offers a heated indoor pool, whirlpool, sauna, exercise room, and conference center. Room rates are $109 to $135 a night. Another good choice in the city is the **Dearborn Inn**, 20301 Oakwood Blvd., 313/271-2700. It offers 222 elegant rooms and some cottages on a 23-acre site, with a heated pool, two tennis courts, an exercise room, and a playground. Rooms cost $109 to $159 a night.

For a more intimate setting, try the **Dearborn Bed-and-Breakfast**, 22331 Morley St., 313/563-2200. An elegant and historic house built in 1927, it has four rooms and is filled with Victorian antiques. The inn offers a smoke-free environment, a heated pool, and, for a quirky twist, horseshoe pits. Rooms cost $85 to $165. The economically minded might consider the **Red Roof Inn-Dearborn**, 24130 Michigan Ave., 313/278-9732, with 112 rooms and nightly rates of $46 to $75.

Hotel and motel construction has boomed near Metropolitan Airport in recent years, so you should find no shortage of rooms there, especially along Merriman Road (the main entrance to the airport) north of I-94. Two of the dozen or so hotels near the airport are the **Baymont Inn**, 9000 Wickham Rd., 734/981-1808, where rooms rent for $48 to $70; and the **Hilton Suites-Detroit Metro Airport**, 8600 Wickham Rd., 734/728-9200, with a heated indoor/outdoor pool, a whirlpool, and a room rate of $114 per night.

CAMPING

Detroit is not famous as a big camping destination, though its annual Boat and Camper Show at Cobo Center is something to see. However, good campgrounds are readily available within an hour's drive of downtown. As is true all over the state, you will find a mix of private and public facilities, virtually all on the periphery of the metropolitan area.

Michigan is justly proud of its state parks and campgrounds, several of which are near Detroit. North of the city, the **Pontiac Lake State Recreation Area**, 7800 Gale Rd., 248/666-1020, has 176 campsites and is open from mid-May through September. Fees range from $10 to $15, and the park has facilities for fishing, waterskiing, horseback riding, and snowmobiling. It also has nature trails and offers boat rentals.

A bit farther north is the **Ortonville State Recreation Area**, 5779 Hadley Rd., 248/627-3828, which has 32 sites and is open all year. Activities include swimming, boating, fishing, waterskiing, horseback riding, snow-skiing, snowmobiling, and hiking on nature trails. Fees are $6 a night. To the northwest, off I-96 near Milford, is the **Proud Lake State Recreation Area**, 3500 Wixom Rd., 248/685-2433, with 110 sites that are open all year. The area offers facilities for swimming, boating, fishing, skiing, and snowmobiling, as well as a playground and nature trails. Fees are $15 a night.

A couple of private campgrounds are the **Detroit-Greenfield KOA Resort Kamp**, near Ypsilanti (see camping listings in Chapter 2) and **Woodland Waters Campground**, near Romeo, 79720 Kidder Rd., 810/798-3422. Woodland Waters is open May through October, with 281 sites, a beach, swimming, a playground, a recreation room, nature trails, canoeing, and fishing. Rates are $11 to $15 a night for up to six.

NIGHTLIFE

From theater to comedy to dance to every kind of music, Detroit and its environs offer an untold variety of entertainment. The fastest-growing center for entertainment is the downtown theater district, along Woodward Avenue near Grand Circus Park. Central to the revival of the district was the restoration in 1988 of the 5,000-seat Fox Theater, 2211 Woodward Ave., 313/396-7600, a gaudy 1928 movie palace whose architecture has been described as Siamese Byzantine. The building is an adventure in itself, but it's even more exciting to see (and hear) a restored epic like *Ben Hur* or *Lawrence of Arabia* splashed across the giant movie screen. The theater also presents legitimate stage shows and concerts.

A couple of blocks away, at the corner of Brush and Madison, are a pair of theaters: **Music Hall Center for the Performing Arts**, 313/963-2366, and the **Gem Theater**, 313/963-9800. The Music Hall presents a variety of music, drama, and dance productions. As for the Gem Theater, its name says it all. This intimate little cabaret specializes in small-scale musical revues and comedies. It was moved from its previous site across Woodward from the Fox Theater to make room for construction of two new athletic stadiums for the **Detroit Tigers** and **Detroit Lions**, the city's professional baseball and football franchises. Those additions are expected to make the district even more popular.

Just north of the Fox is the **Second City Comedy Theater**, 2305 Woodward Ave., 313/965-2222. It's another property of Fox owner Mike Ilitch, who also owns the Tigers and pushed hard for the stadium project. Second City, like its Chicago peer, features improvisational comedy that is cosmopolitan in scope but with a definite Detroit flavor.

A few blocks away, another old movie palace has been reborn as the **Detroit Opera House**, 1526 Broadway, 313/963-7474. It's the home of the Michigan Opera Theatre, one of the nation's best regional opera companies. In addition to operatic productions, the theater has hosted a variety of productions ranging from dance to musical theater, concerts, and lectures.

When Broadway blockbusters visit Detroit, they usually set up shop at the huge **Masonic Temple Theatre**, 500 Temple, 313/832-2232. Masonic is a great old theater and has hosted a couple of recent visits by *Les Misérables* and *Phantom of the Opera*, but be careful to choose seats as close to the center of the fan-shaped auditorium as possible; a considerable portion of seats along the sides have restricted views of the theater's very deep stage.

Other theaters and concert venues dot the city. On the southern edge of the Cultural Center is **Detroit Symphony Orchestra Hall**, 3711 Woodward Ave., 313/833-3700, an exquisite old concert hall that was nearly in ruins a few years back. The hall is now the home of the Detroit Symphony Orchestra, a world-class musical ensemble, and presents a variety of classical, jazz, and other concerts. In the New Center Area's Fisher Building is the **Fisher Theater**, 3011 W. Grand Blvd., 313/872-1000, which regularly hosts national tours of major Broadway plays and musicals. Its stage and auditorium are smaller than those of Masonic or the Detroit Opera House, but it has presented such musicals as *A Chorus Line* and *Chicago.*

For an excellent local theater company, check out the **Detroit Repertory Theater**, 13103 Woodrow Wilson, 313/868-1347, which has a long reputation for producing quality productions in an intimate setting.

The Detroit area has an incredible variety of concert venues. Many of the world's biggest headliners come to perform at local athletic stadiums. For example, the **Pontiac Silverdome**, Hwy. 59 and Opdyke Rd., 248/456-1600, the current home of the Lions, has hosted the Rolling Stones, Bruce Springsteen, Billy Joel, Elton John, and others. A few miles away is **The Palace of Auburn Hills**, Hwy. 24 and I-75, 248/377-0100, home of the Detroit Pistons basketball team and a regular venue for rock concerts and other special events.

More intimate settings are available. For example, **Baker's Keyboard Lounge**, 20510 Livernois Ave., 313/345-6300, is nationally known for its jazz presentations. The **Soup Kitchen Saloon**, 1585 Franklin St., 313/259-1374, also offers live jazz. **The Rhinoceros**, 265 Riopelle St., 313/259-2208, specializes in blues. And in suburban Royal Oak, the **Metropolitan Music Cafe**, 326 W. Fourth St., 248/542-1990, has live rock concerts.

Other areas that are popular for their profusion of restaurants, cafés, and clubs include **Harmonie Park**, a block off Gratiot Avenue near downtown Detroit; downtown **Royal Oak**, which swarms with sidewalk cafés; downtown **Pontiac**, which has developed a lively club scene; and **Ann Arbor** (see Chapter 2).

The biggest new development on Detroit's nightlife scene has been the advent of casino gambling. Windsor, Ontario, on the Canadian side of the Detroit River, was first out of the starting blocks with the **Windsor Casino**, 519/258-7878. It stands directly opposite Cobo Center and has become a hot destination for thousands of gamblers from southeastern Michigan. After much political uproar, three casinos are expected to open in temporary facilities in Detroit by the end of 1999, and permanent casinos are scheduled to be constructed in the city over the next several years.

HELPFUL HINT

The **Detroit People Mover**, 313/961-6446, is an elevated, automated light-rail system with 13 stops on a 2.9-mile circuit that connects a number of key locations as it loops around the downtown area. It is a convenient way to get between Cobo, Joe Louis Arena, RenCen, Greektown, and the Theater District. It's also a cheap (50 cents) and easy way to get a good overview of the downtown area and a glimpse of Windsor, Ontario, across the river. Hours of operation: Mon–Thu 7–11, Fri 7–midnight, Sat 9–midnight, Sun noon–8. Extended hours during special events.

2
ANN ARBOR

Ann Arbor is the home of the University of Michigan, one of the nation's premier public research universities. But while the university is a prime attraction for visitors, the city and surrounding area have much to offer beyond the confines of the campus—there are plentiful shopping opportunities, art galleries, beautiful rolling farmlands, and forested natural areas nearby.

The city is easily accessible from all directions. I-94, the main east-west route between Detroit and Chicago, runs along the city's south side. Detroit Metropolitan Airport, the area's main air hub, is 30 to 40 minutes east on the freeway. North-south travelers approach by way of U.S. 23, which runs along Ann Arbor's eastern edge and connects Flint, about 50 miles north, with Toledo, Ohio, about 50 miles south. A business loop of U.S. 23 and M 14 angles across the northwest side, encircling the city.

Ann Arbor's two central areas—the university's main campus and the downtown shopping district—are within easy walking distance of each other. But the city also has a good bus system that links the two districts with each other and with shopping centers and hotels along the city's outer edge, so getting around town is no problem, even without a car.

Take Dexter Road northwest out of town for a lovely drive along the Huron River to Dexter, about seven miles away. Another eight miles west is Chelsea, gateway to the Waterloo Recreation Area, a huge scenic area of small towns, little lakes, and wooded hills.

A PERFECT DAY IN ANN ARBOR

Begin at the University of Michigan's central campus. A walk along the Diag, which cuts through the heart of campus, will give you a good taste of the university and its active intellectual and social life, as well as of the varied architecture and arching trees that define the city's atmosphere. Browse the bookstores and other specialty shops that surround campus and stop for lunch at one of the many cafés sprinkled through the State Street area and downtown.

A sunny afternoon in any season is a good time for a leisurely excursion to the town of Dexter, a short but lovely drive along the Huron River through rolling hills and farmland northwest of town. After dinner at the Gandy Dancer, take in a concert at one of the downtown clubs or one of the larger auditoriums on campus.

SIGHTSEEING HIGHLIGHTS
★★★★ **EXHIBIT MUSEUM OF NATURAL HISTORY**
Geddes and N. University Avenue, 734/763-6085
This museum on the University of Michigan campus features an extremely broad range of displays on Michigan wildlife, biology, anthropology, dinosaurs and prehistoric life, minerals and fossils, Native American cultures, ecology, and astronomy. The dinosaur section, which includes seven dinosaur skeletons and numerous dioramas depicting the great animals that roamed the region millions of years ago, is one of the most popular parts of the museum. Another series of dioramas traces the evolution of life, starting with the Cambrian Age, nearly 600 million years ago. Other exhibits illuminate technology used to gather information on weather and atmospheric phenomena, and explore the wonders of human anatomy.
Details: Mon–Sat 9–5, Sun noon–5. Museum is free, planetarium $3 adults, $2.50 seniors and children age 12 and under. (1–2 hours)

★★★★ **GERALD R. FORD LIBRARY**
1000 Beal Avenue, 734/741-2218
Anyone interested in the history of the U.S. presidency will want to visit this library on U-M's North Campus. The library houses documents and exhibits from Ford's years as a congressman, vice president, and president, as well as personal memorabilia of the university's most prominent alumnus.
Details: Mon–Fri 8:45–4:45. (1–2 hours)

DOWNTOWN ANN ARBOR

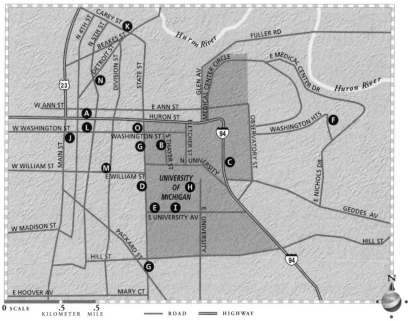

SIGHTS

Ⓐ Ann Arbor Hands–On Museum
Ⓑ Burton Memorial Tower
Ⓒ Exhibit Museum of Natural History
Ⓓ Kelsey Museum of Archeology
Ⓔ Museum of Art
Ⓕ Nichols Arboretum
Ⓖ State Street
Ⓗ University of Michigan
Ⓘ William L. Clements Library

FOOD

Ⓙ Amadeus Cafe Patisserie
Ⓚ Gandy Dancer
Ⓛ Metzger's
Ⓜ Raja Rani
Ⓝ Zingerman's Deli

LODGING

Ⓑ Bell Tower Hotel
Ⓞ Campus Inn

Note: Items with the same letter are located in the same place.

★★★★ STATE STREET

If the University of Michigan is the heart of Ann Arbor, State Street is the aorta, the main artery that circulates traffic through the university area and connects city and campus. Here you'll find bookstores, cafés, and specialty shops that cater to the university community but draw shoppers from all over. This is where the Borders Bookstore chain got its start, though the first Borders store has outgrown its original site and moved to a former department-store building a block away on Liberty Street.

Bibliophiles who love to hunt for special treasures can browse David's Books at the corner of Liberty Street and State Street. It's an upstairs warren of bookshelves where you'll find the eclectic mix of used books you might expect in one of the country's premier university towns.

For music lovers, Schoolkids' Records at Liberty Street and Maynard Street, just west of State Street, offers one of the broader selections you'll find anywhere. It sells the standard pop-rock-rap fare found at mall music stores, but also carries thorough collections of folk, jazz, blues, classical, and international music—something of a rarity these days.

About a block south of Liberty Street, just across State Street from the Diag, is Nichols Arcade. It is a charming, vaulted, two-story passageway lined with antique shops, galleries, clothiers, and other specialty shops.

Details: *2–3 hours.*

★★★★ UNIVERSITY OF MICHIGAN
734/763-4636 (campus information)

U-M is the raison d'être of Ann Arbor, and no visit to the city would be complete without spending at least a little time on campus. In addition to its 30,000-plus student body, U-M brings many thousands of visitors to the city each year for academic conferences, cultural activities, speeches, exhibits, medical research, and athletic events. Every fall for more than 20 years, each home football game alone has drawn more than 100,000 fans to the U-M stadium, and each summer the Ann Arbor Street Art Fairs fill the streets on and near campus with hundreds of thousands more.

The university's borders tend to blur into surrounding residential areas, but the main campus core is bounded by Huron Street, State Street, Washtenaw Avenue, and South University Street. The social and psychological heart of U-M is the Diag, a broad walkway that angles across the center of campus. At the southern edge of the central campus, at State Street and South University Avenue, is the university's Law Quadrangle, where you can stroll through the secluded courtyard and gaze at the handsome ivy-covered Gothic buildings of U-M's Law School.

Details: 1 hour.

★★★★ WATERLOO RECREATION AREA
Bush Road north of I-94, Chelsea, 734/475-3170

About 30 minutes west of Ann Arbor is the Waterloo Recreation Area, nearly 20,000 acres of lakes, wooded hills, marshes, and nature trails. At the Gerald E. Eddy Geology Center, you can see displays of minerals, rocks, and fossils from the Great Lakes region, as well as a slide presentation on Michigan geology. The area is excellent for picnicking, hiking, boating, fishing, and camping. Horse rental is available, and cross-country skiing is popular in the winter.

Details: Daily 9–5. $4 per private vehicle; admission to the geology center is free. (2–6 hours)

★★★ ANN ARBOR HANDS-ON MUSEUM
219 E. Huron Street, 734/995-5439

Housed in an old firehouse built in the nineteenth century, the museum offers more than 200 interactive exhibits on four floors. First-floor exhibits focus on the human body, second- and third-floor displays examine the natural world, and the fourth floor is devoted to computers. You—and your kids—can measure your flexibility and reaction time, observe a working beehive, or use a computer to play three-dimensional tic-tac-toe.

Details: Tue–Fri 10–5:30, Sat 10–5, Sun 1–5. $5 adults; $3 seniors, children ages 3–12, and students with identification. (1 hour)

★★★ KELSEY MUSEUM OF ARCHEOLOGY
434 S. State Street, 734/764-9304

The Kelsey Museum, also on the U-M campus, is small but distinctive. Built in 1891 from local fieldstone, the building itself is worthy of attention for its Romanesque style, elaborate woodwork, and large Tiffany window. The archeological collection housed inside features a variety of artifacts, such as statues, glass, and pottery from university archeological sites in the Mediterranean and Near East.

The items on display are drawn from a permanent collection of more than 100,000 objects. Exhibits include Egyptian masks and sculptures dating back as far as 2400 B.C., rare Roman glass objects, and painted Greek vases.

Details: *Tue–Fri 9–4, Sat–Sun 1–4; closed during the university's Christmas break. Admission is free. (1 hour)*

★★★ MATTHAEI BOTANICAL GARDENS
1800 N. Dixboro Road, 734/998-7060

Just east of Ann Arbor you'll find U-M's Matthaei Gardens. Matthaei's 350 acres offer several outdoor nature trails, ranging in length from about a half-mile to nearly two miles. One of the most interesting is an ethnobotanical trail, with markers that explore the connections between people and plants. The markers note plants that have been used for food, medicine, shelter, and even toys (cattails that once were used to make dolls). A creek, several ponds, and a wetlands area attract birds, small mammals, and other wildlife. A conservatory houses a large collection of unusual cacti, palms, and other exotic plants from all over the world.

Details: *Grounds open daily 8–dusk, conservatory open daily 10–4:30. Grounds admission free; conservatory admission $2 adults, $1 ages 5–12, free children under 5, free to all Mon and Sat 10–1. (2 hours)*

★★★ MUSEUM OF ART
State Street and South University Street, 734/764-0395

The permanent collection of this museum on the U-M campus is an impressive one, with more than 13,000 pieces that are rotated periodically through the museum's galleries. Holdings include Western art from the sixth century to the present, African art, and art of the Near and Far East. Among the most notable artists represented are Picasso, Rembrandt, Monet, Delacroix, Rodin, Miro, Whistler, and Cezanne. The museum also hosts special exhibits, concerts, and other events.

Details: *Sept–May Tue–Sat 10–5 (Thu 10–9), Sun noon–5; June–Aug Tue–Sat 11–5 (Thu 11–9), Sun noon–5. Admission is free. (1 hour)*

★★★ NICHOLS ARBORETUM
734/998-7175

Near the main U-M campus is this 123-acre arboretum, which offers several nature trails that wind through the wooded grounds. A self-guided-tour brochure is available. Within the arboretum, established in 1907 with a historic landscape designed by Ossian Cole Simonds, you will find more than 500 species of woody plants. A peony garden with more than 780 varieties includes more than 260 varieties that predate World War II; bloom time is usually the first two weeks of June. The arboretum also includes a wetland area along the Huron River; a special collection of rhododendron, azalea, and other Appalachian plants; and a 20-acre plot that is a true, unplowed remnant of the prairies that covered much of southern Michigan before the arrival of European settlers.

Details: Gates at 1827 Geddes Rd., Washington Heights, and campus parking lot M-29 near the university medical center. Daily dawn–dusk. (1–2 hours)

★★ BURTON MEMORIAL TOWER
300 block of South Thayer, 734/764-2539

Musically inclined visitors may want to check out Burton Tower, one of the better-known landmarks on the U-M campus. At the top of the tower is the Baird Carillon, whose 55 bells range from 12 pounds to 12 tons. During the half-hour concerts that are offered at noon on weekdays while the university is in session, visitors can climb the tower to watch the player operate the levers and pedals that sound the bells. The tower also provides an excellent view of the campus and surrounding neighborhoods of Ann Arbor.

Details: Mon–Fri noon–12:30. Weekly concerts June–July Mon at 7. (30 minutes)

★★ WILLIAM L. CLEMENTS LIBRARY
909 S. University Avenue, 734/764-2347

If you are interested in Americana, rare books, maps, and original manuscripts, U-M's Clements Library houses excellent collections. The library is one of the nation's leading resources for documents about America up through the nineteenth century. It's also home to some fascinating antiques, including a grandfather clock that once served in George Washington's headquarters and a collection of Amberina glassware. The library building itself, with its Italian Renaissance villa style, is an entertaining sight both inside and out.

Details: Reading room open Mon–Fri 9–noon and 1–5. Exhibits open Mon–Fri noon–4:45. Admission is free. (1 hour)

★★ YPSILANTI

Ypsilanti is home of Eastern Michigan University. The attractive campus features a one-room schoolhouse—a tribute to EMU's history as one of the nation's top colleges of teacher education, and to the university's role in establishing consolidated rural school districts in the 1920s.

Just as interesting is Ypsilanti's abundant supply of Greek Revival architecture, particularly along Huron Street. The Depot Town area, along Cross Street just east of Huron Street, contains a variety of interesting shops and restaurants in vintage buildings, and is home to the annual Frog Island Blues Festival.

Details: *About five miles east of Ann Arbor on Washtenaw Ave. (1–2 hours)*

FITNESS AND RECREATION

In Ann Arbor you will find plenty of outlets for fitness and recreation activities. Bicyclists, in-line skaters, joggers, and walkers are everywhere. The campus area is particularly popular for such activities, and the **Nichols Arboretum** is another fine spot for jogging or walking. The road from Ann Arbor to Dexter along the **Huron River** is a particularly popular spot for bicyclists and long-distance runners.

A bit farther afield, the **Waterloo State Recreation Area** (I-94 exit 157, 734/475-8307) and the **Irish Hills** offer plenty of opportunities for hiking, camping, boating, fishing, swimming, waterskiing, snowmobiling, cross-country skiing, and horseback riding.

FOOD

Ann Arbor has many excellent restaurants, from the quirky to the exotic to the traditionally fancy. Its array of eateries features a cross-section of good ethnic cuisines, low-budget student fare, and all-American standbys.

One of the city's traditionally popular spots is the **Gandy Dancer**, 401 Depot St., 734/769-0592. The restaurant is in a renovated railroad station and offers an American menu with an emphasis on seafood. Dinners cost $15 to $30. Another Ann Arbor standard is **Weber's**, 3050 Jackson Rd., 734/665-3636, a longtime favorite of university students and their parents for family dinners. Weber's serves a standard, if staid, American menu, with dinners in the $10 to $20 range.

Downtown is **Metzger's**, 203 E. Washington St., 734/668-8987, a German restaurant with a reputation for serving large portions of its excellent wurst, potato dumplings, and schnitzel. Dinner costs $10 to $20. A few blocks away, the **Raja Rani**, 400 S. Division St., 734/995-1545, offers traditional Indian cuisine with dinners in the $10 to $20 range.

The best Chinese food in town is at **Szechuan West**, 2161 W. Stadium Blvd., 734/769-5722. The cavelike atmosphere (a carry-over from another restaurant that originally occupied the building) is a bit strange, but the food is excellent, and dinner costs between $10 and $20. For food with a middle-European flavor and some delicious tortes, try the **Amadeus Cafe Patisserie**, 122 E. Washington St., 734/665-8767. Dinner ranges from $10 to $20, and lunches cost under $10.

Perhaps the most entertaining food adventure to be had in Ann Arbor is a trip to **Zingerman's Deli**, 422 Detroit St., 734/663-3354. Zingerman's makes truly great deli sandwiches with an amazing array of combination options. They even make their own bread. Meals are priced from $5 to $15. The deli also contains a gourmet grocery featuring coffees, meats, cheeses, and other unusual items.

For solid meals under $10, cruise Washtenaw Avenue between Ann Arbor and Ypsilanti, where you'll find numerous casual and inexpensive restaurants from which to choose.

LODGING

Ann Arbor is a large, busy city, but it is easy to get around. Your choice of accommodations will depend on your chosen mode of transportation. If you plan to travel mostly by foot while you're in town, you'll probably want to stay at one of the hotels near the central campus, such as the **Campus Inn**, E. Huron St. at State St., 734/769-2200. The location is nearly perfect, about four blocks from the heart of campus and about the same distance from the downtown business district. Rates range from $108 to $123.

The **Bell Tower Hotel**, 300 S. Thayer St., 734/769-3010, is even closer to campus, directly across the street from U-M's Hill Auditorium and about 75 yards from the Diag. It's more elegant, too, and a bit more costly, with rates ranging from $107 to $240 a night.

Around the city's edges are several clusters of hotels and motels that are more moderate in price but are 5 to 10 minutes by car or bus from Ann Arbor's main attractions. One such cluster is on the west side, near Jackson Road and West Stadium Boulevard.

Weber's Inn, the dean of Ann Arbor's hotels, is at 3050 Jackson Rd., 734/769-2500. Easily accessible to I-94 and, via Jackson Road, to the downtown area, Weber's has rates from $95 to $245 a night. The inn has conference

ANN ARBOR

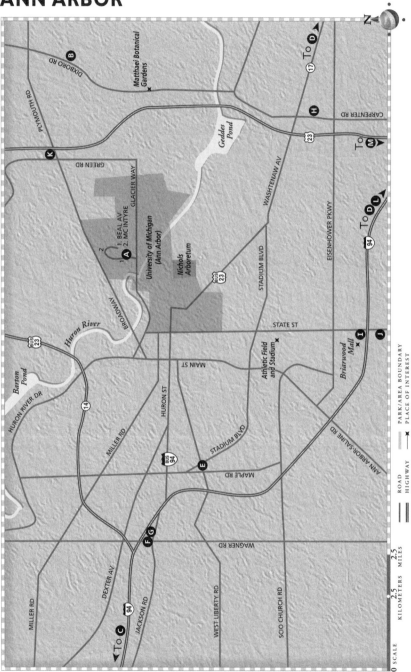

University of Michigan (Ann Arbor)
1. BEAL AV
2. MC INTYRE

Matthaei Botanical Gardens

DIXBORO RD

PLYMOUTH RD

GREEN RD

GLACIER WAY

Geddes Pond

WASHTENAW AV

CARPENTER RD

EISENHOWER PKWY

STADIUM BLVD

Nichols Arboretum

BROADWAY

Huron River

Barton Pond

HURON RIVER DR

MILLER RD

HURON ST

MAIN ST

STATE ST

Athletic Field and Stadium

Briarwood Mall

ANN ARBOR-SALINE RD

STADIUM BLVD

MAPLE RD

DEXTER AV

JACKSON RD

WAGNER RD

WEST LIBERTY RD

SCIO CHURCH RD

MILLER RD

To **G**

To **B**

To **K**

To **D**

To **H**

To **M**

To **D**

To **L**

SCALE
0   2.5
KILOMETERS

0   2.5
MILES

ROAD
HIGHWAY
PARK/AREA BOUNDARY
PLACE OF INTEREST

facilities, a heated indoor pool, a sauna and whirlpool, and one of the city's best restaurants.

Nearby is the **Clarion Hotel Atrium and Conference Center**, 2900 Jackson Rd., 734/665-4444. With 222 rooms, it's one of the largest hotels in town. Like Weber's, it has a full array of luxuries, including a heated indoor pool, sauna, and whirlpool. Rates run from $79 to $159 a night.

The State Street exit off I-94 on the city's south side is the main entryway to the campus area, and a variety of hotels are clustered there. At the high end of the scale is the **Crowne Plaza-Ann Arbor**, 610 Hilton Blvd., 734/761-7800, adjacent to the Briarwood Mall, with room rates from $104 to $145. Nearby, the **Fairfield Inn** by Marriott, 3285 Boardwalk, 734/995-5200, offers mid-priced rooms from $69 to $119 a night. The low end of the price scale is represented by **Motel 6**, 3764 S. State St., 734/665-9900, with rates from $42 to $48 a night.

On the east side, the **Comfort Inn**, 2455 Carpenter Rd., 734/973-6100, has rooms ranging from $64 to $135 a night and is just a short drive from downtown along the Washtenaw Avenue commercial strip near U.S. 23. A couple of exits north on U.S. 23 at Plymouth Road, the **Red Roof Inn**, 734/996-5800, offers inexpensive rooms—$47 to $73 a night—within a five-minute drive of U-M's North Campus and the offices of numerous high-tech companies along Plymouth Road and Huron River Parkway.

CAMPING

The most plentiful and scenic campgrounds are in the Waterloo Recreation Area (see Sightseeing Highlights). The state-operated recreation area has four

SIGHTS
Ⓐ Gerald R. Ford Library
Ⓑ Matthaei Botanical Gardens
Ⓒ Waterloo Recreation Area
Ⓓ Ypsilanti

FOOD
Ⓔ Szechuan West
Ⓕ Weber's

LODGING
Ⓖ Clarion Hotel Atrium and Conference Center
Ⓗ Comfort Inn
Ⓘ Crowne Plaza–Ann Arbor
Ⓙ Fairfield Inn
Ⓙ Motel 6
Ⓚ Red Roof Inn
Ⓖ Weber's Inn

CAMPING
Ⓛ Detroit–Greenfield KOA Resort Kamp
Ⓜ KC Campground
Ⓒ Waterloo Recreation Area campgrounds

Note: Items with the same letter are located in the same place.

separate campgrounds with a total of more than 230 sites. **Portage Lake Campground**, with 194 sites, and **Horsemen's Campground**, with 25 sites, are open all year. **Sugarloaf Campground**, with 190 sites, is open from mid-May to mid-September, and **Green Lake Campground**, with 25 sites, is open from the end of May through November. The two small campgrounds charge $6 a night, Sugarloaf charges $12, and Portage Lake charges $14 (rates are subject to change). Reservations must be made at least seven days in advance with a $4 reservation fee plus the total camping fee. For more information, call 734/475-8307.

At least two private campgrounds are within easy reach of Ann Arbor. **KC Campground**, 14048 Sherman Rd., Milan, is about 12 miles south of town off U.S. 23 near exit 25. The campground has 100 sites and charges $12 to $18 per night for two people, plus $5 for each extra adult. It's open from May 1 through October, and a reservation deposit is required. Call 734/439-1076 for reservations or further information.

The **Detroit-Greenfield KOA Resort Kamp**, 6680 Bunton Rd., Ypsilanti, has 216 sites and is open from April 1 through October 31. Fees range from $22 to $28, with a charge of $2 to $4 for each extra person. A reservation deposit is required, and a cancellation fee applies with less than three days' notice. The campground is south of I-94 near exit 187, which is about three miles east of Ypsilanti. From the exit, go one mile south to Textile Road, one mile west to Bunton Road, then one mile south to the campground. For reservations or more information, call 734/482-7722.

NIGHTLIFE

Ann Arbor is a great place for music. The city comes alive most nights, and especially on weekends, with dozens of bars and clubs offering live entertainment. In addition, the city offers a variety of theater and concert venues, mostly near the U-M campus. The State Street area has numerous small cafés that are popular evening gathering spots, particularly after concerts at one of the nearby theaters (**Hill Auditorium** and **Power Center** on the U-M campus, or the **Michigan Theater** on Liberty Street a block west of State Street).

One of the best and most venerable concert clubs is **The Ark**, 316 S. Main St., 734/761-1451, an acoustic-music mecca for the Midwest. The Ark spotlights the best local, regional, and national performers in folk, blues, bluegrass, and other acoustic genres.

A couple of outstanding jazz clubs also grace the city's night scene: the **Bird of Paradise**, 207 S. Ashley St., 734/662-8310, and **The Earle**, 121 W. Washington St., 734/994-0211.

3
LANSING

Lansing is truly the heart of Michigan, and not simply because it is the state capital. That just makes it the hub of state government. What makes Lansing the heart of Michigan is its unique blend of social, economic, political, and intellectual cultures.

At once urban, suburban, and rural, here business, labor, and farming communities meet. Lansing's atmosphere is casual, no-nonsense, and low-key, but it is also academic and can be competitive and intensely partisan.

Within the city are auto manufacturing plants that connect with the state's industrial southeast. That isn't surprising when you consider that Lansing was the home of Ransom Olds and his Oldsmobile. But a drive of less than 30 minutes from downtown will take you into verdant farmlands at the core of the state's strong agricultural economy.

Everything is close to Lansing. Drive 90 minutes east and you are deep in the urban world of metropolitan Detroit. Drive 90 minutes west and you are on the sandy shores of Lake Michigan. Drive 90 minutes north and you find the vast green forests and blue inland lakes that make northern Michigan a year-round haven for outdoor recreation. Even the Upper Peninsula is just a half day away.

That easy access and government offices draw people from all over the state. Michigan State University in East Lansing makes the area an important international research center as well and attracts visitors from all over the world.

LANSING

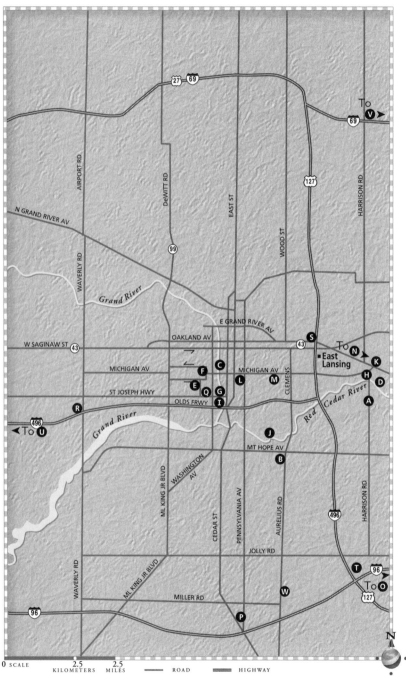

AIRPORT RD

DeWITT RD

EAST ST

HARRISON RD

27 69

To V 69

127

WOOD ST

N GRAND RIVER AV

WAVERLY RD

99

Grand River

E GRAND RIVER AV

W SAGINAW ST 43

OAKLAND AV

43 S

To N K

East Lansing

MICHIGAN AV

F C

MICHIGAN AV

L M

H D

CLEMENS

ST JOSEPH HWY

E

Q G

A

OLDS FRWY

I

496 R

U

To

Grand River

Red Cedar River

J

MT HOPE AV

B

ML KING JR BLVD

WASHINGTON AV

CEDAR ST

PENNSYLVANIA AV

AURELIUS RD

HARRISON RD

496

JOLLY RD

ML KING JR BLVD

T 96

To O

127

WAVERLY RD

MILLER RD

W

96

P

N

0 SCALE 2.5 2.5
KILOMETERS MILES ROAD HIGHWAY

A PERFECT DAY IN LANSING

Start with a tour of the Michigan State University campus in East Lansing. Take a lap—by car or bike—around West Circle Drive, with its Gothic-style dormitories, library, and the landmark Beaumont Tower, whose carillon has recently been restored. If the weather is nice, park near the administration building and stroll along the Red Cedar River, where you can watch and feed the ducks.

Drive south along Farm Lane through the center of campus and out into the lovely woodlots and experimental farms that stretch for several miles. Take Mount Hope Road or Jolly Road west into Lansing where they intersect Cedar Street, which will bring you back north into the downtown area. There you can tour the state capitol, spend a few hours browsing the exhibits at the Michigan Library and Historical Center, or walk through River Front Park, which stretches for three miles along both sides of the Grand River.

In the evening, consider a program at MSU's Abrams Planetarium or the Wharton Center for the Performing Arts. In addition to a regular schedule of university concerts and programs, the Wharton Center regularly hosts national touring companies of major theatrical productions such as *Phantom of the Opera*.

SIGHTS

- **O** Abrams Planetarium
- **O** Beal Botanical Gardens
- **O** Childen's Garden
- **B** Carl G. Fenner Arboretum
- **C** Impression 5 Science Center
- **D** Kresge Art Museum
- **E** Michigan Library and Historical Center
- **F** Michigan State Capitol
- **G** Michigan Women's Historical Center and Hall of Fame
- **H** MSU Museum
- **I** R. E. Olds Transportation Museum

SIGHTS (continued)

- **O** Riverfront Park
- **O** Potter Park and Zoo
- **A** Wharton Center for the Performing Arts

FOOD

- **K** Beggar's Banquet
- **L** Clara's
- **M** Emil's
- **A** State Room
- **N** Travelers Club International Restaurant and Tuba Museum

LODGING

- **O** Comfort Inn
- **K** East Lansing Marriott at University Place
- **P** Holiday Inn South
- **A** Kellogg Center
- **Q** Lansing Radisson Hotel
- **R** Lansing Sheraton Hotel
- **S** Quality Inn University Place
- **T** Red Roof Inn-East
- **U** Red Roof Inn-West

CAMPING

- **V** Hickory Lake Camping
- **W** Lansing Cottonwood Campground

Note: Items with the same letter are located in the same place.

SIGHTSEEING HIGHLIGHTS

★★★★ MICHIGAN LIBRARY AND HISTORICAL CENTER
717 W. Allegan Street, 517/373-3559

The center explains the state's social, cultural, political, and economic development using extensive displays of historical artifacts, photographs, and multimedia presentations. Many displays are visually dramatic, such as the giant lumberman's wheel that was used to haul logs out of the state's northern forests and a life-size replica of a copper mine passage. Video presentations on the state's early days give fascinating views of life in the mining and lumber camps of the nineteenth century. A snack area and museum store are located on the lower level. The building also houses the state library and state archives.

Details: Mon–Fri 9–4:30, Sat 10–4, Sun 1–5. Admission is free. (1–3 hours)

★★★★ MICHIGAN STATE CAPITOL
Michigan and Capitol Avenues, 517/373-2353

Lansing was designated Michigan's capital in 1847, after long and heated debate by the legislature was unable to produce agreement on anyplace else. The decision had the flavor of a bitter joke; at the time

THE CAPITOL OF MICHIGAN

Travel Michigan

Lansing was home to a sawmill and a single log cabin. The current capitol at Capitol Avenue and Michigan Avenue, dedicated in 1879 and the first state capitol designed to look like the U.S. Capitol, underwent a major restoration in the early 1990s.

Details: Tours every half hour Mon–Fri 9–4, Sat 10–3. Admission is free. (1–2 hours)

★★★ ABRAMS PLANETARIUM
Shaw and Farm Lanes, 517/355-4676

On the MSU campus, this planetarium features a variety of exhibits and programs on astronomy. It is small, with a 150-seat auditorium, but it has been popular for decades. The facility offers high-quality family entertainment that appeals to everyone's fascination with the night sky.

Details: Exhibit hall open Mon–Sat 8:30–noon and 1–4:30, Fri–Sat 7:30–10 and Sun 2–5. Planetarium shows Fri–Sat 8, Sun 2:30 and 4. Exhibit hall: free. Planetarium shows: $3 adults, $2.50 seniors and students with identification, $2 children under age 12. (1 hour)

★★★ BEAL BOTANICAL GARDENS
West Circle Drive, 517/355-9582

Founded in 1855 as the nation's first land-grant college, Michigan State University has always been deeply involved in agricultural science. It is no wonder, then, that the campus derives a tremendous amount of its beauty from growing things. At any time of the year it is a joy to walk, bike, or drive about the campus and observe the abundant plant life. West Circle Drive is home to huge old hardwood trees mixed with broad grassy spaces. Here too you'll find the Beal Gardens, which offer a variety of seasonal displays.

Details: Between the MSU Library and the IM Sports Building. Call for information about the plantings or guided group tours. (1 hour)

★★★ CHILDREN'S GARDEN
Bogue Street

The Children's Garden is a delightful place to spend an hour with small children in good weather. In addition to lovely flowers and other plants that will appeal to adults, the garden has a variety of paths, mazes, waterspouts, and noisemakers that keep youngsters entertained.

Details: South of Wilson Rd. on the west side of Bogue St., MSU campus. Open daylight hours. (1 hour)

★★★ IMPRESSION 5 SCIENCE CENTER
200 Museum Drive, 517/485-8116

Next door to the Olds Museum is the center, a hands-on museum aimed especially at children and their parents. Displays cover such topics as physics, energy, chemistry, biology, medicine, and computers. But fun is as big a part of the experience as learning. A giant bubble maker, satellite dishes that let you whisper to friends 50 feet away, a giant walk-through heart, and a chemistry lab that lets kids experiment with their own goopy formulas are just a few of the activities that spin fun out of scientific concepts. The museum also has a gift shop and a deli.

Details: Mon–Sat 10–5, Sun noon–5. $4.50 adults, $3 seniors and ages 3–17. (1–2 hours)

★★★ KRESGE ART MUSEUM
Auditorium Road east of Farm Lane, 517/355-7631

This museum on the MSU campus houses changing exhibits that cover more than 5,000 years of art history. The collection includes art from a wide range of cultures, including Greek and medieval pieces. Modern art is another strong point, especially American works from the 1960s and '70s.

Details: Sept–May Mon–Wed and Fri 9:30–4:30, Thu noon–8, Sat–Sun 1–4; June–July Mon–Fri 11–4, Sat–Sun 1–4. Tours available by appointment. Admission is free. (1 hour)

★★★ MICHIGAN STATE UNIVERSITY MUSEUM
West Circle Drive, 517/355-2370

The museum features full dinosaur skeletons and a variety of exhibits on cultural and natural history. Dioramas on Michigan logging camps, copper mines, and forts illustrate some of the forces that shaped Michigan's early history, while other exhibits examine various natural habitats of North America, woodlands Indian culture, and the state's wildlife and geology. Artifacts from world cultures—from Africa to Asia to South America—also are on display. Next to the museum is Beaumont Tower with its 47-bell carillon, which stands on the site of one of the university's original buildings.

Details: Mon–Fri 9–5, Sat 10–5, Sun 1–5. Donations accepted. (1 hour)

★★★ R. E. OLDS TRANSPORTATION MUSEUM
240 Museum Drive, 517/372-0422

Ransom E. Olds and his Oldsmobile—one of the first truly practical cars—made Lansing one of the top auto-producing cities in America at the beginning of the twentieth century. The Olds Museum, at the south end of River Front Park, documents the history of the transportation industry in the Lansing area. Displays include a variety of antique vehicles, including the first Oldsmobile, built in 1897.
Details: Mon–Sat 10–5, Sun noon–5. $4 adults; $2 seniors, children ages 6–17, and students with identification; $8 families. (1–2 hours)

★★ CARL G. FENNER ARBORETUM
2020 E. Mount Hope Road, 517/483-4224
The arboretum has a nature center, nature trails, and an herb garden. The center offers displays on native birds, reptiles, amphibians, and the environment. Picnicking is permitted, and the arboretum hosts a Maple Syrup Festival in March and an Apple Butter Festival in October.
Details: Grounds open 8–dusk. Nature center open spring–fall Tues–Fri 9–4, Sat 10–5, Sun 11–5; winter Sat–Sun 11–4. Admission is free. (1–2 hours)

★★ MICHIGAN WOMEN'S HISTORICAL CENTER AND HALL OF FAME
213 W. Main Street, 517/484-1880
The center honors the lives and achievements of Michigan women and recognizes their contributions to the state's history and culture. It includes a series of rotating historical exhibits that describe the accomplishments of many outstanding women, and a gallery that displays the work of notable Michigan women artists and photographers. Some of the art and photography, as well as a variety of other gifts, are available for sale.
Details: Wed–Fri noon–5, Sat noon–4, Sun 2–4. $2.50 adults, $2 age 60 and over, $1 students. (30 minutes)

★★ POTTER PARK AND ZOO
1301 S. Pennsylvania Avenue, 517/483-4222
The park is a pleasant family-outing spot in good weather, with picnicking and playground facilities and a small zoo that includes primates, rhinos, lions, kangaroos, penguins, farm animals, and an aviary. In summer, canoe rentals are available, as are pony and camel rides.

Details: *Daily 9–7. $2.50 adults, $1 ages 3–15; vehicle admission $1.50. (1–2 hours)*

★★ RIVERFRONT PARK

A three-mile stretch of green space and boardwalk, the park follows both sides of the Grand River through the downtown area, from just north of I-496 to North Street. A pleasant place for a jog or stroll, it is one of the best urban parks in the state.

Details: *1 hour.*

★★ WHARTON CENTER FOR THE PERFORMING ARTS
Bogue Street and Wilson Road, 517/432-2000

In addition to university plays, concerts, lectures, and other programs, the center regularly hosts touring Broadway shows, concerts, and other attractions. The Great Hall was site of one of the 1992 presidential debates.

Details: *On the east side of the MSU campus. For schedule and ticket information call 517/432-2000. For free backstage tours call 517/353-1982. (1 hour)*

FITNESS AND RECREATION

The Michigan State University campus is the best spot for walking, jogging, in-line skating, or bicycling. The campus has miles of sidewalks and bike paths. One of the most popular routes follows the sidewalks that line either side of the Red Cedar River as it winds its way through campus, stretching from Jenison Fieldhouse on the west to Bogue Street on the east, a distance of nearly two miles one way. Bridges spanning the river at regular intervals make shorter loops easy to arrange. Long-distance runners or bikers can head south from the main campus along Farm Lane into the scenic farmland used by the university for experimental agriculture.

FOOD

Plenty of good restaurants fill the Lansing–East Lansing area, but few are truly remarkable. An exception is **Beggar's Banquet**, 218 Abbott Rd., 517/351-4573. A fixture of the East Lansing scene since the early 1970s, Beggar's specializes in fine American cuisine, with dinners in the $10 to $20 range and lunches under $10. Reservations are suggested, especially on weekends. Also in East Lansing, on the MSU campus, is the **State Room** restaurant at Kellogg

Center, on Harrison Road just south of Michigan Avenue, 517/432-4000. The center is a showplace conference center for the university, which has a School of Hotel, Restaurant, and Institutional Management. The food, which includes steaks as well as lighter fish and chicken entrées (not to mention an award-winning barbecued shrimp appetizer), is excellent, and dinners cost $10 to $20.

A bit farther east, in downtown Okemos, is a truly intriguing eatery called the **Travelers Club International Restaurant and Tuba Museum**, 2138 Hamilton, 517/349-1701. If you think the name is a mouthful, try the food. One of the most diverse menus you're likely to come across at a single restaurant offers African, Asian, Indian, Middle Eastern, Caribbean, and American (North, Central, and South) dishes on a daily basis with a series of regional specials that rotates through the year. The ambiance is suitably quirky, too; the walls are festooned with a collection of 50 or more tubas, sousaphones, baritones, and French horns. Dinners are in the $10 to $20 range, and lunches are under $10.

In Lansing proper, one of the more interesting restaurants is **Clara's**, 637 E. Michigan Ave., 517/372-7120, a casual spot with an extensive American menu in a renovated historic train depot. Meals are in the $10 to $20 range.

For excellent, down-to-earth Italian food in the cozy atmosphere of a traditional neighborhood café, try **Emil's**, 2012 E. Michigan Ave., 517/482-4430. The restaurant has been a local institution for decades. Dinners are in the $10 to $20 range, and lunches are under $10.

LODGING

Between state government and the university, the Lansing area draws thousands of visitors daily. To accommodate these people there is an ample supply of hotels and motels, most representing the familiar national chains. At the upper end of the cost scale is the **East Lansing Marriott at University Place**, 300 M.A.C., 517/337-4440, about a block from the MSU campus, with rooms for $84 to $135 a night. On the west side of town is the **Lansing Sheraton Hotel**, 925 S. Creyts Rd., 517/323-7100. The Sheraton is about four miles from downtown Lansing, off I-496 at the Creyts Road exit. Rooms range from $102 to $138 per night.

The **Lansing Radisson Hotel**, 111 N. Grand Ave., 517/482-0188, is a bit less expensive, with rooms at $79 to $125 a night. The Radisson's location, just two blocks east of the capitol, is convenient, too.

Mid-priced options are readily available along the main arteries into the area. The most centrally located is MSU's **Kellogg Center**, on Harrison Road just south of Michigan Avenue, 517/432-4000. This university conference center has rooms that range from $79 to $207 a night.

The **Comfort Inn** of East Lansing, 2209 University Park, 517/349-8700, for example, is at the Okemos Road exit off I-96, a major access point to the MSU campus for traffic coming from the east. Room rates range from $65 to $120 a night. On the southern rim of Lansing is the **Holiday Inn South**, 6820 S. Cedar St., 517/694-8123, with rooms from $80 to $103 a night. The Holiday Inn is just off I-96 at the Cedar Street exit.

Right on the border between Lansing and East Lansing is the **Quality Inn-University Place**, 3121 E. Grand River Ave., 517/351-1440, with rooms ranging from $69 to $84 a night.

On the inexpensive side, you'll find a pair of Red Roof Inns. The **Red Roof Inn-East** is at 3615 Dunkel Road at the intersection of U.S. 127 and I-496, 517/332-2575. **The Red Roof Inn-West**, 7412 W. Saginaw Hwy., 517/321-7246, is on the far west rim of the I-96 loop around Lansing, at exit 93B. Both have rooms in the $40 to $72 range.

CAMPING

Campgrounds are sparse in the greater Lansing area, and those available are private. The closest to the capital city is the **Lansing Cottonwood Campground**, 5339 S. Aurelius Rd., 517/393-3200, which is open from May 1 through October. The campground has nature trails and fishing, and, for a fee, canoes, kayaks, and paddleboats. Rates begin at $13.50 a night for two, with a $2 to $3 charge per extra person.

Northeast of Lansing, along I-69 at Perry, is **Hickory Lake Camping**, 11433 S. Beardslee Rd., 517/625-3113, a private 108-site campground. It's open from May 1 through mid-October and charges $15 a night for five, $1 per extra person.

4
BATTLE CREEK

Around the nation, Battle Creek is known as the Cereal City, for its long and close connection with companies like Kellogg's, Post, and Ralston Purina. But the area's history is more than nutritional. In the decades before the Civil War, the city and surrounding region were a center of intense abolitionist activity. In fact, an 1846 incident in which white residents of nearby Marshall saved an escaped slave and his family from the agents of a Kentucky slaveholder attracted national attention and fueled a controversy that led to passage of the Fugitive Slave Act in 1850. The area's most famous former resident, ex-slave and abolition activist Sojourner Truth, is buried in Battle Creek's Oak Hill Cemetery.

Today the Battle Creek–Kalamazoo area is a bustling combination of urban and rural activity. Kalamazoo, with more than 80,000 residents, is the larger of the two cities and is home to Western Michigan University, the state's fourth-largest public university. Battle Creek is home to more than 53,000 people. Together, the cities offer a wealth of entertainment and recreation.

The local atmosphere is also influenced by the many small towns and quiet rural areas that cover much of the region. The cities are large enough to offer variety, and the countryside is close enough to provide quick access to nature and tranquility. The area's location along Michigan's main east-west route—I-94, which connects Detroit and Chicago—makes access to those larger metropolitan regions quick and easy.

BATTLE CREEK

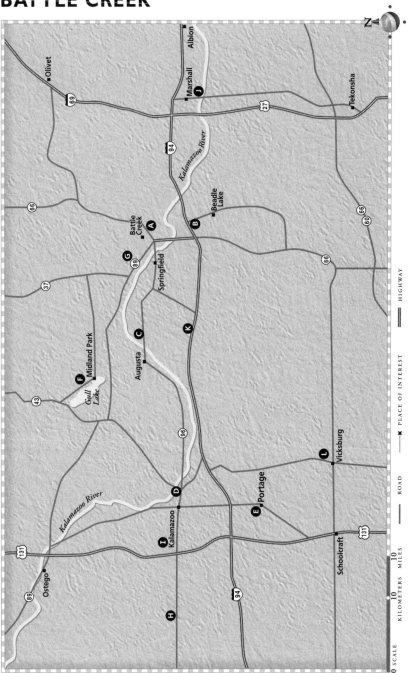

A PERFECT DAY IN BATTLE CREEK AND KALAMAZOO

Spend a few morning hours at the Gilmore Classic Car Museum in Kalamazoo for a taste of Michigan's automotive history, then take a short jaunt west on I-94 to Paw Paw for a taste of something more potable at one of the town's two wineries. You can tour the St. Julian Winery—Michigan's biggest—and have lunch at the adjoining Italian restaurant.

In the afternoon, head back east toward Battle Creek to spend some time exploring the Binder Park Zoo or gazing at birds and other natural wonders at the Kellogg Bird Sanctuary. Then take a quick spin over to the nearby small town of Marshall to see the lovely historic homes and stop for dinner at Schuler's, a regional culinary icon.

SIGHTSEEING HIGHLIGHTS

★★★★ **BINDER PARK ZOO**
7400 Division Drive, 616/979-1351
One of Battle Creek's most remarkable assets is this small but beautiful zoo designed to make you feel like you are encountering the animals in their natural settings. The zoo features a surprisingly large selection of exotic and endangered species, such as Chinese red

---

SIGHTS

- **Ⓐ** Art Center of Battle Creek
- **Ⓑ** Binder Park Zoo
- **Ⓒ** Fort Custer National Cemetery
- **Ⓓ** Gilmore Classic Car Museum
- **Ⓔ** Kalamazoo Aviation History Museum
- **Ⓕ** Kellogg Bird Sanctuary
- **Ⓖ** Leila Arboretum
- **Ⓗ** Michigan Fisheries Interpretive Center

FOOD

- **Ⓞ** Bill Knapp's
- **Ⓘ** Chianti Players Pub
- **Ⓐ** Clara's on the River
- **Ⓓ** Great Lakes Shipping Company
- **Ⓓ** Old Country Buffet
- **Ⓐ** Porter's Steak House
- **Ⓙ** Schuler's
- **Ⓓ** Webster's

LODGING

- **Ⓖ** Appletree Inn
- **Ⓓ** Hall House
- **Ⓐ** Motel 6
- **Ⓙ** National House Inn
- **Ⓐ** Old Lamplighter

LODGING (continued)

- **Ⓐ** McCamly Plaza Hotel
- **Ⓓ** Radisson Plaza Hotel at Kalamazoo Center
- **Ⓘ** Red Roof Inns
- **Ⓓ** Stuart Avenue Inn

CAMPING

- **Ⓚ** Fort Custer Recreation Area
- **Ⓛ** Oak Shores Resort Campground
- **Ⓒ** Shady Bend Campground
- **Ⓙ** Tri-Lake Trails Campground

Note: Items with the same letter are located in the same place.

---

pandas, Mexican wolves, Formosan sika deer, ring-tailed lemurs, and a Siberian lynx. The Miller Children's Zoo also offers a petting zoo and exhibits of domestic animals.

Details: *Apr 26–Oct 13 Mon–Fri 9–5, Sat and holidays 9–6, Sun 11–6; open Wed evenings in summer. $5.45 adults, $4.45 age 65 and over, $3.45 ages 3–12. (2–3 hours)*

★★★★ **KELLOGG BIRD SANCTUARY**
12685 E. C Avenue, 616/671-2510
About halfway between Battle Creek and Kalamazoo, and a little north of both, is a wonderful bird sanctuary established by cereal magnate W. K. Kellogg in 1928. The sanctuary is on the east shore of (appropriately) Gull Lake, and today is part of an experimental biological station operated by Michigan State University. The facility has an observation deck, a 1.5-mile paved walk with interpretive signs, and a variety of displays. You can see dozens of different species, especially waterfowl, including birds of prey, wild turkeys, and rare trumpeter swans.

Details: *May–Oct daily 9–8, Nov–April daily 9–5. $3 adults, $2 age 65 and over, $1 ages 2–12. (1 hour)*

★★★ **ART CENTER OF BATTLE CREEK**
265 E. Emmett Street, 616/962-9511
Battle Creek's Art Center is small but intriguing, focusing primarily (though not exclusively) on established and emerging Michigan artists. The 190-item permanent collection includes paintings, sculptures, photographs, watercolors, and folk art from as far back as 1894.

Every six weeks the center mounts a new rotating exhibition; often including the work of nationally and internationally known artists as well as Michigan artists. Recent exhibits have explored environmental sculpture, the work of Native American masters, interpretations of nature, and a children's art show. An interactive, hands-on children's gallery offers activities that are thematically related to the current exhibit. The center also has an art library with files on Michigan artists that are open to the public.

Details: *Sept–July Tue–Sat 10–5, Thu 10–7, Sun noon–5. Donation requested. (30 minutes)*

★★★ **GILMORE CLASSIC CAR MUSEUM**
6865 Hickory Road, Kalamazoo, 616/671-5089

Car Collector magazine named the Gilmore one of the 10 best automotive museums in the country, and it isn't hard to see why. The museum's collection includes more than 130 antique, classic, and collector cars, bearing such venerable nameplates as Rolls Royce, Packard, and Lincoln. There are Stanley Steamers, Cadillacs, and Model-T Fords, too, as well as a narrow-gauge steam locomotive and a double-decker London bus. Exhibits range from an 1899 Locomobile to a Cadillac designed to explore styling concepts for the year 2002. Also on display are a collection of classic hood ornaments and an assortment of colorful car badges. The museum occupies a lovely 90-acre rural site, with the cars displayed in six large barns that are themselves historic structures.

Details: *May–Oct daily 10–5. $6 adults, $5 age 62 and over, $3 ages 7–15. (1 1/2–2 hours)*

★★★ **KALAMAZOO AVIATION HISTORY MUSEUM**
3101 E. Milham Road, Kalamazoo, 616/382-6555
This museum includes planes used in the Korean and Vietnam Wars, as well as rare aircraft—most of which still fly—from before World War II. Flying demonstrations are offered at 2 daily from May through September, depending on the weather.

Details: *Summer Mon–Sat 9–6, Wed 9–8, Sun noon–6; fall–spring Mon–Sat 9–5, Sun noon–5. $10 adults, $8 age 60 and over, $5 ages 6–15, children under 5 free. (1 hour)*

★★★ **MICHIGAN FISHERIES INTERPRETIVE CENTER**
Fish Hatchery Road, Kalamazoo, 616/668-2876
The center includes exhibits on the life cycle of fish and on some of the record fish caught in the state. Other attractions are a slide show, a hatchery pool, and a pond where visitors can view and feed fish.

Details: *Six miles west of U.S. 131. Mon–Sat 9–5, Sun noon–8. Admission is free. (1 hour)*

★★ **FORT CUSTER NATIONAL CEMETERY**
15501 Dickman Road, Augusta, 616/731-4164
A 770-acre portion of Fort Custer was dedicated as a national cemetery in 1984 to honor military veterans from the Midwest. The lovely cemetery grounds include the burial sites for several German World War II prisoners and the grave of an unknown soldier. The cemetery

entrance is lined with 152 American flags, and nearby is a display of the 50 state flags.

Details: *Daily dawn–dusk, cemetery office open daily 8–4:30.* *(1 hour)*

★★ LEILA ARBORETUM
W. Michigan Avenue and 20th Street, Battle Creek, 616/969-0270

For a leisurely stroll in an attractive wooded setting, visit Battle Creek's Leila Arboretum. This botanical garden covers 72 acres and includes more than 3,000 species of trees and shrubs. Many of the plantings date back to the 1920s, when the arboretum was created and patterned after European gardens. The arboretum includes a beautiful collection of flowering ornamental trees and many varieties of perennials and other flowers. One special area is devoted entirely to rhododendrons.

Details: *Daily dawn–dusk. Admission is free. (1 hour)*

FITNESS AND RECREATION

Probably the best spot in the area for outdoor exercise and activity—winter or summer—is the **Fort Custer Recreation Area**, eight miles west of Battle Creek on Highway 96. The 2,962-acre park has 3.5 miles of marked trails that circle three small lakes; the trails are reserved for cross-country skiers after the snow flies but are excellent hiking trails when the ground is clear. Several more miles of trails—available to horses and snowmobiles as well as skiers and hikers—wind through the park's heavily wooded grounds.

The park's largest lake, **Eagle Lake**, has a good swimming beach and picnic area, and all the park's lakes allow no-wake boating and fishing. If biking or in-line skating is your pleasure, an extensive web of paved roads and bike paths within the park provides ample opportunities for both.

FOOD

The area's most widely known and loved culinary institution is in Marshall. It is **Schuler's**, 115 S. Eagle St., 616/781-0600, a historic restaurant that serves an American menu in an Old World atmosphere. The ambiance is warm and comfortable and dinners cost $15 to $30; lunches are mostly in the $10 to $15 range.

A bit more elegant—and costly—is **Porter's Steak House**, 50 Capital

Ave. S.W., on the 16th floor of McCamly Plaza Hotel, Battle Creek, 616/963-9686. Dinner here runs $20 to $30. Another fine-dining option is **Webster's**, 100 W. Michigan Ave., in Kalamazoo's Radisson Plaza Hotel, 616/343-4444. Dinners cost $15 to $30.

For interesting atmosphere in Battle Creek, visit **Clara's on the River**, 44 N. McCamly St., 616/963-0966. This restaurant features an American menu and casual dining in a remodeled historic train depot. Dinners cost between $15 and $25.

Kalamazoo has numerous mid-priced restaurants. You might try the **Chianti Players Pub**, 4210 Stadium Dr., 616/372-7177, a casual place that features Italian dishes, steaks, and seafood in the $10 to $20 range. Or try the **Great Lakes Shipping Company**, 4525 W. KL Ave., 616/375-3650, which offers steak and seafood in an informal, nautical setting, with dinners priced from $15 to $25.

For dinners under $10, try **Bill Knapp's**, 2810 Capital Ave. S.W., Battle Creek, 616/979-2101; or the **Old Country Buffet**, 5220 W. Main St., Kalamazoo, 616/344-6212.

LODGING

The Battle Creek-Kalamazoo area has a good selection of bed-and-breakfast inns. Among the nicest of these is Marshall's **National House Inn**, 102 S. Parkview Ave., 616/781-7374, in a restored 1835 inn on Fountain Circle on the west edge of downtown. Rooms cost $64 to $130 a night, and the inn offers a smoke-free environment.

In Kalamazoo, **Hall House**, 106 Thompson St., 616/343-2500, is another historic bed-and-breakfast in a restored 1923 residential home, with rooms ranging from $59 to $140 a night. The **Stuart Avenue Inn**, 229 Stuart Ave., 616/342-0230, offers 17 rooms in two lovely Victorian homes with English gardens in the city's historic district. The inn is smoke-free, and rooms cost $45 to $150 a night.

Battle Creek's contribution to the historic bed-and-breakfast scene is the **Old Lamplighter**, 276 Capital Ave. N.E., 616/963-2603. The inn has a smoke-free policy, and rooms cost $60 to $100 a night.

If you prefer a conventional hotel, the **Radisson Plaza Hotel at Kalamazoo Center**, 100 W. Michigan Ave., 616/343-3333, offers luxury accommodations with room rates of $90 to $300 a night. The hotel's lobby is located in a mall for your shopping convenience. The **McCamly Plaza Hotel**, 50 Capital Ave. S.W., 616/963-7050, also is at the luxury end of the spectrum, with a heated indoor pool, sauna, whirlpool, and rates of $89 to $119 a night.

SIDE TRIP: MARSHALL

About 12 miles east of Battle Creek, the small town of Marshall boasts the state's largest collection of Gothic Revival and Greek Revival homes from the 1840s and 1850s. The downtown area has adopted a Victorian theme to complement the tourist appeal of the local homes, and many good antique shops fill the city.

At the Honolulu House, the Marshall Area Chamber of Commerce (109 East Michigan Avenue), or at many of the local inns and shops, you can get a map that outlines a self-guided tour of the town. Marshall also has several quaint and romantic bed-and-breakfast inns for those who want to luxuriate in the nostalgic atmosphere.

Less expensive accommodations are to be had in Battle Creek at the **Appletree Inn**, 4786 Beckley Rd., 616/979-3561, which includes health club privileges with its room rates of $41 to $110 a night; and the **Motel 6**, 4775 Beckley Rd., 616/979-1141, with nightly rates of $34 to $40.

Kalamazoo offers economy seekers a pair of **Red Roof Inns** on the east side of town at 3701 Cork Street, 616/382-6350, where rooms cost $46 to $66 a night; and on the west side at 5425 West Michigan Avenue, 616/375-7400, where rooms cost $38 to $59.

CAMPING

About midway between Battle Creek and Kalamazoo, near Augusta, is the **Fort Custer Recreation Area**, 5163 W. Fort Custer Dr. (see Fitness and Recreation), 616/731-4200 or 800/543-2937, which includes a public campground with 112 sites. Rates are $12 per night, and the campground is open year-round. Note that the park has no showers and facilities are limited in winter.

Also at Augusta is the **Shady Bend Campground**, 15320 Augusta Dr., 616/731-4503, a private facility with 62 sites. Nightly rates are $16 for two, with a fee of $1 to $2 per extra person. The campground is open from May 1 to October 15.

The **Tri-Lake Trails Campground**, 219 Perrett Rd., 616/781-2297, is a private campground near Marshall with 272 sites. Open from May 1 to October 1, Tri-Lake Trails offers miniature golf, shuffleboard, swimming, and a playground. Rates are $15 per night for four people, with a fee of $1 for each additional person.

South of Kalamazoo at Vicksburg is the **Oak Shores Resort Campground**, 13496 S. 28th St., 616/649-4689, a private facility with 117 campsites. The campground has a pool, recreation room, and a playground, and is open from May 1 to October 1. Nightly rates are about $20 for two, with a fee of $1 to $2 per extra person; children ages 3 to 18 pay 50 cents a day.

One of the most intriguing houses you'll find in Marshall is the Honolulu House, just off Fountain Circle at 107 North Kalamazoo Street, built in 1860 by State Supreme Court Justice Abner Pratt after his two-year stint as U.S. consul to the Hawaiian Islands. The house is an exotic mix of Victorian and island styles, with a raised veranda, 15-foot ceilings, elaborate wall murals, and a pagoda-topped tower. It's now a museum, open from noon to five daily May through October. Admission is $3 adults, $2.50 seniors, and $2 ages 12 to 18. Call 800/877-5163 for more information.

GRAND RAPIDS

Grand Rapids is Michigan's Second City, the main hub of economic and political activity in the western half of the Lower Peninsula. It is a major industrial center, most noted for the production of furniture, though it is also the home base of the Amway direct sales empire.

Politically and culturally it is the center of a staunchly conservative region, deeply influenced by its Dutch Reformed roots and intensely proud of its history as the home of President Gerald R. Ford throughout his political career. In a way, the city and the surrounding region mark a divide in the state's orientation. East of Grand Rapids, the state seems to face toward Detroit. But from Grand Rapids south and west, the influence of Chicago—which is about as far away as Detroit—begins to dominate.

The city has seen a lot of growth in recent years, mainly in hi-tech development. Much of that has been connected with the engineering education center established by Grand Valley State University. Grand Rapids also is the gateway to the popular tourist region that stretches along the Lake Michigan shore from Saugatuck north to Ludington.

A PERFECT DAY IN GRAND RAPIDS

Start with a tour of the Gerald R. Ford Museum and perhaps a stroll around the modern downtown district or along the Grand River. In the afternoon visit the

Travel Michigan

Frederik Meijer Gardens to view the exotic plants and excellent bronze sculptures, or walk through the Van Andel Museum Center for a fascinating look at the city's furniture-manufacturing heritage.

If you are adventurous and the weather is nice, take the 30- to 40-minute drive out to the Lake Michigan shore at either Grand Haven or Holland. There are state parks on the shore just outside both cities.

SIGHTSEEING HIGHLIGHTS

★★★★ GERALD R. FORD MUSEUM
303 Pearl Street N.W., 616/451-9263

Although he has long since retired to sunny southern California, Gerald Ford remains Grand Rapids' favorite son, and this museum is a tribute to the former president and longtime congressman. A series of displays explores Ford's life and public career, highlighted by a 28-minute movie, *Gerald Ford—The Presidency Restored.* Exhibits feature personal items from Ford's childhood and his college years at the University of Michigan, where he was a star football player. The museum also holds a replica of the White House's Oval Office as it looked while Ford was president.

> *Details: Daily 9–5. $3 ages 16–64, $2 age 65 and over, under age 16 free. (1–2 hours)*

★★★ FREDERIK MEIJER GARDENS
3411 Bradford N.E., 616/957-1580

The gardens are actually a combination indoor-outdoor complex that includes a five-story, 15,000-square-foot conservatory as well as ponds, wooded areas, and a variety of flower gardens. The conservatory houses exotic plants from all over the world. Some display areas adopt particular themes, such as the Victorian Gardens Parlor, which focuses on the kinds of plants that were popular among the wealthy during the Victorian era. Interspersed among the plants—indoors and out—are sculptures by internationally known artists, most notably Marshall Fredericks. The gardens also include a café and a gift shop that features tools, books, and even specialty plants.

> *Details: June–Aug Mon–Sat 9–5 (Thu 9–9), Sun noon–5. $5 adults, $4 age 65 and over, $2 ages 5–13. (1 1/2–2 hours)*

★★★ GRAND RAPIDS ART MUSEUM
155 Division Street N., 616/459-4676 or 616/459-4677

GRAND RAPIDS

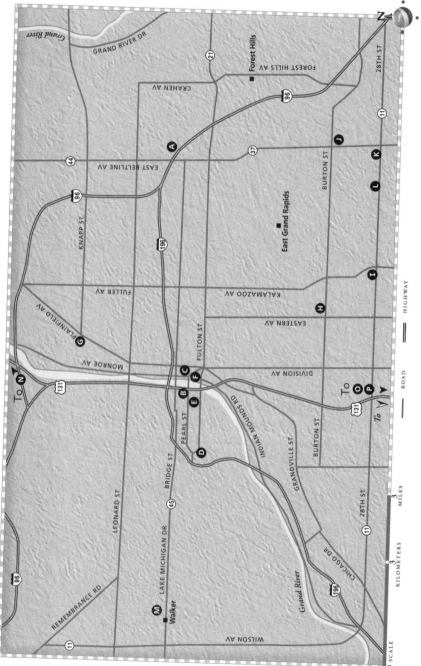

Specializing in nineteenth- and twentieth-century works, the museum collections include sculptures, paintings, photographs, and decorative arts from such artists as Alexander Calder and Max Pechstein. A children's gallery offers hands-on exhibits.

Details: Tue–Sun 11–6, Fri 11–9. $3 adults, $2 seniors and students with identification, $1 ages 6–17. (1–2 hours)

★★★ VAN ANDEL MUSEUM CENTER
272 Pearl Street N.W., 616/456-3977

This museum examines the history and heritage of the Grand Rapids area, with exhibits that include replicas of an 1890s city street and a furniture factory from the early twentieth century. Among other exhibits are the skeleton of a 76-foot finback whale, a working carousel, and a planetarium.

Details: Daily 9–5. $5 adults, $4 age 62 and over, $2 ages 3–17, planetarium charges an additional $1.50 for daytime shows and $5 for evening shows, carousel rides 50 cents. (1–2 hours)

★★ JOHN BALL PARK ZOO
I-196 and Highway 45, 616/336-4300 or 616/336-4301

This zoo is medium in size but distinctive in appearance and atmosphere, built around a large hill with a 60-foot waterfall. It features exhibits that replicate the environments of a northern Michigan stream, the seacoast of the Pacific Northwest, and the rocky

---

SIGHTS
- Ⓐ Frederik Meijer Gardens
- Ⓑ Gerald R. Ford Museum
- Ⓒ Grand Rapids Art Museum
- Ⓓ John Ball Park Zoo
- Ⓔ Van Andel Museum Center

FOOD
- Ⓕ 1913 at the Plaza
- Ⓖ Bill Knapp's
- Ⓓ Canal Street Grill
- Ⓒ Charley's Crab
- Ⓕ Cygnus
- Ⓗ Great Lakes Shipping Company
- Ⓘ Old Country Buffet
- Ⓕ Schnitzelbank
- Ⓙ Seoul Garden

LODGING
- Ⓕ Amway Grand Plaza
- Ⓚ Comfort Inn
- Ⓔ Days Inn-Downtown
- Ⓛ Holiday Inn-Airport East
- Ⓜ Motel 6
- Ⓝ Swan Inn

CAMPING
- Ⓞ Dome World Campground
- Ⓟ Woodchip Campground

Note: Items with the same letter are located in the same place.

---

seashores of southernmost South America where penguins roam. Africa-oriented exhibits focus on zebras, antelopes, and other animals of the savannah, and on the chimps and monkeys of the African forests. One exhibit area enables visitors to view nocturnal animals like bush babies and foxes in darkened conditions.

Details: *Daily 10–6. $3.50 ages 14–62, $2 age 63 and over and ages 5–13, free to all Dec–Feb. (1–2 hours)*

FITNESS AND RECREATION

If you're looking for a pleasant place to walk or jog, try **Comstock Riverside Park** on the city's north side, near the junction of I-96 and Highway 131. Between Memorial Day and Labor Day, **AJ's Family Water Park**, 4441 28th St. S.E., 616/940-0400, offers a wave pool, water slides, play areas, miniature golf, and a video arcade. The park is open daily from 11 to 8; water activities are open from Memorial Day to Labor Day. Admission is $13 for anyone over 48 inches tall, $11 for anyone shorter. Those over age 65 or under age 2 are admitted free.

FOOD

As you might expect in a city as determinedly Middle American as Grand Rapids, local restaurants tend toward standard American fare. You won't find a lot of exceptional ethnic restaurants, a bit surprising for a city this large, until you consider the relatively homogenous local culture.

Despite the limited scope, however, there are a number of good options in a variety of price ranges. For elegant dining, try one of the restaurants at the Amway Grand Plaza Hotel, 616/774-2000, on Pearl Street at Monroe Street—**Cygnus** or **1913 at the Plaza**. Cygnus offers a rooftop dining room with entertainment and dancing, and is the more expensive of the two. 1913 at the Plaza, fashioned in early-1900s decor, also offers fine dining, with meals in the $30 range. Several other restaurants at the hotel, such as the **Canal Street Grill**, offer good meals at more moderate prices.

If seafood is your preference, try **Charley's Crab**, 63 Market St. S.W., 616/459-2500. The atmosphere is casual, with a children's menu and Sunday brunch available, as well as a cocktail lounge and entertainment. Meals run $15 to $25. Another notable Grand Rapids seafood restaurant with meals in the $15 to $25 range is the **Great Lakes Shipping Company**, 2455 Burton St. S.E., 616/949-9440.

For good low-priced food, try **Bill Knapp's**, 3100 Plainfield Rd. N.E.,

---

616/361-7309, or the **Old Country Buffet**, 3545 28th St. S.E., 616/957-0042, both of which offer dinner for less than $10.

Two ethnic eateries are **Schnitzelbank**, 342 Jefferson Ave. S.E., 616/459-9527, and **Seoul Garden**, 2409 E. Beltline, 616/956-1522, in suburban Kentwood. Schnitzelbank is a casual German-style restaurant with an Old World atmosphere. Dinner costs $10 to $20, and some American dishes are available for the gastronomically timid. Seoul Garden offers a variety of Korean and Chinese dishes, with dinners in the $10 to $15 range.

LODGING

Grand Rapids' premier hotel is the **Amway Grand Plaza**, Pearl St. at Monroe St., 616/774-2000, a 30-story downtown tower with an elegant atmosphere. It has 682 rooms, a restaurant, and extensive exercise facilities including a pool, saunas, lighted tennis courts, a racquetball court, a squash court, and an exercise room. Rates start at $99 a night and go up to $365 a night. A few blocks away is the **Days Inn-Downtown**, 310 Pearl St. N.W., 616/235-7611. Rates range from $63 to $90 a night.

A number of moderately priced inns are available in Kentwood, on the southeast side of Grand Rapids. Try the **Comfort Inn**, 4155 28th St. S.E., 616/957-2080, where rates range from $69 to $89 a night; or the **Holiday Inn-Airport East**, 3333 28th St. S.E., 616/949-9222, with rates running from $89 to $99 a night.

The economically minded might want to stay in Walker on Grand Rapids' northwest side, where the **Motel 6**, 777 Three Mile Rd., 616/784-9375, offers rooms for $30 to $36 a night. Another low-priced motel is in Comstock Park, just north of Grand Rapids. The **Swann Inn**, 5182 Alpine Ave., 616/784-1224, has rooms that range from $40 to $65 a night.

CAMPING

The nearest camping is available at a pair of private campgrounds at Byron Center, about 12 miles south of downtown Grand Rapids. **Dome World Campground**, 400 84th St. S.W., 616/878-1518, is open May through September, with 100 sites and a nightly charge of $18 to $20 for two adults and two children. In addition to a heated pool and a playground, the facility offers a variety of activities on a fee basis, such as miniature golf, an indoor driving range, batting cages, and go-carts.

Woodchip Campground, 7501 Burlingame S.W., 616/878-9050, offers 97 sites with a heated pool, playground, basketball court, and shuffleboard court. The campground is open May through September and charges $17 per night.

A 30- to 45-minute drive puts you within range a variety of private and state-park campgrounds on the Lake Michigan shore at Holland and Muskegon (see Chapter 6).

6
THE WESTERN SHORE

Michigan's western shore is famous for its magnificent dune beaches along Lake Michigan. The warm sand and mild lake waters set the relaxed atmosphere for a region of small towns and summer vacationers.

Western Michigan was dominated early by the lumber industry. Its great pine forests were felled to build homes and businesses in booming cities like Chicago and Detroit, not to mention thousands of smaller towns and villages across the Midwest. Not far behind was the tourism industry, as the increasingly affluent upper crust who occupied many of those new houses in the aforementioned booming cities began to look for a summer retreat from the urban swelter.

Michigan towns all along the Lake Michigan shore attracted thousands of summer residents, especially from the Chicago area. Saugatuck, for example, became known as an art colony after a summer art school linked to the Chicago Institute of Art was opened in 1910. Given the miles of windswept sand and sparkling blue water, it is no surprise that artists found the place appealing. But you don't have to be an artist to appreciate the beauty of the region or to find serene escape on one of the many public beaches.

A PERFECT DAY ON THE WESTERN SHORE

Begin in Saugatuck with a leisurely stroll through the galleries and shops of downtown. Drive about 10 miles north to Holland to see the tulip gardens and

THE WESTERN SHORE

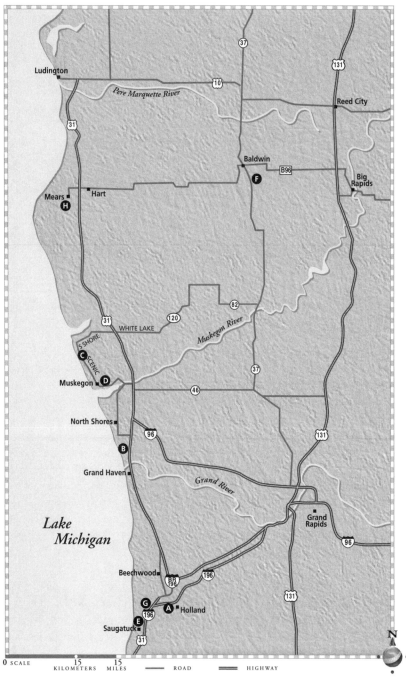

Ludington

Pere Marquette River

31

Reed City

131

37

10

Baldwin

B96

F

Big Rapids

Mears ■ ● H Hart ■

WHITE LAKE

31 120

82

Muskegon River

C S SHORE

● SCENIC

Muskegon ■ ● D

North Shores ■

96

● B

Grand Haven ■

Grand River

37

46

131

Grand Rapids

96

Lake Michigan

Beechwood ■

196

196

196

G ●

A ● Holland

E ●

Saugatuck ■

31

131

N

0 SCALE   15   15
KILOMETERS   MILES   ── ROAD   ══ HIGHWAY

some klompen dancing at Windmill Island or to tour the De Klomp Wooden Shoe and Delftware Factory.

Spend the afternoon in the wave pool or on the water slides at one of the water parks near Muskegon. After dinner drive to Hoffmaster State Park. Visit its nature center to learn about the history and ecology of the dunes, then walk out along the dunes and watch a spectacular sunset over Lake Michigan.

SIGHTSEEING HIGHLIGHTS
★★★★ DUTCH VILLAGE
U.S. 31, Holland, 616/396-1475

This is an excellent family-fun place. Intended to represent the cultural roots of Holland's Dutch immigrants, this village is a mixture of authenticity and fanciful nostalgia. Old World–style brick buildings with tile roofs cluster around four canals and gardens that boast hundreds of varieties of flowers. Central to the village's appeal is an antique street carnival with a carousel and an old-style swing ride. Klompen dancers perform regularly throughout the day and numerous shops and exhibits illuminate such subjects as regional Dutch costumes, cheese making, and wood carving.

SIGHTS
- Ⓐ Baker Furniture Museum
- Ⓐ De Klomp Wooden Shoe and Delftware Factory
- Ⓐ Dutch Village
- Ⓑ Hoffmaster State Park
- Ⓒ Michigan's Adventure Amusement Park
- Ⓓ Muskegon Museum of Art
- Ⓔ Saugatuck
- Ⓕ Shrine of the Pines
- Ⓓ USS Silversides Maritime Museum
- Ⓐ Windmill Island

FOOD
- Ⓓ Finley's
- Ⓐ The Hatch
- Ⓐ Pietros Trattoria
- Ⓐ Sandpiper
- Ⓓ Tony's Club

LODGING
- Ⓔ Bayside Inn
- Ⓓ Comfort Inn-Muskegon
- Ⓐ Dutch Colonial Inn
- Ⓔ Park House Bed & Breakfast Inn
- Ⓐ The Parsonage 1908
- Ⓓ Seaway Motel
- Ⓐ Super 8 Motel

CAMPING
- Ⓕ Bray Creek Campground
- Ⓑ Hoffmaster State Park
- Ⓖ Holland State Park
- Ⓕ Leverentz Lakes Campground
- Ⓓ Muskegon KOA
- Ⓐ Oak Grove Campground Resort
- Ⓗ Sandy Shores Campground and Resort

Note: Items with the same letter are located in the same place.

Details: About a mile north of SR 21. July–Aug daily 9–6, Apr–June and Sept daily 9–5. $6 adults and teens, $4 ages 3–11. (2–3 hours)

★★★★ HOFFMASTER STATE PARK
6585 Lake Harbor Road, Muskegon, 616/798-3711

Hoffmaster is the best place in the state to see and learn about the Lake Michigan dunes. A collection of hands-on exhibits and other displays at the park's Gillette Visitors Center give a fascinating and comprehensive explanation of how the world's longest stretch of freshwater dunes developed and describe the many forms of plant and animal life that the dunes support.

Details: Three miles off U.S. 31 at the Pontaluna Rd. exit. Apr–Nov daily 8–10, Dec–Mar daily 8–6:30. Park admission $4 per vehicle, visitors center free. (2–4 hours)

★★★★ MUSKEGON MUSEUM OF ART
296 W. Webster Avenue, Muskegon, 616/720-2570

This museum, founded in 1912 by local lumber baron Charles Hackley, is widely regarded as the best art museum in western Michigan. Its collection includes works by James Whistler, Winslow Homer, Edward Hopper, and Andrew Wyeth. It also holds a set of etchings by Rembrandt and a large collection of works by Francoise Gilot.

Details: Tue–Fri 10–5, Sat–Sun noon–5. Donations are appreciated. (1–2 hours)

★★★★ SAUGATUCK
616/857-1701 (Saugatuck-Douglas Convention and Visitors Bureau)

Noted for its history as an art colony, which dates to 1910, Saugatuck is a very small but beautiful resort town on Lake Michigan. Saugatuck Dunes State Park offers two miles of sandy beach and 14 miles of hiking trails. Downtown Saugatuck has a solid mix of art galleries, casual clothing stores, and gift shops. There's even a memorial to Burr Tillstrom, who was a summer resident and creator of the puppets on the *Kukla, Fran, and Ollie* TV show of the 1950s.

Details: 2–6 hours.

★★★★ WINDMILL ISLAND
Seventh Street and Lincoln Avenue, Holland, 616/355-1030

This 30-acre park in Holland is filled with tulip gardens, canals, a miniature Dutch village, and a working windmill. The windmill was brought from the Netherlands, where it was originally built in the 1780s. Attractions include a slide presentation, guided tours May through October, and *klompen* dancing demonstrations during summer. Each May the island is a highlight of the city's Tulip Time Festival, which features millions of blooming tulips in remarkable displays throughout the community.

Details: *May–Oct daily; call for hours. $5.50 adults and teens, $2.50 ages 5–12. (2–3 hours)*

★★★ BAKER FURNITURE MUSEUM
100 E. Eighth Street, Holland, 616/392-8761

The furniture industry has long been an important part of the western Michigan economy. At this museum you'll see examples of furniture from various countries, including original pieces made in the sixteenth century.

Details: *Apr–Oct Mon–Fri 10–5, Sat 9–noon. $2 adults, $1 ages 12–16. (2 hours)*

★★★ DE KLOMP WOODEN SHOE AND DELFTWARE FACTORY
12755 Quincy Street, Holland, 616/399-1900

For an inside look at Dutch crafts, visit this factory, where craftspeople demonstrate the art of making wooden shoes and blue-and-white delftware. Delftware originated in the Netherlands during the seventeenth century as an aesthetically appealing but less expensive alternative to the fine Chinese porcelain that was beginning to make its way to Europe. Artisans at the factory show how the delftware is made and explain how to distinguish the real thing from imitations. Delftware and wooden shoes are available for sale.

Details: *May daily 8–dusk; Apr and June–Dec Mon–Fri 8–6, Sat–Sun 9–5; Jan and Mar Mon–Fri 9–5. Admission is free. (1 hour)*

★★★ MICHIGAN'S ADVENTURE AMUSEMENT PARK
U.S. 31 at the Russell Road exit, 616/766-3377

This family outing combines a water park with an amusement park. Three roller coasters are among its 20 rides, and there are water slides, a wave pool, and a water play area for small children.

Details: *Eight miles north of Muskegon. Open daily in summer; call for hours. Admission is $18. (3–6 hours)*

★★★ USS SILVERSIDES MARITIME MUSEUM
1346 Bluff Street, Muskegon, 616/755-1230

At Muskegon's Pere Marquette Park you can tour this restored and highly honored World War II submarine. Walk through the cramped quarters below deck and imagine what it was like to spend nearly two months at a time there while patrolling enemy waters.

Details: *June–Aug daily 10–5:30; May and Sept Mon–Fri 1–5:30, Sat–Sun 10–5:30; Apr and Oct Sat–Sun 10–5:30. $4 adults, $3 age 62 and over and ages 12–18, $2 ages 5–11. (30 minutes)*

★★ SHRINE OF THE PINES
Highway 37, Baldwin, 616/745-7892

The site is one man's memorial to the vast forests of virgin pine that covered much of Michigan before the lumber industry stripped the land in the late 1800s. Raymond W. Oberholzer gathered stumps, roots, and treetops left behind as scrap by the lumberjacks and made from them an astonishing array of beds, chairs, tables, gun racks, chandeliers, and other furnishings as a tribute to the vanished forests. These items, made from the 1930s through the 1950s, are on display in a log hunting lodge on the banks of the Pere Marquette River.

Details: *About two miles south of Baldwin. May 15–Oct 15 daily 10–6. $3.75 adults, $3 over age 59, $1 ages 6–18, $8 families. (30 minutes–1 hour)*

FITNESS AND RECREATION

Whether it is at one of the public state park beaches or at one of the private amusement parks near Muskegon, recreation in western Michigan revolves around water—primarily swimming and boating. Hiking trails are available at several of the state parks, as are miles of sandy **Lake Michigan** beach. What better way to get some exercise than by strolling for a few aimless hours along the beach, gazing at the sand and water?

FOOD

Although western Michigan is a long-standing tourist area, it does not have a great reputation for outstanding restaurants. One of the better choices is the **Sandpiper**, 2225 S. Shore Dr., Holland, 616/335-5866. Serving an

American menu with unusual seafood specials, the Sandpiper offers an especially scenic view over the marina at the west end of Lake Macatawa. Dinners cost $10 to $20.

Also in Holland, **The Hatch**, 1870 Ottawa Beach Rd., 616/399-9120, specializes in steak and seafood, with dinners in the $10 to $20 range; and **Pietros Trattoria**, 175 E. Eighth St., 616/396-1000, offers Italian food and other Mediterranean dishes. Its dinners cost $10 to $15; lunches are under $10.

In Muskegon, moderately priced dinners and lunches under $10 can be had at **Tony's Club**, 785 W. Broadway, 616/739-7196; and at **Finley's**, 3065 Henry St., 616/733-9928. Both restaurants advertise American cuisine and casual family dining.

LODGING

Western Michigan has few outstanding hotels to boast of, but it does have some appealing bed-and-breakfast inns, especially in Holland and Saugatuck. In Holland, the **Dutch Colonial Inn**, 560 Central Ave., 616/396-3664, is a bed-and-breakfast in a lovely 1928-vintage home, with rates from $90 to $175 a night. **The Parsonage 1908**, 6 E. 24th St., 616/396-1316, occupies a historic home built as a church parsonage in 1908, and offers rates of $65 to $100 a night.

Saugatuck has a handful of bed-and-breakfast inns. Try the **Bayside Inn**, 618 Water St., 616/857-4321. It's downtown on the water and offers rooms for $95 to $225 a night. Or stay at the **Park House Bed and Breakfast Inn**, 888 Holland St., 616/857-4535, a restored historic house built in 1857. Its rooms cost $95 to $225 a night.

For a moderately priced motel, consider the **Comfort Inn in Muskegon**, 1675 E. Sherman Blvd., 616/739-9092, with rooms ranging from $64 to $94 a night. Cheaper options include Muskegon's **Seaway Motel**, 631 W. Norton Ave., 616/733-1220, with rooms from $35 to $60 a night; and, in Holland, the **Super 8 Motel**, 680 E. 24th St., 616/396-8822, with rooms from $35 to $58 a night.

CAMPING

Plenty of campgrounds line Michigan's west coast. If a public campground is your preference, try **Holland State Park**, 616/399-9390, seven miles west of Holland on Ottawa Beach Road on the Lake Michigan shore. The campground is open all year, offers 368 sites, and charges $15 a night.

A bit farther north, near Muskegon, is **Hoffmaster State Park**, 6585 Lake

Harbor Rd., 616/798-3711, another large public facility along Lake Michigan. Hoffmaster has 348 campsites. The park is open all year round and charges $15 a night.

If you are looking for something smaller and more secluded, there are a pair of small campgrounds in the Pere Marquette State Forest at Baldwin. The **Bray Creek Campground**, Maryville Rd. at 40th St., has only 10 sites; while the **Leverentz Lakes Campground**, two miles northeast of Baldwin on U.S. 10, has 17 sites. Both are open all year and charge $4 a night. Call 616/775-9727 for information about both.

For those who prefer private campgrounds, the region offers quite a few. Try the **Muskegon KOA**, 3500 N. Strand, 616/766-3900. Offering 96 sites, it's open from mid-May through mid-September. Rates are $17 a night for two, $1 per extra person. Boats, paddleboats, and kayaks are available for rent.

At Holland, the **Oak Grove Campground Resort**, 2011 Ottawa Beach Rd., 616/399-9230, has 127 private sites and features a heated pool and whirlpool. The campground is open from May 1 to October 1, and rates begin at $28 a night for four with a $3 fee for each extra person.

In Mears, the **Sandy Shores Campground and Resort**, 616/873-3003, has 205 sites and is open from May 1 through the end of September. In addition to beach access, the campground offers a heated pool. Rates start at $20 a night for five, with a $3 to $5 charge for each extra person. A reservation deposit is required and seven days' notice is necessary for a refund.

7
GRAND
TRAVERSE BAY

Traverse City is the most popular resort area in Michigan and swarms with tourists in summer. That often makes things a bit crowded, but it's hard to complain in the midst of so much natural beauty. The cherry orchard–studded hills of the Old Mission Peninsula, the endless sand beaches of the Sleeping Bear Dunes, and the mesmerizing blue waters of Grand Traverse Bay obliterate almost any cares and irritations.

The area's resorts make accommodations, meals, and shopping somewhat expensive, but you can save money by camping. You won't find many campgrounds more convenient than Traverse City State Park, practically in the city's downtown.

Recreation comes in all forms and all year-round. Golf is one of the most popular summer pastimes, and the region is home to numerous challenging courses. Boating—especially sailing—is very popular, too, and there is plenty of access to Lake Michigan as well as several small inland lakes. In winter, skiing and snowmobiling predominate. The area is generally less busy and accommodations are more affordable in winter.

A PERFECT DAY ON GRAND TRAVERSE BAY

Spend the morning exploring the Sleeping Bear Dunes National Lakeshore, an awe-inspiring expanse of sand, trees, and water. Stop at the visitors center in

Empire, then drive up the Lake Michigan coast through Leland to Northport. If you have time, take County Road 629 about eight miles north to the tip of the Leelanau Peninsula for a picnic lunch at Leelanau State Park.

In the afternoon play a round of golf at one of the many courses in the Traverse City area or visit the wineries along the Old Mission Peninsula. The drive alone is worth the time, but the wineries are interesting, too, and the views of the lake are spectacular. Afterward, enjoy dinner at any of the restaurants that offer a view of the bay. Watch the sailboats drift by as you relax with your meal.

SIGHTSEEING HIGHLIGHTS

★★★★ SLEEPING BEAR DUNES NATIONAL LAKESHORE
616/326-5134

According to Chippewa legend, a mother bear and her two cubs began swimming across Lake Michigan to escape a forest fire, but only the mother made it safely to shore. There she remains, as a great dark dune, awaiting her cubs, who turned into North Manitou and South Manitou islands a few miles offshore.

The islands and 35 miles of dunes along the lake have been preserved as a national lakeshore. A visitors center at park headquarters on Highway 72 in Empire offers exhibits and slide presentations about the park and the region's natural history. Some of the dunes rise nearly 500 feet above the lake surface, and in places you can see ghost forests of bleached trees that once were covered by the dunes and reappeared as the sand shifted. The islands are accessible by ferry from Leland and are popular backpacking spots.

Details: Call the National Park Service for information, 616/326-5134. (4 hours)

★★★ CLINCH PARK
616/922-4904

Situated along Traverse City's sandy beachfront, this park includes an aquarium and a zoo that both focus on area wildlife. The park is home to the Con Foster Museum, 616/922-4905, which examines local history and offers visitors rides on a miniature steam-powered train. At the park's marina you can tour the *Madeline*, 616/946-2647, a replica of a 56-foot Great Lakes schooner from the 1850s.

Details: Memorial Day–Labor Day daily 9:30–5:30, mid-April–Memorial Day and Labor Day–Oct 31 daily 10–4. Madeline *open*

GRAND TRAVERSE BAY

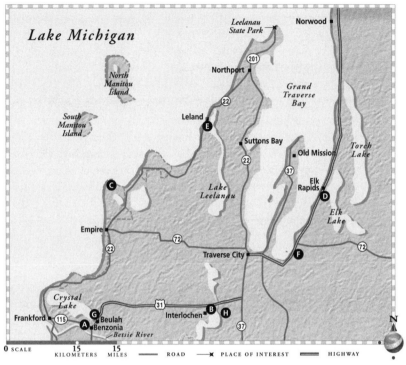

Lake Michigan

Leelanau State Park

Norwood

North Manitou Island

201

Northport

South Manitou Island

Leland

22

E

Grand Traverse Bay

Suttons Bay

Old Mission

Torch Lake

C

Lake Leelanau

22

37

Elk Rapids

D

Elk Lake

Empire

22

72

Traverse City

F

72

Crystal Lake

31

Interlochen

B

H

Frankford

115

G

A

Beulah

Benzonia

Betsie River

37

N

0 SCALE   15 KILOMETERS   15 MILES   ——— ROAD   —✕ PLACE OF INTEREST   ═══ HIGHWAY

SIGHTS

Ⓐ Gwen Frostic Prints
Ⓑ Interlochen
Ⓒ Sleeping Bear Dunes National Lakeshore
Ⓓ Spirit of the Woods Museum

FOOD

Ⓔ The Cove
Ⓔ Leelanau Country Inn
Ⓕ Trillium

LODGING

Ⓕ Grand Traverse Resort
Ⓔ Manitou Manor Bed and Breakfast
Ⓖ Pine Knot Motel

CAMPING

Ⓗ Interlochen State Park

Note: Items with the same letter are located in the same place.

mid-May–Sept 30 Wed–Sun noon–4:30. Admission to park: $2 adults, $1.50 ages 5–13. Admission to Madeline: free. Admission to museum: $1.50 adults, $1 ages 5–13. Train rides: $1 adults, 50 cents ages 5–13. (1–2 hours)

★★★ INTERLOCHEN
Route 137, 616/276-7443

This small village is home to the famous Interlochen Center for the Arts, which includes a summer arts camp, a year-round academy, and a public radio station. The campus covers 1,200 acres and includes two large outdoor concert halls, an art gallery, an indoor auditorium, and a theater. The eight-week summer session includes an arts festival that offers hundreds of concerts, plays, operas, musicals, dance performances, and recitals.

Details: *Just south of U.S. 31 on Rt. 137. (1–4 hours)*

★★ DENNOS MUSEUM CENTER
1701 E. Front Street, Traverse City, 616/922-1055

This museum on the campus of Northwestern Michigan College offers a variety of changing exhibits, including hands-on displays about art, science, and technology. An impressive collection of Eskimo art, one of the largest in the United States, is housed in the Inuit Gallery, one of three permanent exhibits. The other two permanent exhibits are a sculpture gallery and the playful Discovery Gallery.

Details: *Mon–Sat 10–5, Sun 1–5. $2 adults, $1 age 18 and under, $6 families. (1 hour)*

★★ GWEN FROSTIC PRINTS
River Road, Benzonia, 616/882-5505

Along the banks of the Betsie River is a 285-acre wildlife sanctuary that also serves as a studio for Gwen Frostic, a poet and artist who specializes in nature themes. Frostic's original books and artwork are available for sale here.

Details: *Two miles west of U.S. 31 on River Rd. May–Nov daily 9–5:30, Dec–Apr Mon–Sat 9–4:30. (30 minutes)*

★★ SPIRIT OF THE WOODS MUSEUM
U.S. 31, Elk Rapids, 616/264-5597

This museum includes exhibits of Native American artifacts as well as

TRAVERSE CITY

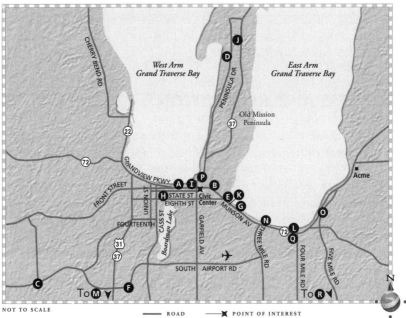

SIGHTS

- **A** Clinch Park
- **B** Dennos Museum Center

FOOD

- **C** Boone's Long Lake Inn
- **D** Bower's Harbor Inn
- **E** Cottage Cafe
- **F** Panda North
- **G** Schelde's
- **H** Top of the Park

LODGING

- **I** Bayshore Resort
- **J** Chateau Chantel Bed & Breakfast
- **K** Days Inn & Suites
- **L** Driftwood Resort
- **M** Econo Lodge
- **N** Economy Inn

CAMPING

- **O** Holiday Park Campground
- **P** Old Mission Inn, Campground, and Marina
- **Q** Traverse City State Park
- **R** Yogi Bear's Jellystone Park Camp-Resort

a variety of North American fish and wildlife. Displays include a collection of early hunting and fishing equipment.

Details: *About two miles south of Elk Rapids on U.S. 31. June–Aug Mon–Sat 9–6, Sun 11–4; Sept–May Mon–Sat 9–5. $3 adults, $2 seniors, $1 students. (1 hour)*

FITNESS AND RECREATION

Opportunities for exercise and physical activity in and around Traverse City are virtually unlimited. The area has more than 30 golf courses, including some designed by Jack Nicklaus and Arnold Palmer. You won't find any better swimming and boating—especially sailing—than that on **Grand Traverse Bay**. Campgrounds abound, and backpackers will find the remote trails of **North and South Manitou Islands** very enjoyable. Winter means plenty of cross-country skiing and snowmobiling, and several downhill-skiing resorts are nearby. And if your idea of exercise is a slow walk along a sandy beach, you can't do better than the endless sands of the **Sleeping Bear Dunes National Lakeshore**.

FOOD

The Traverse City area, as you would expect for the state's most popular resort destination, has a variety of excellent restaurants, ranging from the extravagant to the simple. For elegant dining with a truly spectacular view of the Grand Traverse Bay area, try the Grand Traverse Resort's **Trillium**, 1000 Grand Traverse Village Blvd., 616/938-2100. The menu is American-style, with dinners in the $20 to $30 range. Lunches cost around $10.

Another fine-dining spot is in Traverse City's Park Place Hotel, the **Top of the Park**, 300 E. State St., 616/946-5000. Semiformal attire is required. The restaurant is smoke-free with a lovely view overlooking the city and the bay. American cuisine is the heart of the menu, and dinners cost $20 to $30. **Bower's Harbor Inn**, 13512 Peninsula Dr., 616/223-4222, offers an elegant American menu in the casual atmosphere of a restored historical home on West Bay. Dinners here also cost $20 to $30.

In Leland, a renovated 1891 inn is home to the **Leelanau Country Inn**, 149 E. Harbor Hwy., 616/228-5060, another fine restaurant with dinners in the $20 to $30 range. Here the American menu is augmented with a variety of pasta dishes, seafood, and fresh-baked desserts.

One of the better mid-priced restaurants in the area is Leland's **The Cove**, 111 River St., 616/256-9834. The menu is American fare with an emphasis on fresh seafood, and the atmosphere is casual. In good weather you can eat outdoors overlooking the river. Dinners cost $10 to $20.

In Traverse City, try **Schelde's**, 714 Munson Ave., 616/946-0981, or **Boone's Long Lake Inn**, 7208 Seccor Rd., 616/946-3991. Both specialize in steak and seafood, offer a casual atmosphere, and serve dinners in the $10 to $20 range. One of the few real ethnic-food options is **Panda North**, 2038 S. Airport Rd., 616/929-9722, which serves Chinese dinners for $10 to $20. For inexpensive but good food, visit the **Cottage Café**, 420 Munson Ave., 616/947-9261, a casual spot with an American menu and dinners under $15.

LODGING

Because Traverse City is Michigan's most popular tourist resort area, it should come as no surprise that accommodations here tend toward the expensive, especially during the peak summer season. Room rates vary considerably depending on the time of year, but in summer you should expect to find them near the top of the scales listed below.

The most extravagant accommodations in the area are in Acme at the **Grand Traverse Resort**, 1000 Grand Traverse Village Blvd., 616/938-2100, a luxury resort where rooms range from $100 to $329 a night. The resort has a lot to offer, including 684 rooms, a putting green, a 36-hole golf course, a beach, four pools (all heated and two indoor), saunas, whirlpool, exercise room, racquetball courts, nine tennis courts (five indoor), skate-equipment rental, two dining rooms, and three restaurants. Available activities include fishing, cross-country skiing, ice-skating, snowmobiling, hiking, jogging, and all manner of water sports.

The area offers numerous bed-and-breakfast inns, such as Traverse City's **Chateau Chantel Bed and Breakfast**, 15900 Rue de Vin, 616/223-4110. The inn is small, with just three rooms that cost from $105 to $135 a night, but its location on a high ridge that runs along the Old Mission Peninsula provides a stunning view of the peninsula's vineyards and the bay. The inn offers a smoke-free environment and wine-tasting.

In Leland, the **Manitou Manor Bed and Breakfast**, 147 Manitou Trail W., 616/256-7712, is a refurbished one-story farmhouse with a smoke-free environment and four rooms that run from $85 to $125 a night. If you want a beachfront room, try the **Bayshore Resort**, 833 E. Front St., 616/935-4400. It's smoke-free; offers a heated indoor pool, a whirlpool, and an exercise room; and has rooms for $75 to $320 a night.

More modest accommodations in Traverse City are available at the chain hotels. At **Days Inn and Suites**, 420 Munson Ave., 616/941-0208, rooms cost from $46 to $147 and guests have access to a heated indoor pool, a whirlpool, and a playground. The **Econo Lodge**, 1065 M-37 S., 616/943-3040, also has a heated indoor pool and whirlpool and rooms from $45 to $100 a night.

The **Driftwood Resort**, 1861 Shore Dr., 616/938-1600, has rooms from $40 to $135 a night and offers a beach on the east bay, a heated indoor pool, and a whirlpool. The **Economy Inn**, 1600 U.S. 31 N., 616/938-2080, has rooms ranging from $33 to $110.

Smaller motels farther away from Traverse City and the water are more basic but noticeably less costly. In Beulah, for example, the nine-room **Pine Knot Motel**, 171 N. Center St., 616/882-7551, offers accommodations in the $40 to $60 range.

CAMPING

You will find a good selection of campgrounds, both public and private, in the area. One of the most popular, and probably the best in terms of location, is **Traverse City State Park**, 1132 U.S. 31 N., 616/922-5270. The public park, which is open all year, crams 343 campsites into just 45 acres. It's just two miles from downtown Traverse City on the main tourist route, just across the road from a good beach on the east bay. Rates are $15 a night.

A few miles south of the city is another public campground, **Interlochen State Park**, 616/276-9511. It's one mile south of Interlochen on Highway 137. This campground, snuggled between Duck Lake and Green Lake, was Michigan's first state park and has 550 sites on 187 acres. It offers swimming, fishing, waterskiing, and rental boats, as well as a boat ramp and a playground. Rates are $14 a night.

Private campgrounds are readily available, such as **Yogi Bear's Jellystone Park Camp-Resort**, 4050 Hammond Rd., 616/947-2770, with 221 sites. It's open from May 1 to October 30 and has hiking trails, miniature golf, a playground, a recreation room, a wading pool, and two swimming pools. Rates are $22 a night.

The **Old Mission Inn, Campground, and Marina**, 18599 Old Mission Rd., 616/223-7770, is small but is located in an undeniably scenic area. Open May 15 to October 15, it has 29 sites, offers swimming, fishing, and boating, and has its own beach, boat ramp, and rental boats. Rates are $15 to $18 a night for four, with a charge of $1 per extra person.

Holiday Park Campground, 4860 U.S. 31 S., 616/943-4410, a private facility on Silver Lake with 154 sites, is open all year. Facilities, which are limited in winter, include a beach, playground, and rental boats and paddleboats.

Swimming, fishing, and snowmobiling are available. Rates are $18 to $29 a night for four, with a charge of $1 per extra person.

WINE COUNTRY

The Grand Traverse region is noted for its wine production. Between Traverse City and the Leland area, the region boasts eight vineyards and wineries, all of which are open to the public. The list includes **Boskydel Vineyards**, 7501 E. Otto Rd., Lake Leelanau, 616/256-7272; **Bowers Harbor Vineyards**, 2896 Bowers Harbor Rd., Traverse City, 616/223-7615; **Chateau Chantal**, 15900 Rue de Vin, Traverse City, 616/223-4110; **Chateau Grand Traverse**, 12239 Center Rd., Traverse City, 616/223-7355; **Good Harbor Vineyards**, 34 S. Manitou Trail, Lake Leelanau, 616/256-7165; **L. Mawby Vineyard**, 4519 Elm Valley Rd., Suttons Bay, 616/271-3522; **Leelanau Wine Cellars**, 12683 E. Tatch Rd., Omena, 616/386-5201; and **Old Mission Peninsula Cellars**, 18250 Mission Rd., Traverse City, 616/223-4310.

Scenic Route: Old Mission Peninsula

On a clear day, the 36-mile drive along Highway 37 from Traverse City to Old Mission and back is one of the most breathtakingly beautiful trips in Michigan. When the sun glitters on the blue waters and white sails glide up and down the bay, you'll want to sit and watch forever. In mid-May, when the peninsula's cherry orchards are in bloom, the trip is even more exquisite. The peninsula divides Grand Traverse Bay into two long arms, so there's water everywhere you look. At the tip of the peninsula is a lighthouse and a reconstructed Indian mission, originally built in 1836. Several of the region's wineries sit along the peninsula, offering good opportunities to stop for tours and wine-tasting.

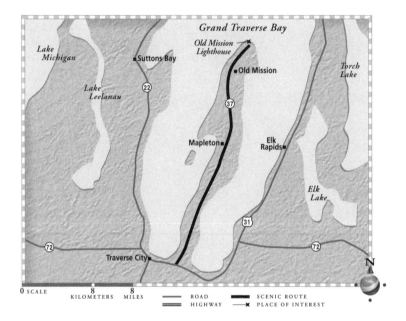

8
LITTLE
TRAVERSE BAY

In a remarkably beautiful state, few places are more lovely than Little Traverse Bay. Stretching along the northern Lake Michigan shore from Cross Village to Charlevoix, the bay region has been one of the most popular resort areas on the Great Lakes for more than 100 years. In Petoskey, Harbor Springs, and Charlevoix you can see the nostalgic old summer homes that provided a hot-weather getaway for the wealthy who came up from Chicago or Detroit by steamer or train in the late nineteenth and early twentieth century. Ernest Hemingway and his parents were among those sojourners, and northern Michigan is the locale for some of Hemingway's most memorable stories.

Lake Michigan is the dominant feature of the region. Its waters attract boaters and anglers from all over the Midwest, and the panoramic views along the shore from Cross Village south to Charlevoix are spectacular. But large inland lakes, particularly Lake Charlevoix, are also very scenic and attract boaters en masse. The area also has excellent golf courses. Winter recreation is a big draw, too, especially for snowmobilers and skiers, who flock to the ski resorts near Boyne City and Harbor Springs.

A PERFECT DAY ON LITTLE TRAVERSE BAY
Start in Charlevoix with a little browsing at the downtown shops and a drive past the charming Earl Young houses in Boulder Park. Then head along the north

shore of Lake Charlevoix on the Boyne City Road to Horton Bay for a brief pilgrimage to the Horton Bay General Store. From there, Horton Bay Road will take you through several miles of scenic, rolling farmland to reconnect with U.S. 31 near the Lake Michigan shore. Stop for a while in Petoskey to wander through the Gaslight Shopping District or to visit the Little Traverse Historical Museum.

After lunch, drive past the historic summer cottages at Bay View and follow U.S. 31 north to Levering. There, take County Road 66 west to Cross Village and follow Highway 119, a beautiful lakeshore drive of 27 miles back to Petoskey. Make a late-afternoon stop in Harbor Springs to browse in a few more galleries and antique shops, or cruise along Beach Drive through Wequetonsing, the best close-quarters view to be had of the area's rich summer-home heritage.

SIGHTSEEING HIGHLIGHTS
★★★★ BAY VIEW ASSOCIATION
U.S. 31, Petoskey, 616/347-6225
Bay View, on Petoskey's north side, was established in 1875 to host Methodist camp meetings during summer. By 1900 most of the 450 graceful summer cottages and public buildings that still stand had been completed, and Bay View was offering extensive summer programs influenced by the Chautauqua movement in New York State. Summer programs continue, with many concerts and other cultural events open to the public. Gazing at the cottages—which are owned by residents on land leased from the association—is a wonderful nostalgic pleasure.

Details: *About two miles north of downtown Petoskey. (1–2 hours)*

★★★★ CHARLEVOIX
616/547-2101 (Convention and Visitor's Bureau)
A small but bustling (that is, congested) resort town in the summer, Charlevoix straddles U.S. 31, the main route from Traverse City to Mackinaw City. It also stretches along a narrow isthmus between three lakes—Lake Michigan on the west, Lake Charlevoix on the east, and Round Lake, the city's boat harbor, in the middle. Bridge Street (U.S. 31) is the only street that passes all the way through town, and a drawbridge downtown opens every half hour in the summer, leading to much of the congestion. But the town is pretty, and it has a fair selection of stores in its four-block shopping district

LITTLE TRAVERSE BAY

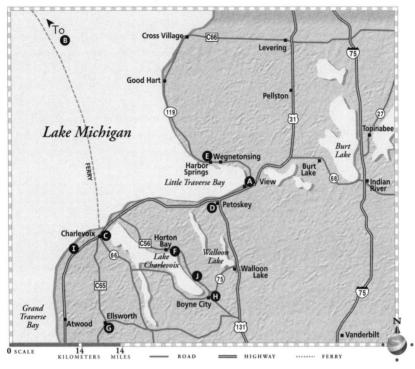

SIGHTS
ⓐ Bay View Association
ⓑ Beaver Island
ⓒ Charlevoix
ⓓ Gaslight Shopping District
ⓔ Harbor Springs
ⓕ Horton Bay
ⓓ Little Traverse Historical Museum

FOOD
ⓒ Grey Gables
ⓒ Juillerette's
ⓔ Mary Ellen's Place
ⓐ Stafford's Bay View Inn

FOOD
(continued)
ⓒ Stafford's Weathervane
ⓖ Tapawingo
ⓔ Turkey's Cafe & Pizzeria
ⓓ Villa Ristorante Italiano

LODGING
ⓓ Apple Tree Inn
ⓓ Baywinds Inn
ⓔ Birchwood Inn
ⓗ Boyne City Motel
ⓓ Econo Lodge
ⓓ Stafford's Bay View Inn
ⓐ Terrace Inn

LODGING
(continued)
ⓗ Water Street Inn
ⓒ Weathervane Terrace Hotel

CAMPING
ⓘ Fisherman's Island State Park
ⓑ Mackinaw State Forest
ⓑ Beaver Island Campground
ⓐ Petoskey KOA
ⓓ Petoskey State Park
ⓙ Young State Park

Note: Items with the same letter are located in the same place.

geared to the tourist trade. One of the best is Koucky Gallery, an unusual and amusing store with decorative artwork from hundreds of artists and artisans.

Although Charlevoix's two venerable summer resort communities—the Chicago Club and the Belvedere Club—are generally closed to the public, one public thoroughfare, Ferry Street, offers fine views of the old homes as it follows the base of the bluff where the Belvedere overlooks Lake Charlevoix. For a real architectural treat, drive out Park Street to Boulder Park on the Lake Michigan shore, where you'll see an attractive but quirky collection of limestone and fieldstone homes with cedar shake roofs. They were built from the 1920s to the 1950s by Earl Young, a self-taught architect. Judging by their appearance, you might expect to see gnomes emerging at any moment.

Details: 2–4 hours.

★★★★ **GASLIGHT SHOPPING DISTRICT**
616/347-4150 (Petoskey Chamber of Commerce)
In a six-square-block area of downtown Petoskey, you will find more than 70 stores, craft shops, and galleries aimed directly at the tourist trade. The stores can provide hours of leisurely enjoyment for the avid shopper. Many are in buildings with well-kept, two-story Victorian facades, and streetlights modeled on turn-of-the-century gas lanterns reinforce the atmosphere. If your feet tire, sit a spell in shady Pennsylvania Park across the street.

Details: 1–3 hours.

★★★★ **HARBOR SPRINGS**
616/526-7999 (Harbor Springs Chamber of Commerce)
Harbor Springs has always been an exclusive resort town for the very rich, but it is much more accessible than one would expect and exudes a relaxing, small-town charm. The huge old summer homes of the Wequetonsing colony that face the bay are not as hidden from general view as similar communities in Bay View and Charlevoix. Drive slowly along Beach Road for a grand view of the big old homes with their broad lawns.

In good weather you'll also see dozens of sailboats reaching down the bay. The town's downtown area is an interesting mix of galleries, restaurants, specialty stores, and antique shops. Waterfront parks border either edge of downtown, and east of Wequetonsing along Beach

Road you'll find several small nature preserves that are open to the public.
Details: *2–4 hours.*

★★★★ LITTLE TRAVERSE HISTORICAL MUSEUM
Lake Street, Petoskey, 616/347-2620

This museum, at the entrance to Bayfront Park, is housed in an old railroad depot that was built in 1892. It contains a variety of historical exhibits, including a collection of quill boxes made by local Indians more than 100 years ago and displays on the area's lumber and tourism industries.

Probably the most popular exhibits at the museum involve two of the area's most famous former residents: Civil War historian Bruce Catton and novelist Ernest Hemingway. Hemingway spent his first 18 summers at his family's summer home on beautiful Walloon Lake.

Details: *Off Lake St. one block south of U.S. 31. May–Labor Day Tue–Sat 10–4, Sun 1–4; Labor Day–Dec Tue–Sat 10–4. $1 adults, age 12 and under free. (30 minutes–1 hour)*

★★★ BEAVER ISLAND
888/446-4095 (ferry schedule and reservations)

You will need to take a $31, two-hour ferry ride from Charlevoix to reach the port of St. James on Beaver Island. But if you are an island lover, or simply an admirer of remote, serene beauty, it is well worth the money and the trip. The 14-mile-long island, located about 18 miles west of the Lower Peninsula in Lake Michigan, lacks the cultivated beauty—and the crowds—of Mackinac Island. In fact, though summer ferry schedules allow a day-trip visit with more than seven hours in which to nose around the island, it is a shame to go so far only to rush back. It is better to plan to spend at least one night at a campground or a small but comfortable lodge in St. James, the island's only town.

You can also say you spent the night in what once was the only kingdom in the United States. James Jesse Strang, leader of a breakaway Mormon group, brought his followers to the island in 1847, where he declared himself king and ruled until the colony dissolved in 1856.

Details: *Round-trip fare: adults $31, ages 5–12 $15.50. Vehicle rates begin at $104. (1–2 days)*

★★ HORTON BAY

616/582-6222 (Boyne City Chamber of Commerce)

About halfway between Boyne City and Charlevoix on Boyne City Road is Horton Bay, a small but necessary stop for any true Ernest Hemingway aficionado. The tiny town was made modestly famous by Hemingway in several of his Nick Adams stories. The Horton Bay General Store looks much as it did when Hemingway knew it, and the little church nearby is where Hemingway married his first wife, Hadley Richardson of St. Louis, who, like Papa, was a summer visitor. As you drive along the Boyne City Road with its gorgeous views of Lake Charlevoix and the surrounding hills, it is not hard to see why Hemingway fell in love with the place.

Details: *30 minutes.*

FITNESS AND RECREATION

Summer or winter, just about any kind of recreation you want is available in the area. There are state parks for camping; lakes for fishing, boating, and swimming; and golf courses have been sprouting up like summer grass all over the area for several years. In fall the area is a popular hunting region, and in winter it attracts thousands of skiers and snowmobilers. The most popular ski resorts are near Harbor Springs and Boyne City.

For a beautiful ambiance while hiking, swimming, or cross-country skiing, check out one of the local state parks: **Young State Park**, 616/582-7523, two miles north of Boyne City on Boyne City Road; **Petoskey State Park**, 616/347-2311, four miles northeast of Petoskey off U.S. 31 on Highway 119; on **Fisherman's Island State Park**, 616/547-6641, three miles southwest of Charlevoix off U.S. 31 on Bells Bay Road.

FOOD

The Little Traverse Bay region is filled with good restaurants that serve traditional—and sometimes not-so-traditional—American cuisine in quaint Victorian houses. The most famous is **Tapawingo**, 9502 Lake St., 616/588-7971, in the small town of Ellsworth, 12 miles south of Charlevoix on County Road 65. The restaurant is in a charming old house on St. Clair Lake and is noted for its elegant presentation of modern American cooking. Its four-course dinners cost from $35 to $45. Partisans say it is the best restaurant in Michigan.

Another charming option is **Stafford's Bay View Inn**, 2011 Woodland

Ave., 616/347-2771. Tucked amid turn-of-the-century summer homes in the historic Bay View Association on the north side of Petoskey, the inn overlooks Little Traverse Bay. The inn offers an elegant Victorian theme, with wicker rockers on its wide verandah and traditional country-inn cuisine. Dinners cost $20 to $30.

A related restaurant (Stafford's dominates the refined dining market, with five good restaurants in the area) is **Stafford's Weathervane**, 106 Pine River Ln., 616/547-4311, in Charlevoix. With its Earl Young boulder design, the restaurant is intriguing and a great spot for boat-watchers along the Pine River Channel, which connects Lake Michigan with the busy boat basin on Round Lake. The food is good, too. The menu features American cuisine in the $15 to $25 range. Also in Charlevoix, try the **Grey Gables**, 308 Belvedere, 616/547-9261, with its cozy setting in an old Victorian house. The Grey Gables offers excellent American food, such as prime rib, stuffed pork chops, and various seafood dishes. Dinners cost $10 to $20.

For the sake of variety—and a very good meal to boot—try the **Villa Ristorante Italiano**, 887 Spring St., 616/347-1440, just south of the U.S. 31–U.S. 131 intersection in Petoskey. This restaurant serves tasty, filling meals of traditional Italian food in a casual setting decorated with grapevines and wicker baskets. Dinners run $15 to $30.

Harbor Springs is known as a summer haven for the wealthy, but it also is home to a pair of inexpensive taste treats: **Mary Ellen's Place**, 145 E. Main St., 616/526-5591, and **Turkey's Cafe and Pizzeria**, 250 E. Main St., 616/526-6041. Both feature an old-fashioned soda-fountain atmosphere and meals for under $10. Mary Ellen's Place does not serve dinner but has excellent breakfasts and lunches. Turkey's Cafe does serve dinner. It specializes in pizza and will allow you to design your own omelet for breakfast.

A good inexpensive restaurant in Charlevoix is **Juillerette's**, 1418 Bridge St., 616/547-9212, with family dining and meals under $10.

LODGING

Petoskey is the best place in the region for both supply and range of accommodations. Keep in mind that because Little Traverse Bay is a prime resort area, rates can change substantially with the season. Rates are usually lowest in the winter, after the holidays.

At the upper end of the price range is **Stafford's Bay View Inn**, 2011 Woodland Ave., 616/347-2771. The inn is housed in an historic 1886 structure in the picturesque Bay View Association on the north side of Petoskey. It boasts an elegant Victorian atmosphere, and the nightly rates of $79 to $210 include health club privileges. Another more moderately priced historic hotel in Bay View is the **Terrace Inn**, 1549 Glendale, 616/347-2410, in a restored 1911 Victorian inn with rates between $49 and $103 a night.

On Petoskey's south side, near the junction of U.S. 31 and U.S. 131, you will find a good selection of hotels. The **Baywinds Inn**, 909 Spring St., 616/347-4193, offers rates between $55 and $150 a night; while the **Apple Tree Inn**, 915 Spring St., 616/348-2900, has rooms from $57 to $141 a night. For less expensive tastes there is an **Econo Lodge**, 1858 U.S. 131 S., 616/348-3324, with rooms from $45 to $90 a night.

In Charlevoix, the **Weathervane Terrace Hotel**, 111 Pine River Ln., 616/547-9955, has an unusual boulder architecture and is located within a block of the city's downtown shopping district. It is also just two blocks from the city park on Round Lake, which hosts numerous festivals and fairs during the summer season. Rooms go for $35 to $199 a night. Harbor Springs' **Birchwood Inn**, 7077 Lakeshore Dr., 616/526-2151, offers rooms for $45 to $110 per night.

Inland, a few miles from Lake Michigan but on the shores of Lake Charlevoix, is Boyne City, another small tourist town. At the **Water Street Inn**, 200 Front St., 616/582-3000, rooms are luxurious but more expensive, running from $70 to $165 a night. An inexpensive option is the **Boyne City Motel**, 110 N. East St., 616/582-6701, with rooms from $43 to $63 nightly.

CAMPING

Good camping is plentiful in the Little Traverse Bay region, mostly in state park campgrounds. The largest and most popular of these campgrounds is **Young State Park**, two miles north of Boyne City on Boyne City Rd., 616/582-7523. The campground has 293 sites, is open all year, and charges $15 a night. Located on the northeastern shore of Lake Charlevoix, the park has excellent facilities for swimming, waterskiing, and fishing, including a boat ramp and rental boats. The park also has a playground and nature trails, as well as access to skiing in the winter.

Along the Lake Michigan shore you'll find **Petoskey State Park**, 616/347-2311. It's four miles northeast of the city, off U.S. 31 on Highway 119. The park has 90 sites, is open all year, and charges $15 a night. It also offers nature trails, boating, fishing, and cross-country or downhill skiing.

Also on Lake Michigan is **Fisherman's Island State Park**, three miles southwest of Charlevoix off U.S. 31 on Bells Bay Rd., 616/547-6641. It has 90 sites, is open all year, and charges $6 a night. Swimming, fishing, and nature trails are available.

For an unusual camping experience, take the ferry from Charlevoix to Beaver Island and spend a night in the Mackinaw State Forest at the **Beaver Island Campground**, 517/732-3541. The campground is located one mile from St. James Harbor on Donegal Bay Road. It has 12 sites, is open all year, and charges $4 a night. An overnight stay will give you time to tour the island, swim, or fish.

If you prefer a private campground, there is a good one just outside Petoskey. The **Petoskey KOA**, 1800 N. U.S. 31, 616/347-0005, has 125 sites, is open May 1 through mid-October, and charges $19 to $26 a night for two. Facilities include a heated pool, whirlpool, playground, and recreation room. Kamping Kabins rent for $38 a night for a one-room cabin, $48 a night for two rooms.

Scenic Route: Cross Village to Charlevoix

If your base is Petoskey, take U.S. 31 north to Levering and then turn west on County Road 66 to Cross Village. From there you follow the Lake Michigan shore south around the rim of Little Traverse Bay to Charlevoix—some of the most beautiful landscape in Michigan. Much of the way from Cross Village to Harbor Springs, the road runs along the side of a bluff that rises high above the lake. Views of the lake from here are spectacular, especially as sunset nears.

Dip down to the harbor at Harbor Springs to ogle the huge yachts at the docks, then continue around to Petoskey. At Bayfront Park you can picnic while you watch the sailboats on the bay.

Lake views are intermittent between Petoskey and Bay Shore, but nearer to Charlevoix the road edges close to the lake again. Lakeside turnoffs provide picnic tables, and you can relax and even put your feet in the water. The entire drive is about 50 miles.

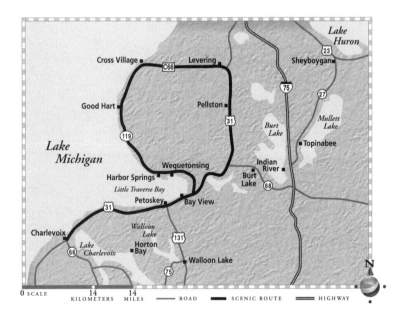

9
MACKINAC ISLAND

Mackinac Island is the crown jewel of Michigan—elegant, down-to-earth, and serene, it is breathtakingly beautiful and just plain fun. The pace of life on the island is slow, in no small part because motorized vehicles are not allowed. Travel on the island happens only by horse, carriage, bicycle, or foot.

Until the late 1700s the Straits of Mackinac were controlled by the French, but in 1780 the English established a fort on the island because of its strategic position in the straits. It remained the dominant military outpost in the area for 115 years.

Today the island is one of the state's dominant tourist attractions and the finish line for two annual yacht races—one up Lake Huron from Port Huron and the other up Lake Michigan from Chicago. An annual Lilac Festival is held in mid-June, one of the loveliest times of year on the island.

High bluffs offer spectacular views of the surrounding waters, the Mackinac Bridge, the Upper Peninsula and Lower Peninsula shores, and the endless stream of sailboats and freighters plying the upper Great Lakes. The island is about three miles long and about two miles wide, with a paved road that follows the shore, so you can easily walk or bike to get where you want to go.

Ferries from both Mackinaw City, in the Lower Peninsula, and St. Ignace, in the Upper Peninsula, offer regular service to and from the island from early morning into the evening, May through October, making flexible-length day trips easy to plan.

MACKINAC ISLAND

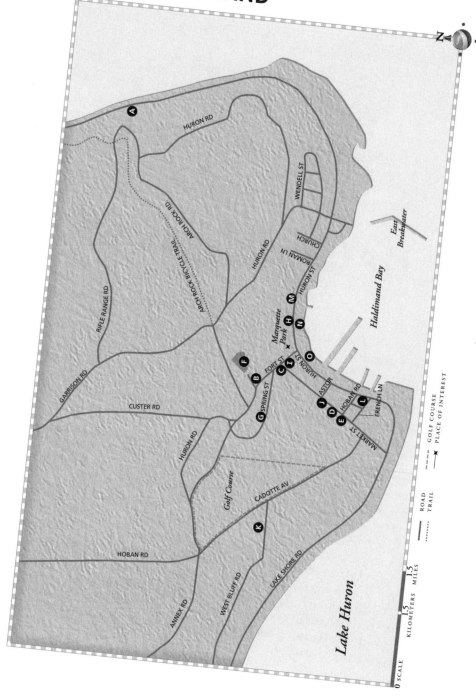

Lake Huron

Haldimand Bay

East Breakwater

HURON RD

WENDELL ST

CHURCH

ROMAN LN

HURON ST

HURON RD

HURON RD

ARCH ROCK RD.

ARCH ROCK BICYCLE TRAIL

RIFLE RANGE RD

GARRISON RD

CUSTER RD

HURON RD

SPRING ST

FORT ST

Marquette Park

HURON ST

ASTOR

HOBAN RD

MARKET ST

FRENCH LN

Golf Course

CADOTTE AV

HOBAN RD

ANNEX RD

WEST BLUFF RD

LAKE SHORE RD

SCALE

0   1.5
KILOMETERS

1.5
MILES

ROAD
TRAIL

GOLF COURSE
PLACE OF INTEREST

A PERFECT DAY ON MACKINAC ISLAND

Half the fun of Mackinac Island is getting there. Plan an early morning ferry ride across from either Mackinaw City or St. Ignace. The ride is a bit shorter from St. Ignace, but unless you plan to spend some time in the eastern Upper Peninsula, Mackinaw City may be more convenient.

Once you're on the island, stroll through some of the galleries and souvenir shops, then take one of the carriage tours that offer a good overall view of the island and its history. By then it should be just about time for lunch. An excellent place to eat is the Fort Mackinac Tea Room, which has tables on an open-air terrace overlooking the harbor. The view from the terrace is spectacular.

Tour the fort after lunch and be sure to take in one of the presentations by costumed guides, which include demonstrations of military music and firings of rifles and cannons.

If you have the extra time and don't mind paying $7 for the privilege of strolling the grounds and sitting in a rocking chair, spend a few minutes on the broad, pillared verandah of the Grand Hotel. It is the most famous and recognizable hotel in Michigan, the ambiance is elegant, and the view of the straits is breathtaking.

Before you catch the ferry back to Mackinaw City or St. Ignace, be sure to stop into one of the many fudge shops for which the island is justifiably famous. It may wreck your diet, but your taste buds will thank you.

SIGHTS
- Ⓐ Arch Rock
- Ⓑ Bark Chapel
- Ⓒ William Beaumont Memorial
- Ⓓ Benjamin Blacksmith Shop
- Ⓔ Biddle House
- Ⓕ Fort Mackinac
- Ⓖ Governor's Mansion
- Ⓗ Indian Dormitory
- Ⓘ McGulpin House
- Ⓙ Stuart House Museum of the Astor Fur Post

FOOD
- Ⓕ Fort Mackinac Tea Room
- Ⓚ Grand Hotel
- Ⓛ Lake View Hotel & Conference Center
- Ⓜ Island House

LODGING
- Ⓚ Grand Hotel
- Ⓝ Inn on Mackinac
- Ⓜ Island House
- Ⓛ Lake View Hotel & Conference Center
- Ⓞ Murray Hotel

Note: Items with the same letter are located in the same place.

ARCH ROCK ON MACKINAC ISLAND

Travel Michigan

SIGHTSEEING HIGHLIGHTS

★★★★ CARRIAGE TOURS
906/847-3573

For a relaxing ride and a view of all the main scenic and historic sites on the island, take a carriage tour. Tours start on Main Street in the center of the shopping district and wind about the island in a two-hour loop. You'll pass the historic Grand Hotel and the **Governor's Mansion**, and make a stop at **Arch Rock**, a strikingly beautiful natural bridge high above the waters of Lake Huron. If you choose, you can end your ride at the upper entrance to Fort Mackinac, which saves you the climb up the hill to the fort.

Details: Tours mid-May–mid-Oct daily 9–4, extended hours in summer. $13 adults, $6.50 ages 4–11. (2 hours)

★★★★ DOWNTOWN
906/847-6418 (Chamber of Commerce)

The island's downtown area, which stretches for several blocks between the fort and the Grand Hotel, is a mixture of shops, hotels, and historic sites, most of which are free. The **Bark Chapel**, in Marquette Park, is a reconstruction based on chapels built on the island by French missionaries in the late 1600s. At the foot of Fort Mackinac is the **William Beaumont Memorial**, dedicated to a pioneer in the study of the human digestive system. Costumed interpreters explain displays that include Beaumont's medical instruments.

Other free downtown sites include the **Benjamin Blacksmith Shop**, with demonstrations that use original nineteenth-century equipment; the **Biddle House**, with displays of nineteenth-century home furnishings and domestic craft demonstrations; the **Indian Dormitory**, an 1838 structure that now holds an Indian museum and antiques; and the **McGulpin House**, which was built around 1780. The **Stuart House Museum of the Astor Fur Post**, 906/847-6418, on Market Street a block from the ferry dock, was the first headquarters of the American Fur Company and now offers displays of the company's records and other artifacts from the early 1800s. The museum has recently been renovated.

Details: 1–6 hours.

★★★★ FORT MACKINAC
616/436-5563

All the buildings of this fort, perched on a bluff above the harbor, are original and date from the eighteenth and nineteenth centuries. They have been restored and now provide an authentic backdrop for interpretive demonstrations and reenactments by guides in period costumes. The fort itself, with stone walls up to eight feet thick, was built in 1780 by the British and was captured by them again in the War of 1812. The fort's bluff-top site gives it a commanding—and spectacularly beautiful—view of the Straits of Mackinac. Take a stroll through more than a dozen restored buildings, including the soldiers' barracks and officers' quarters, or watch daily rifle and cannon demonstrations. The fort offers a multimedia orientation program and hands-on programs and games for children. For a pleasant pause in your day, have lunch on the terrace of the Tea Room overlooking the harbor and the straits.

Details: *Mid-May–mid-Oct daily 10–4, extended hours in summer. $7.25 adults, $4.25 children, $21 per family. (1–2 hours)*

FITNESS AND RECREATION

You'll get plenty of exercise walking around town, but if you are looking for a more intense workout, take a spin around the island on Highway 185. The only traffic you'll have to worry about will be other walkers, joggers, and bicyclists (bicycles are available for rent). The scenery along the way can't be beat, especially along the southwest edge of the island, with its gorgeous vista of the Straits of Mackinac.

FOOD

One of the great joys for visitors to Mackinac Island is to amble about the town, strolling in and out of shops and leisurely selecting from among the many restaurants, food stands, and fudge stores at which you may ease your hunger. For my money, though, the best place for lunch is the **Fort Mackinac Tea Room**, 906/847-3331, inside the fort. So plan your visit to the fort to coincide with the lunch hour. The food is basic but good, prices are moderate, and the view of the harbor from the terrace on a sunny day alone is worth the price of a meal.

For more elegant fare, try one of the major hotel dining rooms. The **Grand Hotel** (it's impossible to miss), 906/847-3331, advertises itself as an American tradition, and the menus in the hotel's four restaurants reflect that tradition— with American cuisine presented in grand fashion. Carlton's focuses on continental breakfasts and light lunches, while the Geranium Bar offers a variety of lunch entrées, especially soups, salads, and fruit. The Grand Strand serves more substantial breakfasts and lunches, while the Main Dining Room offers a vast buffet and five-course dinners costing $65 per person. If that's too steep, you can still absorb the unique atmosphere by taking afternoon tea, served from 3:30 to 5 for $15 per person.

The **Island House**, 1 Lake Shore Dr., 906/847-3347, offers fine dining on such specialties as prime rib and Barbarie Duckling, with dinners priced in the $15 to $25 range. A breakfast buffet is also available, and the hotel's Garden Grill is open for chicken, ribs, and burgers from noon to 3. The **Lake View Hotel and Conference Center**, Main St., 906/847-3384, also offers fine dining in the standard American style, with dinners priced in the $15 to $25 range.

LODGING

Many hotels, lodges, and guest houses fill Mackinac Island, though rooms are generally more expensive and harder to come by than in Mackinaw City or St. Ignace on the mainland. But if you are willing to accept the greater cost and make reservations well in advance, a few days' stay on the island can be a unique pleasure. Any list of options will inevitably be dominated by the **Grand Hotel**, 906/847-3331, a study in opulent luxury. Perched on a bluff overlooking the straits, the hotel's long, white, columned facade exudes an extravagant grace that makes Tara look like a summer cottage. The grounds include an 18-hole golf course, a putting green, and four tennis courts. Room rates range from $285 to $750 a night (a bit less before mid-June and after Labor Day), and the hotel is open from early May through October.

At a somewhat more moderate price, solid options include the **Island House**, 1 Lake Shore Dr., 906/847-3347, a charming, renovated historic hotel that was built in 1852. It's open from early May until late October, and rates range from $140 to $180 a night. The **Lake View Hotel and Conference Center**, Main St., 906/847-3384, is another renovated historic hotel (originally built in 1862), open mid-May to mid-October. Rooms go for $170 to $325 a night.

There are a couple of good lodging options at the lower end of the price range. Try the **Murray Hotel**, directly across from the Arnold Ferry Dock, 906/847-3361. It occupies an historic 1882 building and charges $69 to $225 a night from mid-May to mid-October. Or try The **Inn on Mackinac**, Main St., 906/847-3361, a bed-and-breakfast in a renovated summer guest home built in 1867. The inn is open from mid-May to mid-October, with rates from $79 to $250 a night.

CAMPING

There are no campgrounds on the island; see listings for the Straits of Mackinac in Chapter 10 for nearby camping options.

FERRY SERVICES

Mackinac Island is served by three ferry services: **Arnold Transit**, 906/847-3351, **Shepler's**, 616/436-5023, and **Star Line**, 616-436-5044. All three offer service from Mackinaw City at the tip of the Lower Peninsula and St. Ignace in the Upper Peninsula. The trip from Mackinaw City is about 15 minutes; the trip from St. Ignace takes about 10 minutes. On all three lines, round-trip fares are about $13 for adults and $7 for children. Children age four and under ride free.

10
THE STRAITS OF MACKINAC

The Straits of Mackinac is the state's busiest tourist area outside of south-eastern Michigan. That is because of the area's mixed role as both a tourist destination and the focal point of transportation between Michigan's two great peninsulas. The region has its own historical and natural attractions, such as the reconstructed colonial Fort Michilimackinac in Mackinaw City and Wilderness State Park. But it also is the necessary connecting point for anyone headed for the state's tourism jewel, Mackinac Island. What's more, the giant Mackinac Bridge is the sole roadway link between the Upper and Lower Peninsulas, so all I-75 traffic in either direction passes through the region. But while all that traffic often makes Mackinaw City extremely crowded in the summer, it also is possible, within a very short distance, to find very isolated spots for reflection and relaxation, particularly along the sandy and inviting shores of Lake Michigan.

The location of the Straits, at the convergence of Lake Michigan and Lake Huron, just a few miles from where the St. Marys River links Lake Superior to Lake Huron, has made the area a key transportation hub for centuries. European settlers recognized its importance as long ago as the early 1600s, when French missionaries and explorers—eager to extend their fur trading into the region—began visiting the area by canoe. Today, millions of tons of grain, coal, iron ore, and countless other materials and products pass under the bridge's arching span each year on their way to and from Chicago.

A PERFECT DAY IN THE STRAITS

A perfect day begins in Mackinaw City with a visit to the rebuilt fort, Colonial Michilimackinac, to get a feel for life in the area during the fur-trading era. Be sure to browse the shops downtown, especially the fudge shops, and spend some time at the Bridge Museum, learning about the magnificent steel span that ties Michigan's two peninsulas together. The lakeshore at the northern edge of town offers an excellent view of the bridge, too.

Then it's time for a close-up view of the bridge as you drive across to St. Ignace in the Upper Peninsula. There you can find out about Native American life and the early European explorers at the Father Marquette National Memorial and Museum and the Marquette Mission Park and Museum of Ojibwa Culture.

In the afternoon, drive west along Highway 2 and spend some time on the glorious sand beaches of Lake Michigan. Take a swim, relax on the sand, have a picnic dinner, and watch the sun set over the water, as lumbering freighters roll south and west from the straits toward Chicago.

SIGHTSEEING HIGHLIGHTS

★★★★ COLONIAL MICHILIMACKINAC
I-75 at exit 339, 616/436-5563

This reconstructed fort, just west of the Mackinac Bridge's southern tip, is on the site of the original, which was built by the French in 1715 and was controlled by the British from 1761 to 1781. Buildings inside include a priest's house, a church, a blacksmith shop, barracks, block-houses, a guardhouse, and a trader's house. Costumed interpreters provide reenactments and demonstrations.

Details: Southern tip of the Mackinac Bridge. Mid-June–Labor Day daily 9–6, hours vary mid-May–mid-June and Labor Day-mid Oct. $7.25 adults, $4.25 ages 6–12, $21 families. Combination tickets for Fort Mackinac on Mackinac Island and Mill Creek State Historic Park: $15 adults, $8.50 ages 6–12, $42 families. (2 hours)

★★★★ WILDERNESS STATE PARK
Wilderness Park Road, 616/436-5381

The park is one of the Lower Peninsula's largest tracts of wilderness. It encompasses 26 miles of Lake Michigan shoreline and 16 miles of trails that can provide either leisurely walks or strenuous hikes. Rustic trailside cabins can be rented, but they are usually spoken for months in advance so reservations are an absolute necessity. All but one of the six cabins is isolated near its own stretch of beach. Three other cabins near the park's campgrounds are available for large groups and can sleep up to 24. In winter the hiking trails are excellent for snowmobilers and cross-country skiers.

Details: 12 miles west of Mackinaw City. Open year-round, 24 hours daily. Cabins rent for $40–$55 a night. (2 hours minumum)

★★★ FATHER MARQUETTE NATIONAL MEMORIAL AND MUSEUM
Highway 2, St. Ignace, 906/643-8620
This 52-acre park commemorates the life of the famous French Jesuit missionary and explorer. Displays include artifacts from Marquette's travels. The grounds also have walking trails that lead to lovely views of the straits and the bridge.

Details: Just west of the bridge. Park open daily 9–8, museum open Memorial Day–Labor Day daily 9–5. $4 per vehicle. (1 hour)

★★★ MACKINAC BRIDGE AND BRIDGE MUSEUM
I-75 between Mackinac City and St. Ignace, 616/436-5534
This five-mile-long toll bridge, opened in 1957, links Michigan's Upper

MACKINAC BRIDGE

Travel Michigan

and Lower Peninsulas. It is one of the longest suspension bridges in the world. Scenic views of the bridge are available from all over the Straits area. The museum on Central Avenue in downtown Mackinaw City includes displays and a film that explain the history of the bridge and its construction.

Details: *Museum open Apr–Oct 9–midnight. Free. (30 minutes)*

★★★ MARQUETTE MISSION PARK AND MUSEUM OF OJIBWA CULTURE
500 N. State Street, St. Ignace, 906/643-9161

This museum is located on the presumed site of Father Marquette's grave. The building itself is a restored nineteenth-century Jesuit church, dedicated to the Ojibwa, the original inhabitants of the upper Great Lakes. Some of the museum's artifacts have been dated to 6000 B.C.

STRAITS OF MACKINAC

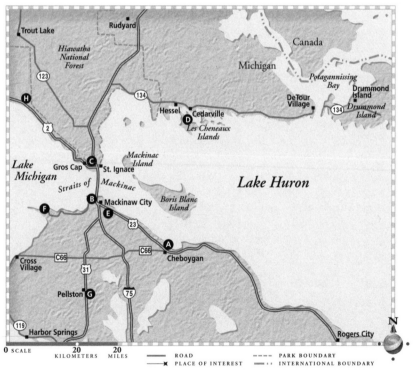

Details: *Memorial Day–Labor Day Mon–Sat 10–8, Sun 1–8; Labor Day–early Oct Mon–Sat 11–5, Sun 1–5. $2 adults, $1 ages 6–12, $5 families. (1 hour)*

★★★ MILL CREEK STATE HISTORIC PARK
Highway 23, Mackinaw City, 616/436-7301

This park features the site of an eighteenth-century industrial complex, thought to be the oldest in northern Michigan. A sawmill here was built in 1790. The park features demonstrations of early industrial techniques and also offers nature trails with scenic overlooks.

Details: *Mid-June–Labor Day daily 9–6, hours vary rest of the year. $6.50 adults, $3.50 ages 6–12, $17 families. Combination tickets that include admission to Fort Mackinac on Mackinac Island and Colonial Michilimackinac: $15 adults, $8.50 ages 6–12, $42 families. (1 hour)*

★★ CHEBOYGAN COUNTY HISTORICAL MUSEUM
404 S. Huron Street, Cheboygan, 616/627-9597

SIGHTS
- **Ⓐ** Cheboygan County Historical Museum
- **Ⓑ** Colonial Michilimackinac
- **Ⓒ** Father Marquette National Memorial and Museum
- **Ⓓ** Les Cheneaux Islands
- **Ⓑ** Mackinac Bridge and Bridge Museum
- **Ⓒ** Marquette Mission Park and Museum of Ojibwa Culture
- **Ⓔ** Mill Creek State Historic Park
- **Ⓕ** Wilderness State Park

FOOD
- **Ⓑ** The Admiral's Table
- **Ⓑ** Audie's
- **Ⓐ** The Boathouse
- **Ⓒ** Galley Restaurant & Bar
- **Ⓐ** Hack-Ma-Tack Inn
- **Ⓑ** Neath the Birches
- **Ⓖ** Dam Site Inn

LODGING
- **Ⓒ** Aurora Borealis Motor Inn
- **Ⓐ** Best Western River-Terrace Motel
- **Ⓑ** Best Western Thunderbird Inn
- **Ⓐ** Birch Haus Motel
- **Ⓑ** Clear Water Lakeshore Motel

LODGING *(continued)*
- **Ⓐ** Hack-Ma-Tack Inn
- **Ⓒ** Days Inn St. Ignace & Suites
- **Ⓑ** Hamilton Inn Select–Beachfront
- **Ⓑ** Ramada Limited Waterfront

CAMPING
- **Ⓐ** Cheboygan State Park
- **Ⓗ** Hog Island Point Campground
- **Ⓑ** Mackinaw City KOA
- **Ⓔ** Mackinaw Mill Creek
- **Ⓒ** Straits State Park
- **Ⓕ** Wilderness State Park

Note: Items with the same letter are located in the same place.

This museum is located in a two-story house with an attached jail that was built in 1882. It was the local sheriff's home until 1969. The house has been restored with period furnishings, and the cells contain exhibits on lumbering, farming, and other topics.

Details: *June 15–Sept 15 Mon–Fri 1–4 and by appointment. $2 adults, $1 ages 3–17, $5 families. (30 minutes)*

★★ CHEBOYGAN OPERA HOUSE
403 N. Huron Street, Cheboygan, 800/357-9408

This Victorian theater was built in 1877 and rebuilt after a fire in 1888. Mary Pickford and Annie Oakley are among the entertainers who performed there.

Details: *Guided tours June–Sept Tue–Fri 1–4, by appointment the rest of the year. $1 adults, age 12 and under free. (30 minutes)*

★★ DRUMMOND ISLAND
906/493-5245 (Drummond Island Tourism Association)

At the eastern tip of the Upper Peninsula at the mouth of the St. Marys River, this huge island is a popular destination for anglers, boaters, and hunters. A ferry from De Tour Village on Highway 134 carries cars to the heavily wooded and very scenic island.

Details: *The ferry leaves De Tour at 40 minutes past the hour and returns from the island at 10 minutes past the hour. The trip takes 10–15 minutes; round-trip fares are $8 per car and driver plus $2 per adult passenger, though campers and other large vehicles cost more, up to $18 for a motorhome or bus. (2–4 hours)*

★★ LES CHENEAUX ISLANDS
906/484-3935 (information center)

These 36 wooded islands in Lake Huron, off the southern shore of the Upper Peninsula, provide an extremely scenic setting for snowmobiling, boating, and fishing. The islands can be reached from Hessel and Cedarville.

Details: *Information center on Hwy. 134 in Cedarville. Open year-round Mon–Fri 9–5, plus Sat in summer. (2–4 hours)*

FITNESS AND RECREATION

One of the best places for getting some exercise around the Straits is at **Wilderness State Park** (see Sightseeing Highlights), where you can walk for miles along the Lake Michigan beaches or hike 12 miles of inland trails. The **Les Cheneaux Islands**, near Hessel and Cedarville, also are an excellent and beautiful place for boating.

FOOD

Good restaurants are found on both sides of the Mackinac Bridge, though the selection is somewhat better south of the bridge. Naturally, seafood is a big draw at these restaurants. And virtually all of the restaurants in the area are moderate or low-priced.

Near Pellston, a half-hour drive south of Mackinaw City, is the **Dam Site Inn**, 616/539-8851. It's just off Highway 31, about a mile and a half south of town. This relaxed and gracious country restaurant is open from mid-April to late October and features all-you-can-eat chicken dinners, as well as steaks and seafood. Dinners cost $10 to $20.

In Cheboygan, along the Lake Huron Shore, is **The Boathouse**, 106 Pine St., 616/627-4316. It's located in a converted former boathouse that has the quirky historic distinction of having once belonged to the notorious Purple Gang. The menu is typically American, and the ambiance is casual, with dinners costing $15 to $20. The restaurant is closed Mondays from early September to late May.

Just outside of town is the **Hack-Ma-Tack Inn**, 8131 Beebe Rd., 616/625-2919, in a rustic, historic lodge built in 1894 and overlooking the Cheboygan River. The restaurant features docking facilities and offers an American menu with steak, prime rib, and whitefish specialties. Dinners are priced in the $10 to $20 range.

Mackinaw City has the largest selection of restaurants in the area. The **Admiral's Table**, 502 S. Huron St., 616/436-5687, is a steak and seafood place, specializing in prime rib and whitefish. Dinner costs between $10 and $20. **Neath the Birches**, one mile south of town on Old U.S. 31, 616/436-5401, also specializes in steak and seafood and is open from May 1 through late October. Dinners cost $15 to $30.

For inexpensive meals, try **Audie's**, 314 Nicolet St., 616/436-5744, which features casual family dining in the Family Room and a more intimate atmosphere in the Chippewa Room. Dinners are $10 to $15 in the Family Room, and $15 to $30 in the Chippewa Room.

North of the bridge, in St. Ignace, you'll find the **Galley Restaurant and Bar**, 241 N. State St., 906/643-7960. It serves fresh lake fish and prime-rib dinners in the $10 to $20 range, has a fine view of the city's harbor, and is open from May 1 through October 15.

LODGING

With a population of just 900 residents, Mackinaw City may have the largest number of motel rooms per capita in the state. The city caters not only to tourists exploring the northern Lower Peninsula and through-travelers to the Upper Peninsula, but also to many Mackinac Island visitors.

Depending on the time of year, many of the several dozen motels in town offer a fairly wide range of room rates. For example, the **Best Western Thunderbird Inn**, 146 U.S. 31, 616/436-5433, has rates of $69 to $119 a night. The motel is open from late April through mid-October and has a heated indoor pool, sauna, whirlpool, and playground.

At the **Clear Water Lakeshore Motel**, 1247 S. Huron St., 616/436-7800, room rates range from $29 to $129 a night. The motel is close to the ferry docks and offers a view of the bridge and Mackinac Island. It has two pools, a whirlpool, and a playground, and is open from May 17 through October 26.

Moving up the price scale, the **Hamilton Inn Select-Beachfront**, 701 S. Huron St., 616/436-5005, has a beach on the lake as well as a heated indoor pool, a whirlpool, and an exercise room. It's open all year and charges $38 to $149 for rooms. Likewise, the **Ramada Limited Waterfront**, 723 S. Huron St., 616/436-5055, is close to the ferry services and offers a heated indoor pool and whirlpool. The motel also has a rooftop sun deck with a whirlpool and is open from late April through late October. Room prices range from $49 to $169 a night.

In St. Ignace, the **Aurora Borealis Motor Inn**, 635 W. U.S. 2, 906/643-7488, is open from April 1 through October and charges $59 to $79 nightly for rooms; while the **Days Inn St. Ignace and Suites**, 1067 N. State St., 906/643-8008, charges $49 to $160 a night. The Days Inn has two heated indoor pools, a sauna, whirlpool, and playground.

Farther south along the Lake Huron shore at Cheboygan is the **Best Western River Terrace Motel**, 847 S. Main St., 616/627-5688. Most rooms overlook the Cheboygan River, and the motel offers a heated indoor pool, whirlpool, exercise room, and a boat dock. Rooms go for $53 to $135 a night, and the motel is open all year. The **Birch Haus Motel**, 1301 Mackinaw Ave., 616/627-5862, is open all year, with rates ranging from $25 to $65 a night.

CAMPING

For campers, hundreds of sites are available at campgrounds close to both ends of the Mackinac Bridge. The largest of these is **Mackinaw Mill Creek Camping**, 616/436-5584, a private facility with 600 sites, open from May 1 through October 31. The campground is about three miles south of I-75 on

Highway 23, and offers a heated pool, playground, recreation room, and miniature golf. Rates are $12.50 to $16 a night for four, plus $2 per extra person. Another fair-sized private campground is the **Mackinaw City KOA**, 566 Trailsend Rd., 616/436-5643, with 110 sites, a heated pool, playground, and recreation room. The campground is open from May 1 through October 15 and charges $19 for two, plus $2 to $3 per extra person.

The area also has plenty of public camping facilities, most notably **Wilderness State Park**, 12 miles west of Mackinaw City at 898 Wilderness Park Dr., 616/436-5381. The park has 210 campsites, is open all year, and charges $15 a night. Recreational opportunities include swimming, fishing, waterskiing, cross-country and downhill skiing, and snowmobiling. The park also has a boat ramp, a playground, and nature trails (see Sightseeing Highlights).

North of the bridge is **Straits State Park**, about a half-mile east of I-75 on the south side of Highway 2, 906/643-8620. The park has 318 sites, is open all year, and is an excellent base from which to tour the region. It's just two miles to the Mackinac Island ferry in St. Ignace, six miles across the bridge from Mackinaw City, and within a 90-minute drive from the Seney National Wildlife Refuge, Tahquamenon Falls, and the Soo Locks. Campsites are $14 a night.

A bit farther afield is the **Hog Island Point Campground**, 906/293-5131, in the Lake Superior State Forest, seven miles east of Naubinway on Highway 2 along the Lake Michigan shore. The campground, with 58 sites, features swimming, fishing, and a boat ramp. Open all year, it charges about $4 a night.

Southeast of the bridge is **Cheboygan State Park**, 4490 Beach Rd., 616/627-2811, four miles east of Cheboygan on Highway 23. The campground has 78 sites, remains open all year, and features swimming, a boat ramp, a playground, nature trails, fishing, waterskiing, and cross-country skiing. Rates are $11 a night.

NIGHTLIFE

Aside from a campfire or a cable movie in a Mackinaw City motel room, the most exciting nightlife in the Straits area is the **Kewadin Shores Casino**, 800/539-2346, at Hessel. Take Highway 134 east about 15 miles from I-75, then drive three miles north on 3 Mile Road. The casino has slot machines, blackjack, video poker, and keno, and is open from 9 a.m. to 1 a.m. daily.

11
THE SUPERIOR
SHORE

There must be something that makes people stay in a region where summers tend to be cool and short and winters tend to be cold, very snowy, and long; where work can be as hard as the winter weather; and the economy tends to be iffy and seasonal. Sure, it's a great place for those who love the outdoors—fishing in the summer, deer hunting in the fall, and plenty of winter for snowmobiling or skiing. But for those who love this region and remain here, the attraction has a lot to do with the hypnotic effects of Lake Superior.

It would be difficult to tire of watching this lake. Some days smooth, graceful, and blue, a comfort to the eye and soul, it is also often gray and angry, crashing hard against the rocky shoreline near Presque Isle Park with a power that leaves you awestruck. The water is too cold for any but the briefest of swims, even at the peak of summer, yet in the frightening churn of a November storm there is still an oddly relaxing and reassuring quality to its character.

Highway 28, which connects Sault Ste. Marie and Marquette on its way across the entire Upper Peninsula, is the region's main street. Sault Ste. Marie is a busy city. Located at the northern tip of I-75, it is a major border crossing into Canada and is home to the Soo Locks, one of the most important shipping hubs in the Great Lakes. It also is an excellent base for exploring the eastern Upper Peninsula. Marquette is larger, though, and serves as the economic and social center of the region.

SUPERIOR SHORE

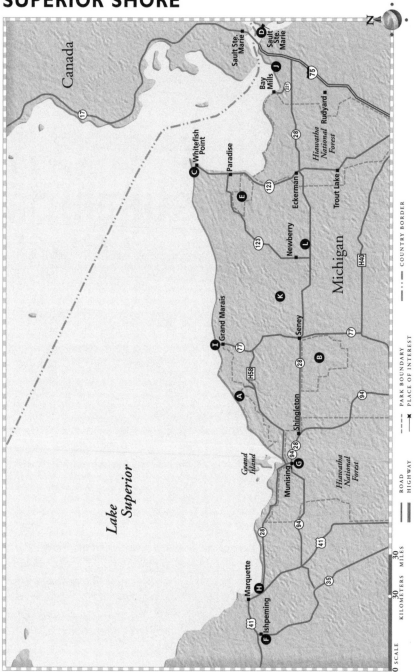

A PERFECT DAY ON THE SUPERIOR SHORE

Begin with a morning jog around Presque Isle Park in Marquette for some exercise and marvelous lakeshore scenery. Drive out to Negaunee for a visit to the Michigan Iron Industry Museum or Ishpeming for the U.S. National Ski Hall of Fame and Museum. Next, take the spectacularly scenic drive along the Lake Superior shore from Marquette to Munising, stopping at Shelter Bay or Au Train for a picnic lunch and some beach lolling.

After lunch, continue east along Highway 28 toward Sault Ste. Marie. At Newberry, take the northern loop on Highway 123 for a short stop at Tahquamenon Falls and reconnect with Highway 28 about 35 miles west of the Soo. If you time it right, you should be able to make the dinner cruise on the Soo Locks tour boats.

SIGHTSEEING HIGHLIGHTS
★★★★ **MICHIGAN IRON INDUSTRY MUSEUM**
County Road 492 at Forge Road, Negaunee, 906/475-7857
Just east of Negaunee, in a secluded wooded area along the banks of the Carp River, this museum occupies the site of the first iron forge in the Lake Superior region. The forge established here in 1848 processed iron ore from nearby mines, and though the forge itself was never a moneymaker, its products convinced investors of the high quality of Michigan's iron ore. The museum exhibits a large number of artifacts and old pieces of mining equipment. Interpretive displays

---

SIGHTS
- **Ⓐ** Pictured Rocks National Lakeshore
- **Ⓑ** Seney National Wildlife Refuge
- **Ⓒ** Shipwreck Historical Museum
- **Ⓓ** Soo Locks Boat Tours
- **Ⓔ** Tahquamenon Falls State Park
- **Ⓓ** Tower of History
- **Ⓕ** U. S. National Ski Hall of Fame and Museum

FOOD
- **Ⓓ** The Antlers
- **Ⓖ** Dogpatch
- **Ⓓ** Freighters
- **Ⓓ** Studebaker's

LODGING
- **Ⓗ** Edgewater Motel
- **Ⓓ** Ojibway Hotel
- **Ⓓ** Skyline Motel
- **Ⓖ** Terrace Motel
- **Ⓘ** Voyageur's Motel

CAMPING
- **Ⓙ** Brimley State Park
- **Ⓚ** Lake Superior State Forest
- **Ⓛ** Newberry KOA Kampground
- **Ⓔ** Tahquamenon Falls State Park
- **Ⓖ** Wandering Wheels Campground

Note: Items with the same letter are located in the same place.

---

inside the museum—and outside along a path that meanders through the old forge site—chronicle the history of the area's iron-mining industry, which still produces nearly a quarter of the iron ore mined in the United States. A slide show in the museum's auditorium illuminates life on Michigan's iron ranges.

Details: *May–Oct daily 9:30–4:30. Admission is free. (1 1/2 hours)*

★★★★ PICTURED ROCKS NATIONAL LAKESHORE
Highway 28 and County Road H58, Munising, 906/387-3700 (visitors center)

This 35-mile stretch of Lake Superior coastline from Munising to Grand Marais includes remarkable wind- and water-carved cliffs. Some of the cliffs rise 200 feet above the lake. Near Grand Marais the cliffs give way to giant sand dunes that once served as skids for sending logs from the forests at the top of the dunes to the lake below.

The parklands along the shoreline contain 21 miles of cross-country ski trails that also are excellent for hiking and backpacking. Good swimming and picnicking sites are plentiful, too. Campgrounds are available in summer, but the roads leading to them are closed by snow from November through April. Although some cliffs are accessible by hiking trails, the most convenient way to see them is by tour boat.

Details: *June–mid-Sept daily 8–6, Mon–Sat 9–4:30 rest of the year. Three-hour boat tours daily in summer and fall. Boats leave from the Munising Municipal Pier, 906/387-2379. $22 adults, $7 ages 6–12, age 5 and under free. (2 hours minimum)*

★★★★ PRESQUE ISLE PARK
Lake Shore Boulevard, Marquette, 906/228-0460

At Marquette's north end, a 328-acre wooded peninsula pokes out into Lake Superior. That's where you will find Presque Isle Park, a delightful place for picnicking, hiking, bicycling, wading in the frigid water, or skipping stones. The park has an outdoor pool with a water slide for summer fun and nature trails that are good for snowshoeing and cross-country skiing in winter. A paved, two-lane drive loops around the whole peninsula, providing an excellent route for bikers and in-line skaters.

Details: *Daily 7–11. Admission is free. (30 minutes)*

★★★★ SOO LOCKS BOAT TOURS
515 E. Portage Avenue and 1157 E. Portage Avenue,
906/632-6301

Sault Ste. Marie is Michigan's oldest city, first visited by Europeans around 1620, when French fur traders began moving into the upper Great Lakes region. Across the St. Marys River is the much larger Sault Ste. Marie in Ontario, Canada. The biggest attraction on either side of the river is the Soo Locks, which enable about 95 million tons of shipborne freight each year to bypass the St. Marys River rapids, where the river drops 21 feet from Lake Superior to Lake Huron. Soo Locks Boat Tours travel through the locks and past the rapids in two-hour narrated tours.

Details: *Cruises May–Oct. Tour fare: $14 adults, $13.50 age 62 and over, $11.50 ages 13–18, $6.50 ages 5–12. Dinner cruises: $34 adults, $32.50 age 62 and over, $25 ages 3–12. (2 hours)*

★★★★ TAHQUAMENON FALLS STATE PARK
Highway 123, 906/492-3415

This 36,000-acre park contains two beautiful falls on the Tahquamenon River. The upper falls are 50 feet high and 200 feet wide. The lower falls are a series of cascades and rapids divided by an island. The falls are popular both for their beauty and their accessibility. A quarter-mile paved path to the Upper Falls leads to the rim of the small gorge through which the river cuts. The paved path splits and continues several hundred yards, upstream and downstream, ending at lovely views at both the top and bottom of the falls. The lower falls are even more accessible, with superb views just 100 yards from the parking lot, near a concession stand that sells food and a large array of souvenirs. The park also offers three campgrounds, more than 25 miles of hiking trails, and a variety of other recreational opportunities.

Details: *About 12 miles west of Paradise. Open 24 hours daily. $4 per vehicle. (1 hour)*

★★★★ U.S. NATIONAL SKI HALL OF FAME AND MUSEUM
Highway 41 between Second and Third Streets,
Ishpeming, 906/485-6323

The museum recognizes the American greats of the skiing world and illustrates the development of the sport through displays of photos, old equipment, trophies, and even a cable car from a ski lift. It is especially interesting to follow the evolution of the sport from the U.S. Army's ski assault team in World War II. Some of these soldiers returned from the war to manage resorts, as recreational interest in skiing began to boom in the late 1940s and 1950s. You'll also learn about the artificial snow-making machine developed by Everett Kirchner at his Boyne Mountain ski resort in the northern Lower Peninsula—a piece of equipment that greatly boosted the ski industry.

Details: *Mid-May–Nov Mon–Sat 10–6, Sun noon–5; rest of the year daily 10–5. $3 adults, $2.50 seniors, $1 students age 10 and over. (1 hour)*

★★★ MARQUETTE HISTORICAL MUSEUM
213 N. Front Street, Marquette, 906/226-3571

This museum explores the area's history through artifacts from early pioneering days as well as exhibits on the mining and lumbering industries that have played such an important part in the region. Displays on the region's significant geological history also are included.

Details: *Mon–Fri 10–5, 10–9 on the third Thu of each month. $3 adults, $1 students with identification, age 12 and under free. (1 hour)*

★★★ MARQUETTE MARITIME MUSEUM
E. Ridge Street and Lakeshore Boulevard, 906/226-2006

The museum features displays on the maritime history of Marquette and Lake Superior. Exhibits include boats and models, charts, photos, and a replica of the dockside offices of the city's first commercial fishing and shipping companies.

Details: *May 31–Sept 30 daily 10–5. $3, age 12 and under free. Lighthouse tours daily 1–4. $2. (1 hour)*

★★★ SENEY NATIONAL WILDLIFE REFUGE
Highway 77, Seney, 906/586-9851

About halfway between Marquette and Sault Ste. Marie on Highway 28, this 95,000-acre refuge is home to more than 200 species of birds as well as beavers, minks, muskrats, otters, coyotes, deer, and bears. One of the largest concentrations of nesting loons in Michigan can be found here, along with bald eagles, ospreys, sandhill cranes, and trumpeter swans. At the refuge headquarters you'll find information for a 1.5-mile self-guided walking tour and a seven-mile self-guided driving tour (over unpaved roads). Early morning and evening are the best times for spotting wildlife.

MARQUETTE

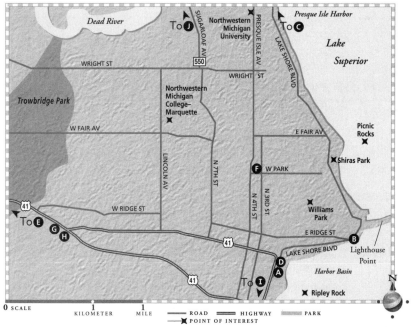

SIGHTS

- **A** Marquette Historical Museum
- **B** Marquette Maritime Museum
- **C** Presque Isle Park

FOOD

- **D** Marquette Harbor Brewery and Vierling Saloon
- **E** Northwoods Supper Club
- **F** The Village Cafe

LODGING

- **G** Comfort Suites
- **H** Days Inn
- **I** Tiroler Hof Motel

CAMPING

- **J** Marquette Tourist Park & Campground

Details: Hwy. 77, about five miles south of its intersection with Hwy. 28. Walking and driving tours open May 15–Oct 15 daily dawn–dusk. Visitors center open May 15–Oct 15 daily 9–5. Refuge office open Mon–Fri 7:30–4. Admission is free. No camping. (1–2 hours)

★★★ SHIPWRECK HISTORICAL MUSEUM
Whitefish Point, 906/635-1742

This museum displays artifacts and pictures of Great Lakes shipping disasters. One of the most famous, the wreck of the *Edmund Fitzgerald* a few miles off Whitefish Point, is described in a video presentation. Nearby is the Whitefish Point Lighthouse, the oldest working lighthouse on Lake Superior, which began guiding ships in 1849.

Details: 11 miles north of Paradise. May 15–Oct 15 daily 10–6. $7 adults, $4 age 12 and under, $20 families. (1 hour)

★★★ TOWER OF HISTORY
326 E. Portage Avenue, Sault Ste. Marie, 888/744-7867

Another worthwhile stop in Sault Ste. Marie, this 21-story tower offers a panoramic view of the Soo Locks, the St. Mary River, and the surrounding area in both the United States and Canada. Displays of artifacts and a slide show depict the area's history. Don't worry, there's an elevator to the top.

Details: Mid-May–mid-Oct daily 10–6. $3.25 adults, $1.75 ages 6–16. (1 hour)

FITNESS AND RECREATION

One of the most popular spots for a walk, jog, skate, or bike ride is **Presque Isle Park** in Marquette (see Sightseeing Highlights). Its trails and rugged shoreline make it easy to set any kind of walking pace, from a gentle amble to a lung-stretching hike. The paved loop around the peninsula is also great for biking.

Not far away, just north of the city along the Big Bay Road, is **Sugarloaf Hill**. From the parking lot at the base you can ascend the quarter-mile trail to the top. The trail rises several hundred feet, a strenuous stroll if you are out of shape. And if the climb doesn't take your breath away, the view from the top will. It is an inspiring panorama, encompassing Lake Superior, Marquette, and mile upon mile of woods and hills stretching inland from the lake.

FOOD

The restaurants in the region are simple and straightforward, with the emphasis on filling portions of basic American cuisine.

One of the best restaurants in the Marquette area is the **Northwoods Supper Club**, just south of U.S. 41 about 3.5 miles west of Marquette, 906/228-4343. This cozy place is a local tradition, family owned and operated since 1934, with a rustic log-frame lounge and a fireplace that is wonderful in cold weather. The food is quite good, and dinners run between $10 and $20.

Downtown is the **Marquette Harbor Brewery and Vierling Saloon**, 119 S. Front St., 906/228-3533, a renovated saloon built in 1883. It offers a warm family atmosphere, with an antique bar and other mementos, and has recently begun serving its own microbrews. The food is excellent, with dinners between $10 and $20. Less expensive and north of downtown toward the Northern Michigan University campus is the **Village Cafe**, 1015 N. Third St., 906/226-6881. The restaurant has a smoke-free policy, and the food is good. For casual family dining in Munising try **Dogpatch**, 325 E. Superior St., 906/387-9948. Dinners are in the $10 to $20 range.

In Sault Ste. Marie, the most elegant restaurant is **Freighters** in the Ojibway Hotel, 240 W. Portage Ave., 906/632-4211. The atmosphere is a bit more than casual, but a bit less than dressy. The dining room overlooks the Soo Locks, and dinners cost $20 to $30. **Studebaker's**, 3583 I-75 Business Spur, 906/632-4262, features family dining, with lunch and dinner buffets and meals costing $10 to $20. **The Antlers**, 804 E. Portage Ave., 906/632-3571, exudes a more traditional U.P. ambiance. Set in a rustic old bar, it has a large collection of mounted animals. Dinners cost $10 to $20.

LODGING

As the Upper Peninsula's biggest city, Marquette has an ample supply of motels, many of them the usual national chains and most of them in the moderate price range. **Comfort Suites**, 2463 U.S. 41 W., 906/228-0028, has a heated indoor pool, sauna, whirlpool, and exercise room, with rates between $68 and $125. The **Days Inn**, 2403 U.S. 41 W., 906/225-1393, also has a heated pool, sauna, and whirlpool, and rooms that cost $50 to $95.

At the less expensive end of the scale are the **Tiroler Hof Motel**, 1880 U.S. 41 S., 906/226-7516, with Austrian-style buildings, a Lake Superior view, and rooms costing $38 to $54; and the **Edgewater Motel**, 2050 U.S. 41 S., 906/225-1305, across the street from Lake Superior, with room rates from $32 to $58.

Options are more limited in Munising. The **Comfort Inn**, a mile and a half east of town on Hwy. 28, 906/387-5292, has a heated indoor pool, whirlpool, and exercise room. Rates are between $50 and $94. The **Terrace Motel**, 420 Prospect, 906/387-2735, has a sauna and recreation room and charges $35 to $52 a night.

For a secluded but scenic getaway, stop at the **Voyageur's Motel** in Grand Marais, 281 E. Wilson St., 906/494-2389. The motel is on a ridge overlooking the harbor and offers—in addition to the lovely view—a sauna, a whirlpool, and even a heated workshop for snowmobiles. Rooms cost $39 to $54 a night.

At the upper end of the price scale in Sault Ste. Marie is the **Ojibway Hotel**, 240 W. Portage Ave., 906/632-4100, a renovated historic hotel built in 1928. The six-story structure has a heated indoor pool, sauna, and whirlpool, and offers a great view of the Soo Locks. Rooms cost $98 to $124 a night. An inexpensive option is the **Skyline Motel**, 2601 I-75 Business Spur, 906/632-3393, with rooms costing $47 to $70 a night.

CAMPING

An abundant supply of campgrounds are found along Highway 28 as it stretches across the Upper Peninsula from Sault Ste. Marie to Marquette. In the eastern region, near the popular tourist area around Tahquamenon Falls, are several excellent state park campgrounds. **Brimley State Park**, one mile east of Brimley on Hwy. 221, 906/248-3422, has 270 sites and is open all year. The campground offers swimming, a playground, nature trails, a boat ramp, and fishing, and charges $12 a night.

Around Whitefish Bay near Paradise are a pair of public campgrounds at **Tahquamenon Falls State Park**: the Lower Falls Campground, 12 miles west of Paradise on Hwy. 123, and the River Mouth Unit, about five miles south of Paradise on Hwy. 123, 906/492-3415. Lower Falls Campground is the larger of the two, with 183 sites. The River Mouth Unit has 136 sites. Both are open year-round and charge $14 a night, and both offer nature trails, fishing, and snowmobiling. The Lower Falls campground also has facilities for cross-country and downhill skiing.

Several more campgrounds are near Newberry. The **Newberry KOA Kampground**, 906/293-5762, is three miles east of Newberry on Highway 28, just east of the junction with Highway 123. It has 146 sites, an indoor pool, sauna, whirlpool, playground, recreation room, and miniature golf. The campground is open from mid-May to mid-October and charges $19.50 a night for two, plus $2 to $3 per extra person. Kamping Kabins are available for about $34 a night.

The **Lake Superior State Forest**, 906/293-5131, has six small public campgrounds in the Newberry area. All are open throughout the year, charge about $4 a night, and provide recreational opportunities such as fishing, boating, and snowmobiling.

The **Wandering Wheels Campground**, 906/387-3315, is a private facility with 88 sites. It's about 3.5 miles east of Munising on Highway 28. The campground includes a heated pool, playground, and recreation room, and is open from May through mid-October. Rates are $17 for four, plus $2 per extra person.

The **Marquette Tourist Park and Campground**, 906/228-0465, is a public facility open from mid-May to mid-October. Its 110 sites cost between $6 and $13 a night. It offers swimming and a playground and has a 15-night maximum stay. The campground is on County Road 550, a half mile north of Wright Street.

NIGHTLIFE

Nighttime entertainment in the region is fairly limited, even in cities like Marquette and Sault Ste. Marie. You'll find a variety of bars with live music (a big emphasis on country and western) and some movie theaters. But other than that, the hot spots are the Indian-run Kewadin Casinos. A small casino in the village of Christmas, just west of Munising, has slot machines, blackjack, video poker, and live poker. Call 906/387-5475 for more information.

The biggest northland casino is the **Kewadin Casino at the Soo**, 2186 Skunk Rd., at I-75 exit 392, 800/539-2346. It has more than a thousand slot machines, roulette, blackjack, video poker, live poker, and craps, and is open 24 hours daily.

Less than 10 miles southeast of Marquette is the **Ojibway Casino of Marquette**, 906/249-4200. It's on the south side of M-28, about four miles east of the intersection with U.S. 41. Open 9 a.m. to 2 a.m. weekdays and 9 a.m. to 4 a.m. Friday and Saturday, it offers slot machines, blackjack, roulette, craps, video poker, and video keno.

Scenic Route: Marquette to Munising

For much of the 50 miles between Marquette and Munising, Highway 28 runs close to the Lake Superior shore, making it a gorgeous drive. In stormy weather the power of the lake is awe-inspiring, and on a quiet, sunny day, the water is so serene that you want to sit and watch it forever.

There are quite a few places to pull off the road and enjoy the scenery, but the most popular, without a doubt, is Au Train. The long beaches there offer plenty of room to stretch out on the warm sand for sunbathing or sand castle–building. For those swimmers not daring enough for the frigid waters of Lake Superior, the shallow pools where the Au Train River empties into the big lake provide a somewhat warmer—or at least less chilly—venue for getting wet.

Another excellent stopping spot is Shelter Bay, a small cove about five miles west of Au Train. A shady roadside park is perfect for a picnic lunch, and on a hot day, the small inland lake near the picnic area makes for good swimming.

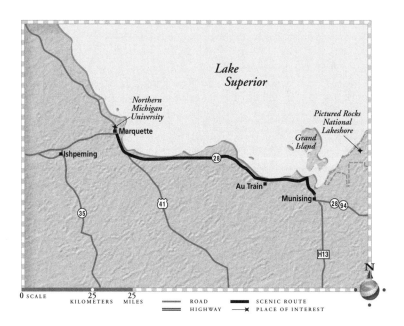

12
COPPER COUNTRY

Michigan's Copper Country is a rare, almost mystical place. It is a region of deep pine forests, rocky terrain, and cold blue waters. Hiking through the dense woods of the Porcupine Mountains or along the rugged Lake Superior shore of the Keweenaw Peninsula, primeval America seems close at hand.

The area's heritage of copper and iron mining has given most of the towns a gritty feel, born of generations of hard labor in a harsh environment. Summers are beautiful but fairly short. Hardwood trees often begin turning color in mid-August, and annual snowfall often exceeds 150 inches. The region is dominated by the presence of Lake Superior, but numerous inland lakes and rivers provide great fishing, and the area is studded with hunting camps and cottages. Campgrounds are ample.

Houghton, in the center of the Keweenaw Peninsula, is the largest city in Copper Country and the area's economic center. With a population of just 7,500 it is not a large city, but it has a variety of restaurants and accommodations, largely because it is home to Michigan Technological University, one of the country's finer engineering colleges.

A PERFECT DAY IN THE COPPER COUNTRY

Setting out from Houghton, take the scenic drive up to Copper Harbor and back through Eagle Harbor and Eagle River. Stop in Copper Harbor long

COPPER COUNTRY

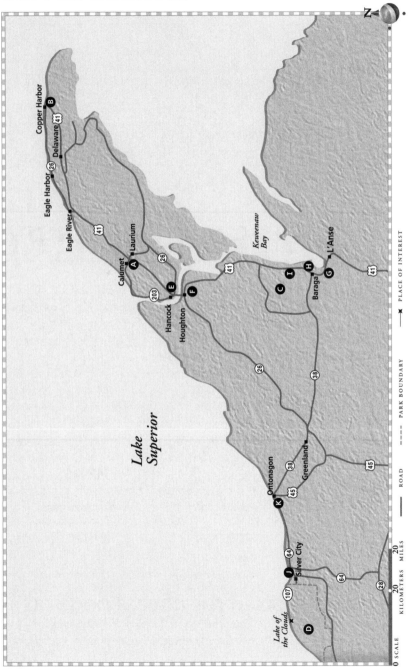

N

Lake Superior

Copper Harbor
Delaware
Eagle Harbor
Eagle River
Calumet
Laurium
Hancock
Houghton
Kewenaw Bay
L'Anse
Baraga
Greenland
Ontonagon
Silver City
Lake of the Clouds

A B C D E F G H I J K

26
41
203
26
41
38
26
45
38
45
64
107
64
28

PLACE OF INTEREST
PARK BOUNDARY
ROAD

0 SCALE
KILOMETERS MILES
20
20

enough to visit Fort Wilkins State Park and have lunch, then begin the return toward Houghton. Pause in Calumet to stroll past the ornate nineteenth-century buildings and see the elegant old theater there.

Heading south and west from Houghton, aim for Ontonagon and Silver City, and take a short hike in the Porcupine Mountains Wilderness State Park. Finish the day with a visit to the Lake of the Clouds Scenic Overlook to watch the sun set beyond the mountains.

SIGHTSEEING HIGHLIGHTS
★★★★ DELAWARE COPPER MINE TOUR
U.S. 41, 906/289-4688

This attraction is small and out of the way (just south of Copper Harbor at the tip of the Keweenaw Peninsula) but it is well worth the stop. The Delaware mine was opened as part of the early local copper rush in the 1840s. It never made much profit and was sealed up in the late 1870s.

A few years ago it was reopened to give tourists a chance to go

---

SIGHTS
- **A** Calumet Theater
- **A** Coppertown U.S.A.
- **B** Fort Wilkins State Park
- **C** Hanka Homestead Museum
- **D** Porcupine Mountains Wilderness State Park
- **E** Quincy Mine Hoist
- **F** Seaman Mineral Museum
- **G** Shrine of the Snowshoe Priest

FOOD
- **H** Baraga Lakeside Inn
- **I** Carla's
- **F** Hunan Gardens
- **F** The Library

FOOD
(continued)
- **D** Porcupine Mountain Lodge Restaurant
- **D** Rainbow Motel Restaurant
- **B** Tamarack Inn

LODGING
- **B** Astor House Motel-Minnetonka Resort
- **H** Best Western Baraga Lakeside Inn
- **E** Best Western Copper Crown Motel
- **D** Best Western Porcupine Mountain Lodge

LODGING
(continued)
- **F** Charleston House Historic Inn
- **G** Downtowner Motel
- **F** Holiday Inn Express
- **B** Norland Motel
- **D** Rainbow Motel & Chalets

CAMPING
- **H** Baraga State Park
- **B** Ft. Wilkins State Park
- **A** McLain State Park
- **D** Porcupine Mountains Wilderness State Park
- **K** River Pines RV Park & Campground
- **J** Union River Campground

Note: Items with the same letter are located in the same place.

underground and experience the miners' world firsthand. Stroll around the grounds on the surface and examine the remains of original buildings and examples of mining equipment, as well as cutaway displays that show how the mine functioned. Then put on a hard hat and climb 110 feet down a stairway through the No. 1 shaft to the mine's first level, where you can explore—with or without a guide—900 feet of horizontal tunnels and two large rooms created by the removal of the ore. Veins of copper are still visible. The mine's nine deeper levels have long since filled with water, but the one level with its intersecting shafts, rooms, and passages gives an excellent view of how the region's copper mines worked.

Details: *12 miles south of Copper Harbor. Mid-May–mid-Oct daily 10–5, extended hours in summer. Guided tours: $8 adults, $4 ages 6–12. Self-guided tours: $7 adults, $4 ages 6–12. (1 hour)*

★★★★ FORT WILKINS STATE PARK
U.S. 41, Copper Harbor, 906/289-4215
The park contains restored buildings of an army post established in 1844 to prevent conflict between miners and local Indians. The fort was never involved in any hostilities and was abandoned by the army in 1870. The fort's buildings are open to the public and contain a variety of exhibits on the area's history and wildflowers. From late June until late August, costumed interpreters help explain the fort's history. The park also has camping facilities.

Details: *Park open 24 hours daily, fort open mid-May–mid-Oct daily 8–dusk. $4 per vehicle. (1 hour)*

★★★★ PORCUPINE MOUNTAINS WILDERNESS STATE PARK
Highway 107, Silver City, 906/885-5275
This park, one of the few large wilderness areas remaining in the Midwest, covers 63,000 acres of wooded mountains in the western Upper Peninsula. It offers outstanding facilities for camping, skiing, and backpacking. Its visitor center provides a variety of natural history programs. Be sure to visit the Lake of the Clouds Scenic Overlook for a spectacular panoramic view of the mountains and the lake far below.

Details: *Park open 24 hours daily; visitors center open late May–mid-Oct daily 10–6. $4 per vehicle. (2 hours)*

★★★ CALUMET THEATER
Sixth and Elm Streets, Calumet, 906/337-2610

This theater, opened in 1900 for staged theatrical performances, also served as a movie house. It was one of the top theaters in the country during its heyday, and luminaries such as Sarah Bernhardt graced its stage. This exquisite theater with nearly perfect acoustics now presents a variety of concerts and stage performances. After your visit, be sure to duck into the bar next door for a view of its turn-of-the-century interior.

Details: Tours late May–mid-Sept Tue–Sun 11–2. $3 adults, $1.50 ages 6–12. (30 minutes)

★★★ COPPERTOWN U.S.A.
Red Jacket Road and Fourth Street, Calumet, 906/337-4354

This museum is in a former pattern shop for the Calumet and Hecla Mine, which ran underneath much of the town of Calumet. Displays, which examine mining techniques, miners' equipment, company management, and even medical facilities, focus mainly on the C & H mine but also give an overview of copper mining and the area's history. A short videotape provides an excellent introduction to the area and to copper mining, and a gift shop has a good selection of books on mining and local history.

Details: June–Oct Mon–Sat 10-5. $3 adults, $1 ages 12–18, under age 12 free. (30 minutes)

★★★ QUINCY MINE HOIST
U.S. 41, Hancock, 906/482-5569

The hoist at Quincy Mine is believed to be the largest steam-powered hoist ever made. It weighs more than 880 tons, has a four-story hoist house, and was used from 1920 to 1931. It could lift 10 tons of ore at a speed of more than 36 miles per hour. Underground mine tours are available.

Details: Late May–Labor Day daily 9:30–5. Surface tour, tram ride, and underground tour: $12.50 adults, $7.50 ages 6–13, under age 6 free. Surface tour and tram ride: $7 adults, $2.50 children, under age 6 free. (1 hour)

★★ HANKA HOMESTEAD MUSEUM
Arnheim Road near Baraga, 906/334-2601

The Upper Peninsula, particularly the Copper Country, once attracted many Finnish immigrants, who worked in the mines and also tried to farm the rocky land. This museum is a restored, century-old Finnish farming homestead that looks as it did during the 1920s.

Details: *About seven miles west of U.S. 41. Memorial Day–Labor Day Tue, Thu, Sat, and Sun noon–4; open by appointment the rest of the year. $3 adults, $1 ages 6–12. (1 hour)*

★★ **SEAMAN MINERAL MUSEUM**
Fifth floor, Electrical Energy Resources Center, Michigan Technological University, 906/487-2572
Michigan Technological University began as a mining college, so it makes sense that it houses the state's official mineralogical museum. The Seaman Museum, with its wide array of specimens of ores and minerals from Michigan's Upper Peninsula, is a must-stop for any serious rockhound. Displays include varieties of iron and copper ores as well as gold and silver, datolites, agates, and fluorescent minerals and crystals. The museum also includes samples of greenstone, the state's official gemstone, commonly found on Isle Royale.

Details: *June–Oct Mon–Fri 9–4:30, Sat noon–4. Guided tours available by appointment throughout the year. $4 adults, $6 per couple, $7 families, $2 age 55 and over, age 12 and under free. (30 minutes)*

★★ **SHRINE OF THE SNOWSHOE PRIEST**
Off U.S. 41, Baraga
On a hill overlooking Keweenaw Bay is a 35-foot statue paying tribute to Bishop Frederic Baraga, a Catholic priest and missionary who came to the region in 1830. Baraga devoted his life to spreading Christianity among Native Americans and traveled as much as 700 miles by snowshoe to visit various tribes.

Details: *Just off U.S. 41, about 3.5 miles south of Baraga. (30 minutes)*

FITNESS AND RECREATION
The best recreation spot in the Copper Country is the **Porcupine Mountains Wilderness State Park**. There are plenty of trails here, with various ranges of difficulty, to provide truly enjoyable exercise for people in any physical condition, from the casual walker to the dedicated backpacker. What's more, the scenery can't be beat.

FOOD

If you are looking for elaborate or elegant restaurant meals, you won't find much to choose from in the Copper Country. That is not to say the food isn't good. But like the region itself, the food here is simple and served without a lot of frills.

In Copper Harbor, at the northern tip of the Keweenaw Peninsula, is the **Tamarack Inn**, 512 Gratiot St., 906/289-4522, which serves chicken, prime rib, whitefish, and trout in a casual atmosphere, with dinners costing $10 to $20. Farther south, in Houghton, you will find **Hunan Gardens**, 301 Sheldon Ave., 906/482-8588, one of the area's few ethnic restaurants. It serves a variety of Chinese dishes, with dinners also in the $10 to $20 range.

The Library, 62 N. Isle Royale in Houghton, 906/487-5882, is a popular local spot for lunch and dinner. The restaurant serves a diverse menu of steaks, pasta, and Mexican dishes and is also a brewpub.

Near Baraga, at the foot of the Keweenaw Bay, are several more good restaurants. Try **Carla's**, six miles north of Baraga on U.S. 41 in Carla's Lake Shore Motel, 906/353-6256. The American-style menu features steaks and fresh local fish, the atmosphere is casual, and the dining room has a lovely view of the bay. Dinners are in the $10 to $15 range. At the **Baraga Lakeside Inn**, 900 U.S. 41 S., 906/353-7123, you will find a fairly standard American menu, with dinners costing $10 to $20.

Near the Porcupine Mountains at Ontonagon are a pair of good motel restaurants: the **Rainbow Motel Restaurant**, 2900 M-64, 906/885-5348, which offers dinners under $10 but is closed from mid-October to mid-May; and the **Porcupine Mountain Lodge Restaurant**, 120 Lincoln St., 906/885-5311, which serves meals in the $10 to $15 range.

LODGING

As with food, accommodations in the Copper Country tend toward the basic—comfortable but not luxurious. That also means that prices tend to be moderate, but a fair number of motels, particularly the smaller ones, close for at least part of the winter.

In Copper Harbor, the **Astor House Motel-Minnetonka Resort**, located at the junction of U.S. 41 and Highway 26, 906/289-4449, is open from May 10 to October 20. The resort has 25 rooms, including a few small cabins and cottages. Rates are $46 to $63 a night for rooms, but up to $85 a night for the cottages. About two miles east of town, past the entrance to Fort Wilkins State Park on U.S. 41, is the **Norland Motel**, 906/289-4815, with nine rooms and rates between $32 and $48 a night. The Norland is open from May 1 through October.

The Houghton-Hancock area has the best selection of motels in the region. In Hancock, the **Best Western Copper Crown Motel**, 235 Hancock, 906/482-6111, is open all year, with 47 rooms, a heated indoor pool, saunas, and a whirlpool. Rates are $40 to $44 nightly. Houghton offers the **Downtowner Motel**, 110 Sheldon Ave., 906/482-4421, with 27 rooms and rates of $40 to $78 a night; and the **Holiday Inn Express**, 1110 Century Way, 906/482-1066, a new 61-room facility with heated indoor pool, sauna, whirlpool, exercise room, and rates from $59 to $139 a night. Both are open all year.

For a more unusual setting, try the **Charleston House Historic Inn**, 918 College Ave., 800/482-7404. Situated about a block from the city's waterfront, near a beach and boat dock, this bed-and-breakfast has six rooms, a smoke-free environment, and prices between $98 and $165 a night. At Baraga, you'll find the **Best Western Baraga Lakeside Inn**, 900 U.S. 41 S., 906/353-7123. All of its rooms feature a view of the Keweenaw Bay, and facilities include a heated indoor pool, sauna, whirlpool, and marina. The inn is open year-round, with rates of $65 to $75 a night.

Close to the Porcupine Mountains you will find accommodations at Silver City. The **Best Western Porcupine Mountain Lodge**, 120 Lincoln St., 906/885-5311, is on Lake Superior near the mouth of the Big Iron River. The lodge features its own beach, heated indoor pool, sauna, and whirlpool. The lodge's 71 rooms are priced at $65 to $100 a night. Not far away, the **Rainbow Motel and Chalets**, 2900 M-64, 906/885-5348, offers 16 rooms for $38 to $67 a night, and two chalets, which hold up to 12 people and rent for up to $250 a night. The motel is close to Lake Superior and features beach access, a sauna, whirlpool, and playground. Mountain bikes are available for rent.

CAMPING

State park campgrounds are larger, more popular, and more numerous than private facilities in the region. One of the most popular is at Silver City. The **Porcupine Mountains Wilderness State Park**, 412 Boundary Rd., 906/885-5275, has 183 campsites, a boat ramp, nature center, nature trails, and excellent opportunities for fishing, cross-country and downhill skiing, and snowmobiling. The park is open all year and features many scenic attractions, most notably the Lake of the Clouds overlook. Rates are $9 to $14 a night. A private facility, **Union River Campground**, 492 M-107, 906/885-5324, also serves the area with 60 sites, beach access, swimming, fishing, and a playground. Rates are $16 a night for two, plus $1 per extra person, but the campground is open only from May 15 to October 15.

Another private facility at Ontonagon is the **River Pines RV Park and Campground**, 600 River Rd., 906/884-4600, with 32 sites. It's open all year but has limited facilities in winter. Rates are $12 to $17 a night for four, plus $2 to $4 per extra person.

Further north and east into the Keweenaw Peninsula are several other state park campgrounds. At **Baraga State Park**, 1300 U.S. 41 S., 906/353-6558, you will find 137 campsites as well as swimming, fishing, boating, nature trails, and a playground. Nightly rates are $11. About seven miles west of Calumet on Highway 203 is **McLain State Park**, 906/482-0278, a 90-site campground open all year, with swimming, nature trails, and a playground, as well as opportunities for boating, fishing, and cross-country and downhill skiing. Rates are $14 a night. Finally, a mile east of Copper Harbor on U.S. 41 is **Fort Wilkins State Park**, 906/289-4215, which has a 165-site campground with a playground and nature trails. It also offers swimming, boating, fishing, waterskiing, and rental boats. Rates are $14 a night.

13
ISLE ROYALE

Isle Royale National Park may be the least-visited national park in the 48 contiguous states—with fewer visitors in a year than Yellowstone gets in a day. But that statistic is simply a reflection of the 134,000-acre island's remoteness, not a comment on its natural wonders or scenic appeal, which are considerable. An Isle Royale sunset that paints clouds in red and peach pastels, reflected like a Monet canvas on the smooth face of Lake Superior, is a sight never to be forgotten.

Established as a national park in 1931, Isle Royale is a 45-mile-long stretch of jagged rock and lush forest wilderness located on the western end of Lake Superior. It is open from mid-April through October. The only access to the park is by boat or floatplane, with one-way boat trips taking a minimum of two and a half hours from Grand Portage, Minnesota, four and a half hours from Copper Harbor, and six and a half hours from Houghton.

The island's 165 miles of hiking trails are rocky and rugged, blackflies and mosquitoes can be intense, and the frigid waters of Lake Superior make swimming an adventure for the hardy—or foolhardy. Still, the view from Mount Ojibway alone is more than worth the inconveniences of the journey. And that is to say nothing of the thrill of spotting wildlife, waterfowl, and forest birds; enjoying some 100 varieties of wildflowers; or boating, canoeing, and fishing on any of the 42 inland lakes. The National Park Service has recently initiated a user fee of $4 per day per visitor.

ISLE ROYALE

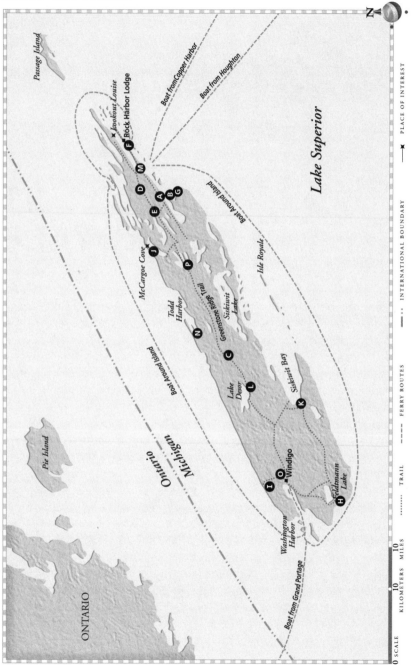

A PERFECT DAY ON ISLE ROYALE

The long boat ride forces a choice between an overnight stay or a frustratingly short visit. Take the Isle Royale Queen from Copper Harbor to Rock Harbor. You'll have about three hours before the boat returns to Copper Harbor, enough time to check out the visitors center across from the dock or walk the short trail to the Old America Dock for beautiful views of the harbor, the rocky island shore, and the lake. You might also spend some time on the nearby nature trail—a variable loop of up to four miles.

For an overnight stay you'll need to make reservations at the lodge or take along your sleeping bag and tent. If you move quickly as you get off the boat, you can claim one of the three-sided wooden shelters at the Rock Harbor campground. Take a ranger-guided stroll on one of the nature trails around Rock Harbor or hike along the shore to the Three Mile Campground.

SIGHTSEEING HIGHLIGHTS
★★★★ GREENSTONE RIDGE TRAIL

This is the main thoroughfare of Isle Royale. It stretches from Windigo at the west end of the island to Lookout Louise, which is across Tobin Harbor from the floatplane dock that serves Rock Island Lodge. Greenstone Ridge is the trail to take if you want to get a good overall view of the island in a one-week trip.

Take a floatplane to Windigo and hike the ridge from west to east

---

SIGHTS
Ⓐ Daisy Farm
Ⓑ Edisen Fishery
Ⓒ Greenstone Ridge Trail
Ⓓ Mount Franklin
Ⓔ Mount Ojibway
Ⓕ Rock Harbor
Ⓖ Rock Harbor
   Lighthouse

FOOD AND LODGING
Ⓕ Rock Harbor Lodge

CAMPING
Ⓐ Daisy Farm
   Campground
Ⓗ Feldtmann Lake
   Campground
Ⓘ Huginnin Cove
   Campground
Ⓙ McCargoe Cove
   Campground
Ⓕ Rock Harbor
   Campground
Ⓚ Siskiwit Bay
   Campground
Ⓛ South Lake Desor
   Campground

CAMPING (continued)
Ⓜ Three Mile
   Campground
Ⓝ Todd Harbor
   Campground
Ⓞ Washington Creek
   Campground
Ⓟ West Chickenbone
   Campground

Note: Items with the same letter are located in the same place.

---

until you reach Mount Ojibway or Mount Franklin, where you can drop down the ridge to the shoreline trail that leads directly into Rock Harbor. If your time on the island is limited to a couple of days, take the water taxi to Daisy Farm and hike the five-mile circuit by way of Mount Ojibway, which includes a one-mile stretch of the Greenstone Ridge Trail.

Details: *half–7 days*

★★★★ ROCK HARBOR
906/482-0984 (park headquarters)

Rock Harbor is the focal point of Isle Royale, especially for visitors on short stays. Not only is it home to the sole lodge on the island, but a wide range of scenery and hiking terrain is nearby. Moose and red foxes are often seen here, as well as an array of waterfowl and other birds. A visitors center near the boat dock provides information about the island's history and its flora and fauna. At the lodge you can link up with a number of guided hiking excursions or rent a canoe to explore the shoreline and small adjacent islands. You can also arrange passage on a water taxi to various trailheads and campgrounds. One such boat takes you to the **Edisen Fishery**, which was owned by one of the last commercial fishermen on the island. From the fishery, a short trail leads to the **Rock Harbor Lighthouse**, which was built in 1855 to guide ore ships to the island. Ironically, the copper mine that was to supply the cargo for those ships closed that same year.

Daisy Farm is another lovely attraction that is accessible by water taxi or via a seven-mile shoreline trail from Rock Harbor. The shoreline campground was once the site of a vegetable farm that served the lodge. It offers glorious views of the western end of Rock Harbor, has abundant wildlife, and is at the head of two trails that lead to the crest of the Greenstone Ridge. Take the 1.7-mile trail to **Mount Ojibway**. At 1,136 feet, the mountain is one of the high points along the ridge and offers spectacular views of the island and Lake Superior. If the weather is good you can easily see the bluffs along the Lake Superior shore at Thunder Bay, Ontario, on the Canadian side of the lake. On especially clear days you can make out the faint shape of the Keweenaw Peninsula, far to the south.

Mount Franklin, another scenic high spot on the ridge at 1,074 feet, is a good day hike from the lodge. Take the Rock Harbor Trail to Three Mile Campground, then follow a two-mile trail up

---

the ridge to the crest. The round trip from the lodge is about 10 miles.

Details: *(half–5 days)*

FITNESS AND RECREATION

Hiking and boating are the primary forms of recreation on Isle Royale. The park has trails for virtually every level of skill and physical endurance, from short, easy nature trails at Rock Harbor and Windigo to the 40-mile **Greenstone Ridge Trail** that connects the two ends of the island. The **Stoll Loop Trail** at Rock Harbor is an easy four-mile stroll that alternates between forest and shoreline; a connecting path shortens the loop to about a mile and a half if you are making a whirlwind day trip. The shorter loop omits some of the most dramatic shoreline scenery. At the west end of the island, the **Windigo Nature Walk** and the **Washington Creek Trail** are easy, and both are two miles or less.

The best of the moderate day hikes is a triangular path that begins at Daisy Farm, climbs the **Mouth Ojibway Trail** to the crest of the Greenstone Ridge, then follows the Greenstone Ridge Trail west to where it connects with the Daisy Farm Trail. It then descends back to the campground. The distance is a little over five miles, with a moderately strenuous climb to the top of 1,136-foot Mount Ojibway.

For avid backcountry hikers, the Greenstone Ridge Trail is moderately strenuous, so plan to spend four to five days to cover the length of the island in either direction. The **Minong Trail** is shorter—about 27 miles from McCargoe Cove to Windigo—but it is also more difficult and takes four to five days. You can get to McCargoe Cove by boat to begin your hike, but plan a couple of extra days on the trail if you go on foot from Rock Harbor to McCargoe Cove.

The waters around the island's shores and on many of the 42 inland lakes are excellent for canoeing and kayaking. In fact, some of the park's most beautiful areas can only be reached by water. Canoes are available at Windigo and Rock Harbor on a day-rental basis, but if you plan extended canoe or kayak trips you will need to bring your own. It is dangerous to cross Lake Superior to Isle Royale in craft less than 20 feet long. But you can take your outboard, canoe, or kayak to the island—for a fee—on the *Ranger III* out of Houghton. Park headquarters can be reached at 906/482-0984.

FOOD AND LODGING

The emphasis on Isle Royale is on camping. **Rock Harbor Lodge**, 906/337-4993 (502/773-2191 from October–April), an 80-room lodge with motel-style rooms and housekeeping cottages, is the only such facility on the island. The lodge also has a Laundromat and the island's only restaurant and coffee shop, though there are two camp stores (one at Rock Harbor and the other at Windigo) that sell food and other supplies for campers.

Rock Harbor Lodge is open from late May to mid-September, and a reservation deposit is necessary at least five days in advance. Rooms are comfortable and include combination showers and baths, though they have no air-conditioning, phones, or televisions. Rates begin at $119 for two people in a housekeeping unit and $186 for two in a motel-style room. The restaurant and coffee shop are open from 7 to 8:30 a.m., noon to 1:30, and 5:30 to 7:30.

CAMPING

The most heavily used campgrounds are at the main entry points to the park: **Rock Harbor Campground**, at the east end of the island, and **Washington Creek Campground**, near Windigo at the west end. Other popular campgrounds within a day's hike from the entry points are **Three Mile** and **Daisy Farm**, west along the shore from Rock Harbor; and **Hugginin Cove** and **Feldtmann Lake Campgrounds**, at the west end of the island near Windigo.

Along the Greenstone Ridge Trail, key campgrounds include **West Chickenbone** and **South Lake Desor**. **Todd Harbor** and **McCargoe Cove Campgrounds** are important stops on the Minong Ridge Trial, which runs along the northern edge of the island.

Some of the campgrounds, such as Daisy Farm, McCargoe Cove, and **Siskiwit Bay**, are accessible by boat as well as by trail. Two dozen other campgrounds—some reachable only by boat—dot the island.

TRANSPORTATION

Getting to Isle Royale takes careful planning; it isn't an excursion you make on a whim while you are in the area. Whether you travel by boat—as most do—or floatplane, you'll need to make reservations. Flights in particular need to be scheduled well in advance.

Ranger III, a 165-foot, government-operated ferry, sails from Houghton to Rock Harbor and is large enough to carry private boats and canoes up to 20 feet long. The trip is about six and a half hours one way, but the boat stays the night in Rock Harbor before returning to Houghton and, because it is the largest boat serving the island, its schedule is less vulnerable to bad weather on the lake. The ferry operates early June to mid-September. Call 906/482-0984 for more information.

The *Isle Royal Queen*, a 65-foot privately owned ferry, travels between Copper Harbor, at the tip of the Keweenaw Peninsula, and Rock Harbor. The trip takes four and a half hours one way, with a layover of about three hours before the return to Copper Harbor. The service operates mid-May through September; call 906/289-4437 (summer) or 906/482-4950 (winter) for more information. Fares for adults are $40 one way and $80 round-trip; children 12 and under pay $20 and $40. Additional charges apply for transporting boats or canoes and gear in excess of 100 pounds per person.

Boat service also is available on the 64-foot **Wenonah** or the 60-foot **Voyager II** out of Grand Portage, Minnesota, from mid-May through October. Call 218/728-1237 for more information.

Regularly scheduled flights by the **Isle Royale Seaplane Service** connect Houghton with both Windigo and Rock Harbor. Hikers can fly to Windigo, hike the length of the island, and return from Rock Harbor by plane or on the *Ranger III*. Call 906/482-8850 for more information. Fares per person are $149 one way and $215 round-trip.

14
THE SUNRISE COAST

Michigan's Sunrise Coast of Lake Huron is a world away from the more famous resort region around Traverse City and Petoskey, and not just because it sits on the opposite side of the Lower Peninsula. The Lake Michigan coast caters to the affluent crowd from Detroit, Grand Rapids, and Chicago, with big marinas, expensive resorts, and fancy restaurants. The Sunrise Coast is a blue-collar haven, filled with summer cottages and hunting camps that belong to working-class families. The pace is a bit slower here. It's less crowded, without the trendy restaurants and fancy resorts.

The main route in the region is U.S. 23, a two-lane highway that hugs the Lake Huron shore from shortly after it splits from I-75 at Standish until the two routes reconnect at Mackinaw City. In the intervening 185 miles, it winds through a dozen or so small towns, past a half-dozen superb state parks, and offers many glorious vistas of lakeshore and northern forest.

These days, I-75 is the most popular route to northern Michigan. But if freeway speeds aren't your idea of vacation pace, the Sunrise Coast route offers an alternative that is much more relaxing and satisfying.

A PERFECT DAY ON THE SUNRISE COAST

It's a leisurely day's drive from Standish to Mackinaw City by way of U.S. 23. (I-75 would get you between the same two points in about two and a half

SUNRISE COAST

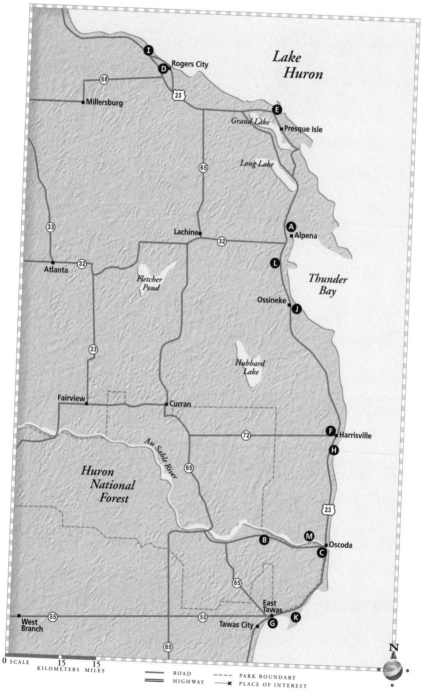

Lake Huron

Rogers City

68

Millersburg

23

Grand Lake

Presque Isle

65

Long Lake

Lachine

32

Alpena

Atlanta

32

Fletcher Pond

Thunder Bay

Ossineke

33

Hubbard Lake

Fairview

Curran

Harrisville

72

Huron National Forest

Au Sable River

65

23

Oscoda

West Branch

55

55

Tawas City

East Tawas

65

0 SCALE

15

15

KILOMETERS   MILES

ROAD

HIGHWAY

PARK BOUNDARY

PLACE OF INTEREST

N

hours.) Allow plenty of time to stop at Tawas Point State Park or Harrisville State Park to swim, stroll along the shore, or just sit and watch the water. Picnic at lakeside or stop for lunch in Alpena.

In the afternoon, stop to see the Presque Isle lighthouses and the small museums nearby. Then continue north, with more time to pause along the lakeshore. Stop for a while at Rogers City to watch freighters take on loads of stone from the world's largest limestone quarry. A stand alongside the U.S. 23 Business Route just south of town offers an amazing view of the 6,000-acre quarry.

SIGHTSEEING HIGHLIGHTS
★★★★ NEW PRESQUE ISLE LIGHTHOUSE AND MUSEUM
Presque Isle peninsula, 517/595-9917

This site is the centerpiece of a small township park that also has nature trails, restrooms, and picnic tables. The tower is 100 feet high, making it one of the tallest lighthouses on the Great Lakes. Unlike the older lighthouse (see next page), the tower itself is open to the public only on the afternoons of July 4 and Labor Day. The museum is in a former Coast Guard station adjacent to the lighthouse.

SIGHTS
- **A** Jesse Besser Museum
- **B** Lumberman's Monument
- **C** Paddlewheel River Boat
- **D** Presque Isle County Historical Museum
- **E** Presque Isle Lighthouses and Museums

FOOD
- **D** The Buoy
- **F** Fieldstones Restaurant
- **A** Hunan Chinese Restaurant

FOOD (continued)
- **A** Thunderbird Inn
- **C** Wiltse's Brew Pub & Family Restaurant

LODGING
- **G** Dale Motel
- **A** Days Inn
- **A** Dew Drop Inn
- **D** Driftwood Motel
- **A** Holiday Inn
- **C** Redwood Motor Lodge
- **C** Rest-All Inn
- **G** Tawas Motel

CAMPING
- **C** Acres & Trails KOA Kampground
- **A** Campers Cove
- **H** Harrisville State Park
- **I** Hoeft State Park
- **J** Paul Bunyan Kampgrounds
- **K** Tawas Point State Park
- **L** Thunder Bay River Campground
- **M** Van Etten Lake Campground

Note: Items with the same letter are located in the same place.

Details: *Mid-May–mid-Oct daily 9–6. Donations appreciated. $2 fee to climb the tower. (30 minutes)*

★★★★ **OLD PRESQUE ISLE LIGHTHOUSE AND MUSEUM**
Presque Isle Harbor, 517/595-2787
The lighthouse was built in 1840, when the harbor was an active lumber port, to guide Great Lakes ships. It was replaced in 1870 by the taller lighthouse a mile away, at the northern tip of the Presque Isle peninsula (see above). The old lighthouse tower and the keeper's house have been restored and turned into a museum. You can even climb to the top of the two-story tower for a beautiful view of the lake and harbor. The keeper's house is filled with antiques.
Details: *About halfway between Alpena and Rogers City. Mid-May–mid-Oct daily 9–5, extended hours in summer. $2 adults, $1 ages 6–12. (30 minutes)*

★★★★ **PRESQUE ISLE COUNTY HISTORICAL MUSEUM**
176 W. Michigan Avenue, Rogers City, 517/734-4121
Once the home of Michigan Limestone and Chemical's first president, Carl Bradley, this restored 1914 home in Rogers City now houses a variety of displays on local history, including Indian artifacts and exhibits on Great Lakes shipwrecks. Some of the building's rooms display period furniture and clothing from the 1920s and earlier. Another display features an Indian birch-bark canoe.

The backbone of the museum is its exhibit on Great Lakes maritime history. The exhibit focuses on famous shipwrecks like the *Edmund Fitzgerald*, the *Cedarville*, the *John G. Munson*, and the *Carl D. Bradley*, a freighter which sank near Beaver Island in Lake Michigan in 1958. A gift shop includes books on shipwrecks as well as maps of the Great Lakes that identify the sites of shipwrecks and lighthouses.
Details: *June–Oct Mon–Fri noon–4, also Sat July–Aug. Donations appreciated. (30 minutes)*

★★★ **JESSE BESSER MUSEUM**
491 Johnson Street, Alpena, 517/356-2202
This Alpena museum combines history, natural history, and art with rotating exhibits in three galleries, a re-creation of an 1890s street, and a planetarium. Also on the grounds are several restored nineteenth-

century buildings, including a homesteader's cabin, a one-room school, a church, and a bank building.

Details: Mon–Fri 10–5, Thu 10–9, Sat–Sun noon–5. Planetarium shows Sun 1 and 3, also July–Aug Thu 7:30. Museum: $2 adults, $1 over age 60 and ages 5–17, $5 families. Planetarium: 75 cents. (1 hour)

★★★ PADDLEWHEEL RIVERBOAT
Foote Dam, West River Road, Oscoda, 517/739-7351

The Au Sable River Queen of Oscoda offers daily 19-mile scenic cruises on the Au Sable River from Memorial Day weekend until late October. The Au Sable is one of Michigan's most beautiful rivers, popular especially among canoeists, who follow its winding path through the central Lower Peninsula, from Grayling to Oscoda on Lake Huron. This river cruise reverses direction, heading upstream in leisurely fashion from the eastern end of the river through the region's lush forests—a great way to soak up some of Michigan's natural outdoor ambiance. The cruise is especially lovely in fall during the peak of the leaf-color season.

Details: About six miles west of Oscoda. Cruises daily Memorial Day–late Sept. Fall-color tours in Sept and Oct. Cruises: $9 adults, $8 age 60 and over, $4 ages 5–12. Color tours: $12 adults, $6 age 12 and under. Reservations suggested at all times and required for fall-color tours. (2 hours)

★★ LUMBERMAN'S MONUMENT
River Road

This large bronze statue of three loggers was built in 1931 to honor the men behind the state's first big economic boom. Nearby is a museum and interpretive center with displays that focus on the timber industry and the life of the logger, a much-mythologized but often misunderstood figure.

Details: About 16 miles west of Au Sable, along River Rd. (30 minutes)

FITNESS AND RECREATION

Recreation in the region revolves around outdoor activities like fishing, swimming, boating, canoeing, and snowmobiling. The **Lake Huron** shore, with its selection of state parks, is very popular. Several large inland lakes—most notably **Grand Lake** and **Long Lake** north of Alpena—offer excellent boating and swimming opportunities.

FOOD

You won't find a lot of fancy restaurants and accommodations along the northern Lake Huron shore. In fact, you won't even find very many of the widely known chain hotels and restaurants. There are a few in Alpena, the region's largest town, but elsewhere most motels and restaurants are small, plain, one-of-a-kind outfits. Tastes are simple in this part of Michigan.

For food, Alpena offers the largest selection. Alpena's **Thunderbird Inn**, 1100 State Ave., 517/354-8900, serves standard American fare with an emphasis on steaks and fresh seafood. Dinners usually cost $10 to $20 but lunches are under $10. One of the few ethnic eateries in the area is the **Hunan Chinese Restaurant**, 1120 S. State Ave., 517/356-6461, which features a great view of the Lake Huron beach and offers dinners under $10.

Other interesting options include **Fieldstones Restaurant**, 676 N. Huron Rd. in Harrisville, 517/724-6338, open from May 1 to November 1, which has a menu that includes steaks, seafood, pasta, and Old World specialties, with dinners in the $10 to $15 range; **Wiltse's Brew Pub and Family Restaurant**, 5606 N. F-41 in Oscoda, 517/739-2231, which specializes in steaks, has its own bakery and brewery on site, and offers lunches under $10 and dinners from $10 to $17; and **The Buoy**, 530 W. Third St. in Rogers City, 517/734-4747, which has a marvelous view of Lake Huron and serves lunches under $10 and whitefish and prime-rib dinners in the $10 to $20 range.

LODGING

Once again, Alpena has the largest selection in the region, with familiar names like the **Days Inn**, 1496 Hwy. 32 W., 517/356-6118, with a heated indoor pool, sauna, and whirlpool, and room rates of $65 to $75; and the **Holiday Inn**, 1000 Hwy. 23 N., 517/356-2151, which has a heated indoor pool, sauna, whirlpool, putting green, and indoor recreation area, with rates from $69 to $109 a night. A low-cost option in Alpena is the **Dew Drop Inn**, 2469 French Rd., 517/356-4414, with rooms from $32 to $46 a night.

At Rogers City, the **Driftwood Motel**, 540 W. Third St., 517/734-4777, offers medium-priced accommodations—$50 to $80 a night—with a heated indoor pool, sauna, and whirlpool.

Toward the southern end of U.S. 23's route along the shore, there are several motels at Oscoda and Tawas City. At Oscoda, try the **Redwood Motor**

Lodge, 3111 N. U.S. 23, 517/739-2021, which has a heated indoor pool, sauna, and whirlpool, as well as a beach on Lake Huron and a playground. Rates are $56 to $77 a night. The **Rest-All Inn**, 4270 N. U.S. 23, 517/739-8822, has the beach and playground but not the pool and charges $39 to $90 a night. A couple of two-person efficiencies also are available for $80 nightly.

Accommodations at Tawas City include the **Dale Motel**, 1086 U.S. 23 S., 517/362-6153, with rates of $32 to $70 a night; and the **Tawas Motel**, 1124 U.S. 23 S., 517/362-3822, with a heated pool, sauna, whirlpool, and playground, with nightly rates of $40 to $70.

CAMPING

The northeast coast of Michigan's Lower Peninsula is a popular camping area with an ample supply of public and private campgrounds all along the Lake Huron shore. Toward the northern end of U.S. 23, about five miles northwest of Rogers City, is **Hoeft State Park**, 517/734-2543, a public campground with 144 sites that is open all year. The campground charges $11 a night and offers nature trails, boating, fishing, and cross-country and downhill skiing.

A few miles south, at Alpena, is **Campers Cove**, 5005 Long Rapids Rd., 517/356-3708, a private campground with 80 sites. It's open from May 1 through September and offers a recreation room, playground, miniature golf, rental boats, canoes, and paddleboats. Rates begin at $10 per night for two, with a charge of $2 per extra person. A reservation deposit is required, and five days' notice is necessary for a refund.

In the Mackinaw State Forest Area you'll find a 10-site facility at the **Thunder Bay River Campground**, 517/732-3541, nine miles southwest of Alpena on Indian Reserve Road. The campground is open all year, charges $4 a night, and offers canoeing and fishing.

Continue south on U.S. 23 and you'll reach Ossineke and **Paul Bunyan Kampgrounds**, 6969 N. Huron St., 517/471-2921, a private facility with 80 sites. The campground is open from mid-April through November and has a heated pool, recreation room, and a playground. Rates are $12.50 a night for two, plus $1 per extra person.

Harrisville State Park, a half-mile south of Harrisville on U.S. 23, 517/724-5126, has 229 campsites. It's open all year, charges $14 a night, and offers swimming, trails, fishing, and a boat ramp.

Oscoda is another big tourist center on the Lake Huron coast, and it has both public and private campgrounds nearby. **Acres and Trails KOA Kampground**, 3591 Forest Rd., 517/739-5115, is a private facility with 100 sites open from mid-April through November. Facilities include hiking trails, a playground, a recreation room, and rental bicycles. Rates are $18 a night for two, with a charge of $1 to $3 per extra person.

Van Etten Lake Campground, 517/826-3211, about five miles northwest of Oscoda on Highway 171 in the Au Sable State Forest, is a public campground with 62 sites. It's open all year, charges $4 a night, and offers swimming, fishing, and a boat ramp.

Tawas City and East Tawas form another major tourist center with a wealth of campgrounds. The largest is **Tawas Point State Park**, 517/362-5041, about four miles northeast of East Tawas off U.S. 23. The 210-site public campground has nature trails, fishing, and rental boats. It's open all year and charges $15 a night. There are five other smaller public campgrounds in the Tawas City–East Tawas area.

Scenic Route: Au Sable River Road

From Tawas City, drive west about a mile on Highway 55, then turn north on Wilber Road. A little more than a mile later, turn left on Monument Road, which will take you through wooded hills and backcountry to River Road. Head west about two miles, past the Canoe Race Monument, to Largo Springs, where you can walk down almost 300 steps to see the secluded springs seep out of mossy bluffs into the Au Sable River. Turning back east, drive slowly along River Road, which follows the Au Sable back to Lake Huron at Oscoda. The drive is about 16 miles from the springs and is particularly lovely during the fall-color season. The Lumberman's Monument also is along the way.

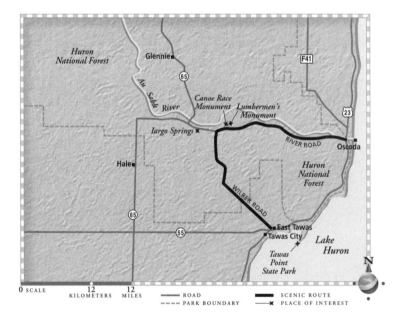

15
MID-MITTEN

If you don't love the outdoors, don't bother with the middle of Michigan's Mitten. In the cities of southern Michigan or the resort areas around Grand Traverse Bay, Little Traverse Bay, and Mackinac Island, you'll find shopping, museums, fine restaurants, and other indoor diversions. But from Mount Pleasant north through the center of the state to Gaylord and beyond, nearly all that's fun goes on outside. Unless you like to hunt, fish, hike, camp, boat, canoe, golf, ski, snowmobile, or at least bird-watch, there isn't much here for you to do.

While the region is relatively isolated from the Great Lakes shores, it has its own dominant waters. Houghton Lake, which is 16 miles long and 8 miles wide, is the state's largest inland lake, and nearby Higgins Lake isn't a lot smaller. Two of Michigan's most popular canoeing rivers, the Au Sable and the Manistee, flow through the area.

Grayling, in the center of the region, is the connecting point of the two main north-south routes in the eastern half of the state: I-75, which funnels traffic to and from the urban areas of southeastern Michigan; and U.S. 27, which comes north from Jackson and Lansing. The entire region is filled with summer cottages and hunting camps, with Grayling and Gaylord as the main tourist centers. Grayling has the more rustic flavor, with its emphasis on fishing and canoeing, while Gaylord, whose focus is on golf and skiing, has more of a resort feel.

MID-MITTEN

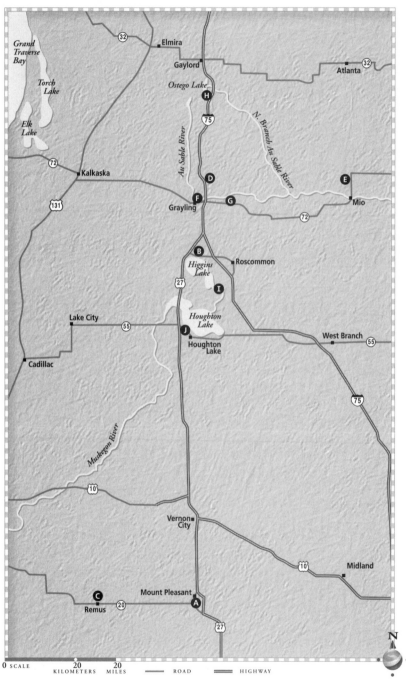

Grand
Traverse
Bay

Torch
Lake

Elk
Lake

Elmira

Gaylord

Atlanta

32

32

Ostego Lake

H

75

N. Branch Au Sable River

72

Kalkaska

Au Sable River

D

E

131

F

G

Mio

Grayling

72

B

Roscommon

Higgins
Lake

27

I

Houghton
Lake

Lake City

55

J

West Branch

55

Houghton
Lake

Cadillac

75

Muskegon River

10

Vernon
City

10

Midland

C

Mount Pleasant

Remus

20

A

27

N

0 SCALE   20   20
     KILOMETERS   MILES   ——— ROAD   ═══ HIGHWAY

A PERFECT DAY IN THE MID-MITTEN

Start off in Grayling with a half-day canoe excursion on the Au Sable River. Several canoe liveries in town offer outings that range from two and a half hours to a week or more. For pure relaxation, it's hard to beat a few hours spent floating gently on the water, listening to the soft rush of the stream and watching the pine forests that line the banks.

After lunch, head north toward Gaylord and make a short visit to Hartwick Pines State Park. Take in the visitors center presentations on the logging industry, then spend an hour strolling through the stand of virgin white pine that soars overhead.

You should make it to Gaylord in time for a late-afternoon round of golf on one of the many good local courses. Make the 19th hole a stop at the Big Buck Brewery and Steakhouse, where you can try one of their special brews—and tour the brewery, too.

SIGHTSEEING HIGHLIGHTS
★★★★ HARTWICK PINES STATE PARK
Hartwick Pines Road, Grayling, 517/348-7068

This park is among the best of the many natural treasures of Michigan. Although the park covers more than 9,000 acres, the awesome stand of virgin pine and hemlock consists of less than 50 acres. These giant trees, which grow up to 200 feet high and live as long as 500 years, once covered much of the state. Those that remain instill sobering

SIGHTS
- Ⓐ Center for Cultural and Natural History
- Ⓑ Civilian Conservation Corps Museum
- Ⓒ Dreamfield Farm
- Ⓓ Hartwick Pines State Park
- Ⓔ Kirtland's Warbler Tour

FOOD
- Ⓕ Albie's

LODGING
- Ⓕ Aquarama Motor Lodge
- Ⓔ Hinchman Acres Resort
- Ⓖ Holiday Inn
- Ⓕ Hospitality House

CAMPING
- Ⓖ Au Sable State Forest Campgrounds
- Ⓓ Hartwick Pines State Park

CAMPING
(continued)
- Ⓑ North Higgins Lake State Park
- Ⓗ Otsego Lake State Park
- Ⓘ South Higgins Lake State Park
- Ⓙ Wooded Acres Campground
- Ⓕ Yogi Bear's Jellystone Park-Heart of the North

Note: Items with the same letter are located in the same place.

reflection on what was lost when millions of acres of virgin pine were logged in the nineteenth century.

Park facilities include a visitors center, where displays and audio-visual presentations describe the history of Michigan's logging industry, the biology of trees, forest management, and other natural science topics. From the center, take a foot trail through the big pines. Guided walks, an hour or more long, are available, and the trails are wheelchair accessible. A logging museum on the grounds includes re-creations of a logging camp kitchen, mess hall, bunkhouse, and a chapel. The park also includes a campground (see Camping).

Details: *Seven miles northeast of Grayling. Park open 24 hours daily. Visitors center open Memorial Day–Labor Day daily 9–7, 9–4 the rest of the year. $4 per private vehicle. (2–3 hours)*

★★★ CIVILIAN CONSERVATION CORPS MUSEUM
Roscommon Road, Roscommon, 517/821-6125 or 517/373-1979

At the entrance to North Higgins Lake State Park is a replica of the barracks used by the Civilian Conservation Corps during the 1930s. The building contains displays on the history and accomplishments of the corps, and the museum offers interpretive programs on forest-fire fighting and the cultivation of pine nurseries. Two original CCC buildings also stand on the grounds. Hiking trails and picnic areas are nearby.

Details: *About five miles west of Roscommon. Open in summer daily 10–6, by appointment the rest of the year. $4 per private vehicle. (30 minutes)*

★★★ KIRTLAND'S WARBLER TOUR
Highway 33, Mio, 517/826-3252 (Forest Service office)

In a state remarkable for its plentiful wildlife, no wild creature has a more unusual tale than the Kirtland's warbler. Fewer than 200 breeding pairs of this endangered species are known to exist, and all make their nests under young jack pines in the forests around Grayling and Mio. The birds begin arriving from their winter home in the Bahamas in mid-May and leave in July. While the birds are in Michigan, U.S. Forest Service guides lead early morning walking tours of one to two miles. Kirtland's warblers are small and reclusive, but most tours spot them.

Details: *Tours May 15–July 3 Wed–Fri at 7 a.m., Sat–Sun at 7 and 11. (2–3 hours)*

★★ CALL OF THE WILD MUSEUM
850 S. Wisconsin Street, Gaylord, 517/732-4336

This museum in Gaylord is a worthwhile, if conventional, tourist stop. Displays include more than 150 stuffed wild animals and birds of North America, including elk, beavers, bears, and various game birds.

Details: Mid-June–Labor Day daily 8:30–9, 9:30–6 the rest of the year. $5 adults, $3 ages 5–13, under age 5 free. (1 hour)

★★ CENTER FOR CULTURAL AND NATURAL HISTORY
Rowe Hall, Central Michigan University, Mount Pleasant, 517/774-3829

This museum on the Central Michigan University campus houses a variety of displays, including Victorian and Civil War artifacts; dioramas on the birds, fish, and mammals native to the state; and the skeletal remains of an American mastodon.

Details: Mon–Fri 8–noon and 1–5. Admission is free. (1 hour)

★★ DREAMFIELD FARM
50th Street and Pierce Road, Remus, 517/967-8422

About 20 miles due west of Mount Pleasant at the town of Remus is a 110-acre Michigan Centennial Farm offering a wide range of hands-on farm activities. Visitors have the opportunity to hand-feed such barnyard animals as sheep, lambs, goats, calves, pigs, and rabbits. Kids can have fun playing in haystacks and driving mini-tractors. The farm also features nature trails and a picnic area, and hayrides are offered in October.

Details: Memorial Day–mid-Sept Tue–Sat 10–5, Oct Sat–Sun 10–5, summer holiday weekends. $4. (1–2 hours)

FITNESS AND RECREATION

Recreation is to be found everywhere outdoors in this region. The various state parks contain dozens of lakes for swimming, boating, and fishing and plenty of nature trails for hiking. Canoeing is an extremely popular activity, especially around Grayling, a key starting point for canoeists on the **Manistee River**, which flows west to Lake Michigan, and the **Au Sable River**, which flows east to Lake Huron. In fact, the Au Sable is one of the most popular canoeing and fishing rivers in the state.

If golf is your idea of exercise, head for Gaylord, where you will find close to a dozen good courses that are open to the public, some of them among the most challenging in the state.

November is hunting season, and the region is one of Michigan's prime deer-hunting areas. In winter you can ski in Gaylord and Grayling and snowmobile just about everywhere. Outdoor winter recreation is so popular that each January Houghton Lake hosts the **Tip-Up Town U.S.A. Festival** for ice-fishing enthusiasts.

FOOD

Restaurants in the region tend toward the small, the basic, the casual, the predictable, and the moderately priced. A notable exception to that rule is Gaylord's **Big Buck Brewery and Steakhouse**, a new and dramatic addition to the local food scene. As its full name suggests, Big Buck, 550 S. Wisconsin St., 517/732-5781, specializes in steaks and its own special beers, which are brewed on site. (Free brewery tours are available.) The setting is warm and modern, with carved wooden fish on the bar and deer-antler chandeliers. In addition to steaks, the menu offers fish, ribs, pasta, and an array of salads. They even make their own soft drinks—root beer (naturally), black-cherry pop, and cream soda. Dinners average $15 to $25.

Gaylord offers several other excellent dining spots. The most venerable—established in 1919 and one of the state's oldest family-owned restaurants—is the **Sugar Bowl** restaurant, 216 W. Main St., 517/732-5524, which features a variety of Greek dishes as well as such standard American entrées as prime rib and whitefish. Dinners cost between $10 and $20.

Jac's Place, at the Marsh Ridge Resort, 4815 Old U.S. 27 S., 517/732-6794, offers an interesting mix of seafood, steak, and pasta dishes and a lovely view of the resort grounds. Dinners cost $15 to $30. For a good, filling meal under $10, try **Gobbler's Famous Turkey Dinner Restaurant**, 900 S. Otsego, 517/732-9005. Known for its generous portions, Gobbler's also serves fresh breaded fish and barbecued ribs.

For inexpensive, hearty meals in Grayling, try **Albie's**, 5604 M-72 W., 517/348-2240. Its specialty is pasties, the traditional Upper Peninsula pastry stuffed with meat and vegetables. If you like them, Albie's will ship them to you anywhere in the United States. Meals cost about $5.

LODGING

Gaylord and Grayling are the main centers for motel accommodations in the region. Gaylord is the larger and busier of the two towns, and the motels there

GAYLORD

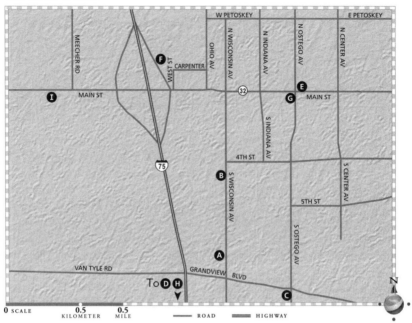

SIGHTS
Ⓐ Call of the Wild Museum

FOOD
Ⓑ Big Buck Brewery & Steakhouse
Ⓒ Gobbler's Famous Turkey Dinner
  Restaurant
Ⓓ Jac's Place
Ⓔ Sugar Bowl

LODGING
Ⓕ Comfort Inn
Ⓖ Downtown Motel
Ⓗ Marsh Ridge Resort

CAMPING
Ⓘ Gaylord Alpine RV Park &
  Campground

tend to be larger and a bit more expensive, though few are what anyone would call fancy.

One that is, however, is the **Marsh Ridge Resort**, 4815 Old U.S. 27, 517/732-6794, where room rates range from $68 to $160 a night. The resort is relatively small, with 59 rooms, but it offers its own 18-hole golf course, driving range and putting green, a sauna, heated pool, whirlpool, tanning booth, and playground.

A moderately priced motel is the **Comfort Inn**, east of I-75 at 137 W. St., 517/732-7541, with rates from $69 to $105 a night. It's larger, too, with 117 rooms, a heated indoor pool, and a whirlpool. The **Downtown Motel**, 208 S. Otsego Ave., 517/732-5010, is one of the least expensive in Gaylord, with rates of $42 to $62 a night. It has only 13 rooms, but it is close to the downtown shopping area.

In Grayling, a couple of good options are the **Hospitality House**, 1232 I-75 Business Loop, 517/348-8900; and the **Holiday Inn**, 2650 S. I-75 Business Loop, 517/348-7611. The Hospitality House has a heated indoor pool and whirlpool, and room rates from $45 to $175 a night. The Holiday Inn has two pools, as well as a wading pool, sauna, whirlpool, playground, and domed recreation area. Rates here range from $69 to $109 a night. The **Aquarama Motor Lodge**, 2307 I-75 Business Loop, 517/348-5405, has rates from $45 to $95 a night.

About 30 miles east of Grayling is Mio, a popular canoeing and winter skiing area, where you will find the **Hinchman Acres Resort**, 702 N. Morenci St., 517/826-3267. The resort, along the Au Sable River, is small—with just 13 rooms—but it offers a beach, playground, and indoor recreation area, as well as trails for hiking and cross-country skiing. Fishing equipment, skiing equipment, and canoes are available for rent. Room rates at the restort range from $50 to $120 a night.

CAMPING

The central part of the northern Lower Peninsula is studded with campgrounds, most of them public, especially in the busy summer tourist area between Houghton Lake and Gaylord.

Just north of Houghton Lake, on Higgins Lake, are a pair of huge state park campgrounds, **North Higgins Lake** and **South Higgins Lake**. Both campgrounds are open all year, and both charge $15 a night. North Higgins Lake State Park, 11252 N. Higgins Lake Dr., 517/821-6125, about five miles west of Roscommon, is the smaller of the two, with 218 sites. South Higgins Lake State Park, 106 State Park Dr., 517/821-6374, is about six miles southwest of Roscommon and offers 512 campsites, a testament to the popularity of the area. Both parks offer good swimming, playgrounds, nature trails, and boat ramps for access to fishing and waterskiing on the lake. The south park also has rental boats, while the north park has a nature center and offers cross-country and downhill skiing as well as snowmobiling opportunities in the winter.

Much smaller and landlocked, but with its own spectacular beauty, is **Hartwick Pines State Park**, 517/348-7068. The park is located seven miles northeast of Grayling at 4216 Ranger Road. Its stands of virgin pine and hemlock are the biggest attractions. The park has 62 campsites, is open all year, and charges $14 to $18 a night. It also has a museum with interesting displays on the local lumbering industry, a playground, nature trails, and a nature program. Visitors have access to nearby downhill and cross-country skiing and snowmobiling trails.

Also near Grayling, at various sites along the Manistee and Au Sable Rivers, are six small **Au Sable State Forest Campgrounds**, ranging in size from 12 to 45 campsites. These campgrounds cater mainly to canoeists but are open year-round and charge $4 a night. Information about all of them can be obtained by calling 517/826-3211.

Just south of Gaylord is another large public campground at **Otsego Lake State Park**, seven miles south of town on Old U.S. 27, 517/732-5485. The park has 203 sites, with swimming, boating, fishing, and waterskiing. Rates are $14 a night. Rental boats are available. Private campgrounds, which offer somewhat more refined amenities at more expensive rates, also are plentiful in the area.

At Houghton Lake is **Wooded Acres Campground**, 997 Federal Ave., 517/422-3413, open all year with 94 sites. Rates start at $13 for four people, with a fee of $2 per extra person. The campground offers a pool, playground, recreation room, miniature golf, and snowmobiling, though facilities are limited in winter.

Yogi Bear's Jellystone Park-Heart of the North, 370 Four Mile Rd., 517/348-2157, is the largest campground in the Grayling area with 218 campsites. The campground is open from May 1 through September 30 and charges $22 a night for two, plus $2 to $3 per extra person. Facilities include a swimming pool, wading pool, playground, recreation room, and miniature golf. Some cabins also are available at $35 a night.

At the **Gaylord Alpine RV Park and Campground**, 1315 M-32 W., 517/731-1772, rates range from $18.50 to $23.50 a night, plus a fee of $3 per extra person. The campground has 130 sites, a heated pool, playground, recreation room, and miniature golf.

NIGHTLIFE

Except for Mount Pleasant, which caters to the CMU student population, nightlife is awfully sparse in the region. For the risk-oriented, however, the Isabella Indian Reservation just east of Mount Pleasant offers the **Soaring Eagle Casino**, 6800 Soaring Eagle Blvd., 888/732-4537. Games include blackjack, live poker, video poker, bingo, and more than a thousand slot machines. It's open 10 a.m. to 2 a.m. Sunday through Thursday, and 24 hours Friday and Saturday.

16
SAGINAW VALLEY

The Saginaw Valley is known for its automaking, industrial cities, and broad, flat farm country. Although Detroit is called the Motor City, Saginaw and Flint have contributed much to the state's auto-industry reputation. Flint in particular played an important role in labor history; a sit-down strike at a General Motors plant there in 1936 boosted the United Auto Workers and galvanized the labor movement. The area has other industrial ties as well. Midland, a few miles west of Bay City, is the home of the Dow Chemical Company.

But much natural beauty can be found here as well, along the gentle rivers that converge on Saginaw Bay and along the bay itself, whose waters and nearby marshlands host hundreds of different species of birds. The bay is also a good boating spot and, in the winter, a popular place for ice fishing.

Saginaw Valley lies along the state's main north-south thoroughfare, I-75. That location can lead to some traffic congestion, particularly around Flint. But it also puts the area within about an hour's drive of metropolitan Detroit, Ann Arbor, Lansing, Port Huron, and the northern vacation areas around Roscommon and Tawas City.

A PERFECT DAY IN THE SAGINAW VALLEY

Start at the southern end of the region, around Flint. If you're in a recreational mood, take in Crossroads Village and Huckleberry Railroad. If shopping and

SAGINAW VALLEY

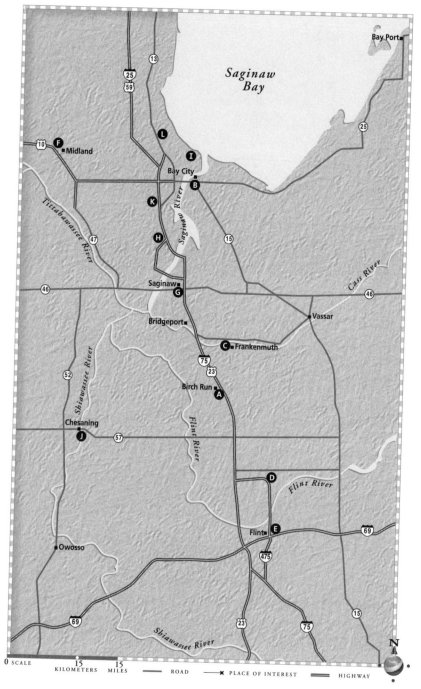

Saginaw Bay

Bay Port

Midland

Bay City

Saginaw

Bridgeport

Frankenmuth

Vassar

Birch Run

Chesaning

Flint

Owosso

Tittabawassee River

Saginaw River

Cass River

Shiawassee River

Flint River

Flint River

Shiawassee River

N

0 SCALE 15 15
KILOMETERS MILES ROAD ✕ PLACE OF INTEREST HIGHWAY

strolling are your cup of tea, head straight for Birch Run and its vast outlet malls. You can easily spend the morning collecting bargains from the more than 175 stores there. Then cruise eight miles over to Frankenmuth, for a pilgrimage to Bronner's Christmas Wonderland and lunch at one of the town's excellent restaurants.

After lunch, continue north on I-75 to Saginaw to visit the Japanese Cultural Center and Tea House and the Marshall M. Fredericks Sculpture Gallery. Finish the day with a leisurely dinner at the Chesaning Heritage House, a fine restaurant in an historic old mansion along the Shiawassee River.

SIGHTSEEING HIGHLIGHTS

★★★★ BRONNER'S CHRISTMAS WONDERLAND
25 Christmas Lane, Frankenmuth, 517/652-9931

If you have a warm spot in your heart for Christmas decorations, don't miss Bronner's, which offers a year-round display (and, of course,

---

SIGHTS

- ⓐ Alpine Mountain Golf
- ⓑ Bay County Historical Museum
- ⓒ Bronner's Christmas Wonderland
- ⓓ Crossroads Village and Huckleberry Railroad
- ⓔ Flint Children's Museum
- ⓔ Flint Institute of Arts
- ⓖ Frankenmuth Riverboat Tours
- ⓗ Herbert H. Dow Historical Museum
- ⓖ Japanese Cultural Center and Tea House
- ⓔ Longway Planetarium
- ⓗ Marshall M. Fredericks Sculpture Gallery
- ⓕ Midland Center for the Arts

SIGHTS
(continued)

- ⓐ Prime Outlets at Birch Run
- ⓘ Saginaw Bay Visitors Center
- ⓔ Sloan Museum

FOOD

- ⓕ Bamboo Garden
- ⓖ Bavarian Inn
- ⓙ Chesaning Heritage House
- ⓔ Don Pablo's
- ⓚ Players Restaurant
- ⓑ Krzysiak's House Restaurant
- ⓒ Zehnder's

LODGING

- ⓓ Ashman Court Hotel
- ⓖ Bavarian Inn Lodge

LODGING
(continued)

- ⓚ Bay Valley Hotel & Resort
- ⓑ Clements Inn
- ⓒ Delta Motel
- ⓔ Frankenmuth Motel
- ⓔ Holiday Inn Gateway Centre
- ⓖ Montague Inn
- ⓔ Red Roof Inn
- ⓒ Super 8 Motel
- ⓒ Zehnder's Bavarian Haus

CAMPING

- ⓛ Bay City State Park
- ⓒ Frankenmuth Jellystone Park Camp Resort
- ⓐ Pine Ridge RV Resort & Campground
- ⓕ Valley Plaza RV Park

Note: Items with the same letter are located in the same place.

---

sales) of more than 50,000 Christmas ornaments, lights, and other decorations. This family-owned business was established in 1945 and is Frankenmuth's most widely advertised attraction. Displays include 200 styles of nutcrackers and 260 Christmas trees decorated in religious, traditional, and toyland themes. Photographers are welcome. **Details:** *Jan–May Mon–Thu and Sat 9–5:30, Fri 9–9, Sun noon–5:30. June–Dec Mon–Sat 9–9, Sun noon–7. (1¹/₂–2 hours)*

★★★★ **CROSSROADS VILLAGE AND HUCKLEBERRY RAILROAD**
6140 Bray Road, Flint, 810/736-7100
This popular family outing spot revolves around a restored mid-1800s village with 30 historic structures along the peaceful shores of Mott Lake. The village has a variety of operating shops—a cider mill, blacksmith shop, print shop, doctor's office, lumberyard, and lawyer's office—where costumed interpreters demonstrate traditional crafts. The Huckleberry Railroad offers 35-minute rides on a steam train, and the *Genesee Belle*, a paddlewheel riverboat, gives 45-minute rides on the lake as well as cruises to Stepping Stone Falls, a manmade waterfall across the lake from the park. Other rides include a 1910 Ferris wheel, a 1912 carousel, and antique Venetian swings. **Details:** *Memorial Day–Labor Day Mon–Fri 10–5, Sat, Sun, and holidays 11–5:30; Labor Day–late Sept and Thanksgiving–Dec weekends only. Village only: $5.25 ages 13–59, $5 age 60 and older, $4 ages 4–12. Village and railroad: $9, $8, and $6 respectively. (4 hours)*

★★★★ **FLINT CHILDREN'S MUSEUM**
1602 W. Third Avenue, Flint, 810/767-5437
The museum is a hands-on learning center with exhibits on the arts, science, and technology. But the atmosphere is different from your typical science and technology museum, because the emphasis is as much on pure fun as it is on learning. Exhibits are aimed at children from preschool to about age 10, with a miniature grocery store with realistic food goods, a fully furnished playhouse, a full-size stagecoach, a mock fire engine, and a weather station where kids can make their own weather forecasts. Kids also have a chance to get an up-close look at—and compare themselves in size to—large stuffed animals, such as a moose, grizzly bear, lion, tiger, leopard, and polar bear. **Details:** *Mon–Sat 10–5, Sun noon–6. $3 adults, $2.50 ages 2–12, $2 age 60 and over. (2 hours)*

★★★★ PRIME OUTLETS AT BIRCH RUN
I-75 at the Birch Run exit, 517/624-7467

Devoted shoppers and bargain hunters will not want to miss this wonderland of more than 175 outlet stores. You can spend an hour—or even a weekend if you are on a concerted, holiday-shopping campaign. Numerous restaurants and several hotels are nearby.

Details: *Mon–Sat 10–9, Sun 11–6. (1 hour minimum)*

★★★ FLINT INSTITUTE OF ARTS
1120 E. Kearsley Street, Flint, 810/234-1695

Also in the Cultural Center, the institute displays a variety of paintings, sculpture, and Renaissance tapestries. It has built a strong reputation for contemporary painting and sculpture as well as nineteenth-century French paintings from such masters as Renoir, Toulouse-Lautrec, and Pissaro. Other well-known artists represented include Benjamin West, John Singer Sargeant, and Goya. A good collection of Chinese and Japanese sculpture and pottery is presented in the Asian Gallery. A museum shop sells books, handmade jewelry, toys, and other items.

Details: *Tue–Sat 10–5, Sun 1–5. Admission is free. (1 hour)*

HUCKLEBERRY RAILROAD IN FLINT

Travel Michigan

★★★ JAPANESE CULTURAL CENTER AND TEA HOUSE
Ezra Rust Drive at S. Washington Avenue, Saginaw, 517/759-1648

Saginaw's relationship with Japanese sister city Tokushima led to the establishment of the Friendship Garden, which includes a variety of trees, bridges, and other decorations brought from Japan, as well as a teahouse where tea and sweets are served. A traditional tea ceremony is presented at two in the afternoon on the second Saturday of each month.

Details: *Gardens open June–Sept Tue–Sat 9–8, Apr–May and Oct–Nov 9–4. Teahouse open Mar–Nov Tue–Sat noon–4. Gardens are free. Teahouse tour: $3, $2 age 12 and under. Full tea ceremony $6. (1 hour)*

★★★ LONGWAY PLANETARIUM
1310 E. Kearsley Street, Flint, 810/760-1181

This is the largest planetarium in Michigan, with a 60-foot domed screen that rivals some of the nation's best in New York and Chicago. Every few months the planetarium presents a new multimedia show that examines such topics as astronomy, space travel, science fiction, and mythology. Exhibit areas offer educational displays about space, astronomy, scientific exploration, and related issues. T-shirts, books, posters, and assorted educational items are available for purchase at the gift counter.

Details: *Display areas open Mon–Fri 9–4, Sat–Sun 1:15–4:30. Laser-light shows Wed, Fri, and Sat evenings. Star shows Sat and Sun afternoon. Display areas free. Star shows and laser-light shows: $4 and $6 adults, $3 and $5 under age 12. (1 hour)*

★★★ MARSHALL M. FREDERICKS SCULPTURE GALLERY
7400 Bay Road, Saginaw Valley State University, Saginaw, 517/790-5667

The Arbury Fine Arts Center on the Saginaw Valley State University campus is home to a remarkable collection of more than 200 original plaster models made by the famous sculptor for artwork on display around the world. The collection also includes portraits, drawings, and photographs of finished stone and bronze sculptures by Fredericks. Nearby is a sculpture garden with other pieces by Fredericks.

Details: *Tue–Sun 1–5. Admission is free. (1 hour)*

★★★ SLOAN MUSEUM
1221 E. Kearsley Street, 810/760-1169

The most interesting of the museums that inhabit Flint's Cultural Center is the Sloan Museum, which features a variety of exhibits that explore the history of the area. Displays include a 10,000-year-old mastodon skeleton as well as exhibits on Flint's automotive industry.

Details: Mon–Fri 10–5, Sat–Sun noon–5. $4 adults, $3.50 age 65 and over, $3 ages 5–12. (1 hour)

★★ ALPINE MOUNTAIN GOLF
Highway 54/83, 517/624-4848

Birch Run has been booming as a destination for families because of its huge outlet malls. But the truth is that shopping is about the last thing on many kids' agendas. Alpine Mountain is one of a growing number of local activities that can help keep peace—and sanity—in the family. While mom and or dad are shopping, this small amusement park can entertain the kids with miniature golf courses, bumper boats, paddleboats, go-carts, and a game room.

Details: Two miles east of I-75 at the Birch Run exit. Memorial Day–Labor Day daily 10–10, Easter–Memorial Day and Labor Day–Oct Sat–Sun 11–9. Activities individually priced. (1–3 hours)

★★ BAY COUNTY HISTORICAL MUSEUM
321 Washington Avenue, Bay City, 517/893-5733

This museum at the foot of Saginaw Bay traces the history of the area. Exhibits on Indian culture, the early fur trade, lumbering, and shipbuilding are included. The museum also has a research library and a gift shop.

Details: Mon–Fri 10–5, Sat–Sun noon–4. Admission is free. (1 hour)

★★ FRANKENMUTH RIVERBOAT TOURS
445 S. Main Street, Frankenmuth, 517/652-8844

For a relaxing change of pace, try a 45-minute cruise on the Cass River aboard the *Riverview Queen*. The diesel-powered, two-deck paddlewheeler lets you take in some of the lovely local countryside—the river is especially scenic during the fall-color season—while lounging on deck and listening to Dixieland music or interesting commentaries about local history and folklore.

Details: Trips depart hourly on the half-hour June–Labor Day

11:30–4:30 and 6; May, Sept, and Oct 12:30, 2:30, 4:30, and 6, depending on weather. $6 adults, $3 ages 3–12. (1 hour)

★★ HERBERT H. DOW HISTORICAL MUSEUM
3100 Cook Road, Midland, 517/832-5319
About 15 miles west of Bay City in Midland, this museum is dedicated to the life and work of the Dow Chemical Company founder. The museum is in a replica of a gristmill near the shed where Dow performed his early experiments.

> **Details:** *Wed–Sat 10–4, Sun 1–5. $2 adults, $1 ages 5–12, $5 families. (1–2 hours)*

★★ MIDLAND CENTER FOR THE ARTS
1801 W. St. Andrews Road, Midland, 517/631-5930
The center offers concerts, musicals, and plays, as well as a hands-on museum with displays on science, technology, history, and art. The center also sponsors two arts festivals during the summer.

> **Details:** *Daily 10–6. $3 adults, $1 under age 25, $8 families. (1 hour)*

★★ SAGINAW BAY VISITORS CENTER
Beaver Road and Route 247, Bay City, 517/667-0717
About three miles north of town in the Bay City State Park, this center offers a variety of exhibits describing life in the area's wetlands. Paved nature trails provide opportunities to observe more than 100 species of birds and migratory waterfowl.

> **Details**: *Tue–Sun noon–5, $4 per private vehicle. (1 hour)*

FITNESS AND RECREATION
For a peaceful afternoon, try canoeing one of the three rivers that converge at Midland—the **Chippewa**, the **Pine**, and the **Tittabawassee**—or paddle around the lake at **Bay City State Park**, which has an excellent sand beach. The park also has nature trails for those who prefer to hike.

FOOD
The best known area eating spots, and often the most fun, are the German-influenced restaurants in Frankenmuth. The **Bavarian Inn**, 713 S. Main St., 800/652-9941, offers German specialties along with steaks, seafood, and very popular chicken dinners in the $10 to $20 range. The town's other famous eat-

ing institution, **Zehnder's**, 730 S. Main St., 800/863-7999, specializes in all-you-can-eat chicken dinners and bills itself as America's largest family-style restaurant. Dinner costs $10 to $20.

For a combination of Polish and American dishes, there's **Krzysiak's House Restaurant**, 1605 S. Michigan Ave., Bay City, 517/894-5531. Dinners range from $10 to $20. Just outside of town is **Players Restaurant**, 2470 Old Bridge Rd. at the Bay Valley Hotel and Resort, 517/686-3500. The menu features American cuisine, with dinners between $10 and $20, and most tables offer a view of the resort's golf course.

Other ethnic options include **Don Pablo's**, G-3145 Miller Rd., Flint, 810/235-2262, with Mexican food, a cantina atmosphere, and dinners under $10; and **Bamboo Garden**, 2600 N. Saginaw Rd., Midland, 517/832-7967, with dishes from various Chinese regions, especially Szechuan and Shanghai. Dinners at Bamboo Garden cost $10 to $20.

If you are looking for a good meal in a particularly charming atmosphere, visit the **Chesaning Heritage House**, 605 W. Broad St., Chesaning, 517/845-7700, an historic mansion built in 1908. The main dining room serves an American menu, such as prime rib, pork dishes, and seafood; the Rathskeller lounge offers pizza and sandwiches. Dinners cost $12 to $22.

LODGING

Accommodations are plentiful along I-75 from Flint to Bay City, especially the usual chains. At the upper end of the price scale are Frankenmuth's two big lodges, **Zehnder's Bavarian Haus** and the **Bavarian Inn Lodge**. Zehnder's, 1365 S. Main St., 800/863-7999, has two heated pools, saunas, a whirlpool, an exercise room, and an 18-hole golf course. Rooms cost $49 to $205 a night. The Bavarian Inn Lodge, 1 Covered Bridge Ln., 888/775-6343, has jogging and walking trails on its spacious grounds along the Cass River, as well as tennis courts, a children's play area, and an 18-hole indoor miniature golf course. Rates are $69 to $300 a night.

At Flint, the **Holiday Inn Gateway Centre**, 5353 Gateway Centre, 810/232-5300, offers a heated indoor pool, sauna, whirlpool, and exercise room, with rates from $99 to $139 a night.

Somewhat less expensive is Bay City's **Bay Valley Hotel and Resort**, 2470 Old Bridge Rd., 517/686-3500, with a heated indoor-outdoor pool, saunas, a whirlpool, exercise room, playground, golf course, and indoor and outdoor tennis courts. Rooms cost $59 to $109. Bay City also has an historic bed-and-breakfast, the **Clements Inn**, 1712 Center Ave., 517/894-4600, housed in an 1889 Victorian-style mansion with antique furnishings. The three-story building has no elevator but offers smoke-free rooms for $70 to $175 a night.

Saginaw's **Montague Inn**, 1581 S. Washington Ave., 517/752-3939, is an historic country inn housed in a lovely restored Georgian mansion overlooking Lake Linton, with rooms ranging from $71 to $176 a night. In Midland, the **Ashman Court Hotel**, 111 W. Main St., 517/839-0500, has rooms from $75 to $150 a night and offers a heated indoor pool, whirlpool, exercise room, jogging trail, and rental bicycles and in-line skates. The **Frankenmuth Motel**, 1218 Weiss St., 517/652-6171, has rooms from $59 to $80 a night.

Inexpensive motels include such standards as the **Super 8 Motel**, 9235 E. Birch Run Rd., Birch Run, 517/624-4440, with rooms from $38 to $58 a night; and the **Red Roof Inn**, G-3219 Miller Rd., Flint, where rooms cost $37 to $57. Even less costly is the **Delta Motel**, 1000 S. Euclid Ave., Bay City, 517/684-4490, with rooms from $27 to $50 a night.

CAMPING

The urban nature of the Saginaw Valley means campgrounds are more scarce than in other regions of the state. However, both public and private facilities are available.

Bay City State Park, 517/684-3020, five miles north of Bay City on Highway 247 along Lake Huron, is open all year and has 263 sites. Activities include swimming, boating, fishing, and nature trails. The nightly rate for camping is $12.

A few miles west, at Midland, is the **Valley Plaza RV Park**, 5215 Bay City Rd., 517/496-9333, a private facility with 96 sites. The campground is open from early April until late October and features swimming, a playground, a recreation room, and health-club privileges. Rates are $22 to $28 for two, plus $1 per extra person.

Two private campgrounds are available in the Frankenmuth area just north of Flint. The **Frankenmuth Jellystone Park Camp Resort**, 1339 Weiss St., 517/652-6668, is open all year with 223 sites. The resort has a heated pool, playground, recreation room, and a miniature golf course. Facilities are limited in winter. Rates start at $27 for two, with an additional fee of $2 to $3 per extra person.

A few miles west, at Birch Run, is the **Pine Ridge RV Resort and Campground**, 11700 Gera Rd., 517/624-9029, with 90 sites. The campground, which features a playground and recreation room, is open from April 1 through mid-November. Rates are $25 a night for two, with a $3 fee per each extra person.

17
THE THUMB

For all its relative closeness to the busy metropolitan Detroit area, the Thumb is an under appreciated commodity—even by Michiganders. The main tourism and recreation routes lead north up I-75 and west along I-94 and I-96, bypassing the Thumb on their way to popular resort towns like Traverse City and Mackinaw City.

The biggest attraction in the Thumb is the Lake Huron shore, which considerable, even though Lake Michigan and Lake Superior receive a lot more attention and publicity. Inland from the lake, the Thumb is primarily a vast sea of flat, open farmland, dotted by small towns.

But that open, uncluttered atmosphere and the slower, relaxing pace give the Thumb considerable appeal for those who quickly tire of crowded tourist havens. You'll find plenty of attractive parks and beaches where you can sit for a while in the sun and watch the freighters glide by on the big lake. And a drive down Highway 53, the Thumb's axis, offers not only lovely rural scenery but also a chance to examine the only known Native American petroglyphs in Michigan.

A PERFECT DAY IN THE THUMB

A day cruising Highway 25 as it follows the Lake Huron shore is a day well spent. Start in Port Huron at the base of the Thumb, about an hour's drive from

THE THUMB

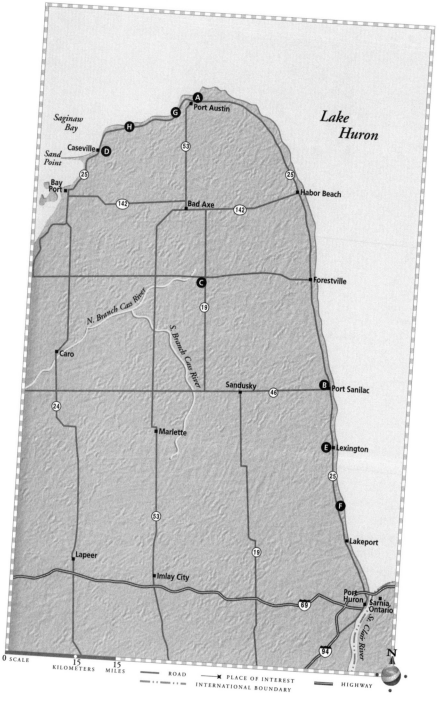

Lake
Huron

Saginaw
Bay

Port Austin Ⓐ
Ⓖ
Ⓗ
Caseville Ⓓ
Sand
Point
53
Bay
Port
25
Habor Beach
25
142
Bad Axe
142

N. Branch Cass River
Forestville
Ⓒ
19

S. Branch Cass River
Caro

Sandusky
46
Ⓑ Port Sanilac
24

Marlette
Ⓔ Lexington
25

Ⓕ

53
Lakeport

Lapeer
Imlay City
19

Port
Huron
Sarnia,
Ontario
69
St. Clair River
94
N

0 SCALE
15
KILOMETERS
15
MILES
ROAD
PLACE OF INTEREST
INTERNATIONAL BOUNDARY
HIGHWAY

Detroit. Get a taste of the state's history—with a nautical emphasis—at the Huron Lightship Museum and the Port Huron Museum. Then head north along Highway 25, which hugs the Huron shoreline all the way around the Thumb to Bay City at the foot of Saginaw Bay.

At least a half-dozen state and county parks line the lake in the 90 miles between Port Huron and Port Austin at the tip of the Thumb. Stop at one of them for a picnic lunch. Port Sanilac's Sanilac County Museum also is worth a short stop.

At Port Austin, you need to make a choice. If you are returning to Port Huron or the Detroit area, head back south on Highway 53, stopping to see the petroglyphs near Bad Axe. At Imlay City you can connect with I-69 to return to Port Huron or continue south on Highway 53, through Romeo, toward Detroit. If your destination is north, continue on Highway 25 from Port Austin, perhaps stopping to swim at Sleeper State Park or driving out to Sand Point, southwest of Caseville, for a beautiful view of Saginaw Bay. Then link up with I-75 at Bay City.

SIGHTSEEING HIGHLIGHTS
★★★★ SANILAC STATE HISTORIC PARK
Forestville and Germainia Roads, 517/373-3559

About 100 years ago a forest fire cleared a patch of land southeast of Bad Axe, revealing a 20-by-40-foot slab of sandstone decorated with carved figures of animals, humans, hunting scenes, and other designs. The carvings were made nearly 1,000 years ago by local Indians.

SIGHTS
- ⓐ Miss Port Austin Perch Party Boat
- ⓑ Sanilac County Museum
- ⓒ Sanilac State Historic Park

LODGING
- ⓐ Castaways Motor Inn
- ⓐ Garfield Inn
- ⓔ Governor's Inn
- ⓐ Lake Vista Motel and Cottages
- ⓑ Raymond House Inn

CAMPING
- ⓕ Lakeport State Park
- ⓖ Port Crescent State Park
- ⓗ Sleeper State Park

FOOD
- ⓐ The Bank 1884
- ⓓ Bay Window
- ⓑ Bellaire Hotel

Note: Items with the same letter are located in the same place.

Similar prehistoric petroglyphs adorn other, smaller rocks in the 240-acre park, which offers an interpretive program and a one-mile nature walk.

Details: Memorial Day–Labor Day Wed–Sun 11:30–4:30. Admission is free. (1 hour)

★★★ HURON LIGHTSHIP MUSEUM
Pine Grove Park, Port Huron, 810/982-0891

For 50 years, from 1920 until 1970, the *Huron* was used as a floating lighthouse to guide Great Lakes freighters from Lake Huron into the shipping channel at the upper end of the St. Clair River just north of Port Huron. The last Great Lakes lightship to retire, it is now a nautical museum, docked at the north end of Pine Grove Park. The self-guided tour allows you to visit the engine room, galley, and crew's quarters below decks of the 97-foot vessel. You can also pause on the deck to watch freighters and other ships glide nearby on the river.

Details: May–Sept Wed–Sun 1–4:30. Admission, which includes the Port Huron Museum, is $2, $1 students and adults over age 55, age 6 and under free. (30 minutes)

★★★ PORT HURON MUSEUM
1115 Sixth Street, Port Huron, 810/982-0891

This city museum focuses on local history over the last 300 years, although it also includes Indian artifacts that date back as much as 9,000 years. You'll find a range of exhibits on the Native American and nautical influences on the city's heritage. Other exhibits describe the early life and endeavors of Port Huron's most famous son, Thomas Edison. In recent years, archeologists have excavated the site of Edison's boyhood home, which once stood on a bluff overlooking the St. Clair River a few blocks north of the museum. Artifacts uncovered there, including objects from the great inventor's boyhood laboratory, are now on display in the museum. On the museum's second floor is a restored pilothouse from a Great Lakes freighter, as well as displays of objects recovered from ships wrecked on Lake Huron.

Details: Wed–Sun 1–4:30. Admission, which includes the Huron Lightship Museum, is $2 adults, $1 students and over age 55, age 6 and under free. (30 minutes)

★★★ SANILAC COUNTY MUSEUM
228 S. Ridge Road (Highway 25), 810/622-9946

PORT HURON

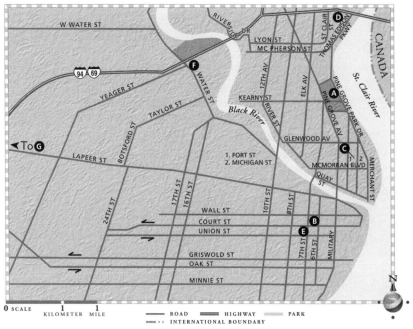

SIGHTS
- **A** Huron Lightship Museum
- **B** Port Huron Museum

FOOD
- **C** Fogcutter
- **D** Thomas Edison Inn
- **E** Victorian Inn

LODGING
- **F** Knights Inn
- **D** Thomas Edison Inn

CAMPING
- **G** Port Huron KOA Kampground

Note: Items with the same letter are located in the same place.

In a restored Victorian house built in 1872 you'll find a variety of antiques, including the home's original furnishings, glassware, medical instruments, and other artifacts. Other structures on the grounds hold dairy, fishing, lumber, and blacksmithing exhibits as well as antique carriages.

Details: *Mid-June–Labor Day Tue–Fri 11–4:30, Sat–Sun noon–4:30. $6 adults, $5 age 55 and older, $2 age 12 and under. (1 hour)*

★★ **MISS PORT AUSTIN PERCH PARTY BOAT**
Port Austin State Dock, East Pier, 517/738-5271
Whether you are an avid angler or just want to spend a few hours on the water, you'll enjoy a 4.5-hour excursion on the 20-passenger *Miss Port Austin*. You'll need to bring your own bucket and stringer for keeping your catch, but bait is provided, and fishing poles can be rented for $2. Anyone over 17 must have a valid state fishing license, but one-day licenses can be purchased at nearby bait-and-tackle shops.

Details: *Trips mid-May–Sept Wed and Sun 7:30 a.m., Sat 7:30 and 2:30. $28, $22 age 55 and over and families on Wed. (5 hours)*

FITNESS AND RECREATION

Recreation in the Thumb revolves around fishing, boating, and swimming at the various parks along the **Lake Huron** shore. Snowmobiling and cross-country skiing also are popular in winter.

FOOD

Although the Thumb is one of the less populous areas in southern Michigan and boasts relatively few restaurants, it has several excellent ones, mainly clustered around Port Austin at the northern tip and Port Huron to the south.

Port Austin is home to the **Garfield Inn**, 8544 Lake St., 517/738-5254, a graceful old Victorian inn that has a reputation for superb American and continental cuisine. Dinner usually costs $15 to $25. Nearby is **The Bank 1884**, 8646 Lake St., 517/738-5353, a century-old bank renovated into a fine restaurant with a continental menu and a very relaxing atmosphere. Dinner normally runs about $15 to $25, but the restaurant closes for the winter.

In Port Huron, the **Victorian Inn**, 1229 Seventh St., 810/984-1437, serves fine American fare, such as prime rib and rack of lamb, in a refined ambiance of lace and antiques. Dinners are in the $15 to $25 range, and lunch costs around $10. At the **Thomas Edison Inn**, 500 Thomas Edison Pkwy., 810/984-8000, you will find excellent American food, a romantic setting, and a fantastic view of the Blue Water Bridge and the St. Clair River. Dinners cost $15 to $25.

Port Huron also offers less pricey restaurants, such as the **Fogcutter**, 511 Fort St., 810/987-3300, with a rooftop view of the river and dinners in the $10 to $20 range; lunch is usually under $10.

About halfway between Port Huron and Port Austin is Port Sanilac, where you will find the **Bellaire Hotel**, 120 S. Ridge Rd., 810/622-9981, an old Victorian home that is most noted for its fish dinners. Meals are in the $10 to $20 range.

In Caseville, southwest of Port Austin along Saginaw Bay, is another inexpensive restaurant, the **Bay Window**, 6750 Main St., 517/856-2676, which offers family dining with meals from under $10 to about $15.

LODGING

The Thumb draws most of its visitors in the summer, and being the sparsely populated area that it is, it should come as no surprise that accommodations are less plentiful in winter, when some motels close for several months. But among the inns with the longest seasons are several intriguing bed-and-breakfast lodges.

The most interesting is Port Austin's **Garfield Inn**, 8544 Lake St., 517/738-5254, a three-story red mansion built in the French style in the 1830s for one of the area's lumber tycoons. The inn got its name from President James A. Garfield, who, as a congressman, delivered a speech supporting Ulysses S. Grant for president from the building's balcony. The inn is on the State and National Registers of Historic Places. It is closed in January and February and has only six guest rooms, which rent for $80 to $110 a night.

Farther south, at Port Sanilac, is another bed-and-breakfast, the **Raymond House Inn**, 111 S. Ridge Rd., 810/622-8800, a red-brick Victorian house just south of town on Highway 25. Rooms go for $75 to $95 a night, but the inn is closed in January and February. About 10 miles farther south is Lexington, where you will find the **Governor's Inn**, 7277 Simons St., 810/359-5770, a bed-and-breakfast that, 80 years ago was the summer retreat of Governor Albert E. Sleeper. The house was built in 1859 and was a summer retreat for Sleeper and his wife, Mary, after Sleeper became governor in 1917. The house, which has three rooms (each with a private bath) and charges $55, $65, or $75 a night, is on the National Register of Historic Places.

The best selection of year-round hotels is at Port Huron. At the expensive end is the **Thomas Edison Inn**, 500 Thomas Edison Pkwy., 810/984-8000, where rooms range from $89 to $205 a night. The inn, which has a sauna, heated indoor pool, and whirlpool, overlooks the St. Clair River. The **Knights**

Inn, 2160 Water St., 810/982-1022, has room rates ranging from $40 to $119 a night.

Port Austin has a couple of moderately priced motels. The **Castaways Motor Inn**, 1404 Port Austin Rd., 517/738-5101, charges $72 to $87 a night (depending on the season) and is open all year. **Lake Vista Motel and Cottages**, 168 W. Spring St., 517/738-8612, has room rates from $70 to $150 a night but is closed from December through March. Cottages are rented mid-June through mid-September at rates of $500 to $540 per week.

CAMPING

The Thumb has a rich supply of campgrounds along the Lake Huron shore, including three state parks and several other public facilities.

About nine miles northeast of Caseville on SR 25, which follows the Lake Huron shore from Bay City to Port Huron, is **Albert E. Sleeper State Park**, 517/856-4411. The park is open all year and has 280 campsites in a wooded area with dunes and a sandy beach. The park also offers nature trails and is a good spot for swimming, fishing, and snowmobiling. Sites are $15 a night.

Not far away, about three miles southwest of Port Austin on SR 25, is **Port Crescent State Park**, 517/738-8663, which is open all year and has 181 sites. The park offers swimming, fishing, a playground, nature trails, cross-country and downhill skiing, and snowmobiling. Rates are $15 a night.

At the southern end of SR 25 is **Lakeport State Park**, 313/327-6224, 11 miles north of Port Huron. The park is open all year, has 300 sites, and offers nature trails, swimming, fishing, and boating. Rates are $14 a night.

The **Port Huron KOA Kampground**, 5111 Lapeer Rd., 810/987-4070, is a private facility with 245 sites and extensive recreational facilities. The campground has a pool, playground, recreation room, basketball court, baseball and soccer fields, go-carts, miniature golf, bumper boats, hiking trails, horseback riding, and rental bicycles. It is open from April through October. May through September rates are $19 a night for two, with a $2 charge per extra person. In April and October, rates are $17 a night for two, plus a $2 charge per extra person.

APPENDIX

Consider this appendix your travel tool box. Use it along with the material in the Planning Your Trip chapter to craft the trip you want. Here are the tools you'll find inside:

1. **Mileage Chart.** This chart shows the driving distances (in miles) between various destinations throughout the state/region. Use it in conjuction with the Planning Map.

2. **Planning Map.** Make copies of this map and plot out various trip possibilities. Once you've decided on your route, you can write it on the original map and refer to it as you're traveling.

3. **Special Interest Tours.** If you'd like to plan a trip around a certain theme—such as nature, sports, or art—one of these tours may work for you.

4. **Calendar of Events.** Here you'll find a month-by-month listing of major area events.

5. **Resource Guide.** This guide lists various regional chambers of commerce and visitors bureaus, state offices, and other useful sources of information.

MICHIGAN MILEAGE CHART

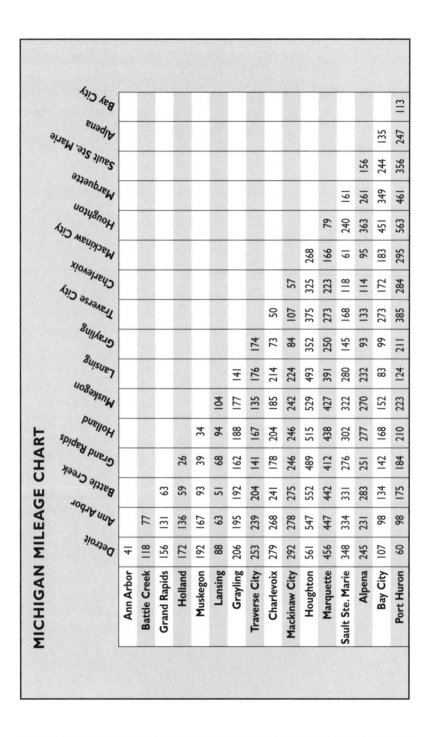

	Detroit	Ann Arbor	Battle Creek	Grand Rapids	Holland	Muskegon	Lansing	Grayling	Traverse City	Charlevoix	Mackinaw City	Houghton	Marquette	Sault Ste. Marie	Alpena	Bay City
Ann Arbor	41															
Battle Creek	118	77														
Grand Rapids	156	131	63													
Holland	172	136	59	26												
Muskegon	192	167	93	39	34											
Lansing	88	63	51	68	94	104										
Grayling	206	195	192	162	188	177	141									
Traverse City	253	239	204	141	167	135	176	174								
Charlevoix	279	268	241	178	204	185	214	73	50							
Mackinaw City	292	278	275	246	246	242	224	84	107	57						
Houghton	561	547	552	489	515	529	493	352	375	325	268					
Marquette	456	447	442	412	438	427	391	250	273	223	166	79				
Sault Ste. Marie	348	334	331	276	302	322	280	145	168	118	61	240	161			
Alpena	245	231	283	251	277	270	232	93	133	114	95	363	261	156		
Bay City	107	98	134	142	168	152	83	99	273	172	183	451	349	244	135	
Port Huron	60	98	175	184	210	223	124	211	385	284	295	563	461	356	247	113

USING THE PLANNING MAP

A major aspect of itinerary planning is determining your mode of transportation and the route you will follow as you travel from destination to destination. The Planning Map on the following pages will allow you to do just that.

First, read through the destination chapters carefully and note the sights that intrigue you. Then, photocopy the Planning Map so you can try out several different routes that will take you to these destinations. (The mileage chart on page 196 will allow you to calculate your travel distances.) Decide where you will be starting your tour of Michigan. Will you fly into Detroit, Grand Rapids, or Flint, or will you start from one of the state's smaller cities? Will you be driving from place to place or flying into major transportation hubs and renting a car for day trips? The answers to these questions will form the basis for your route design.

Once you have a firm idea of where your travels will take you, copy your route onto one of the additional Planning Maps in the Appendix. You won't have to worry about where your map is, and the information you need on each destination will always be close at hand.

PLANNING MAP: Michigan

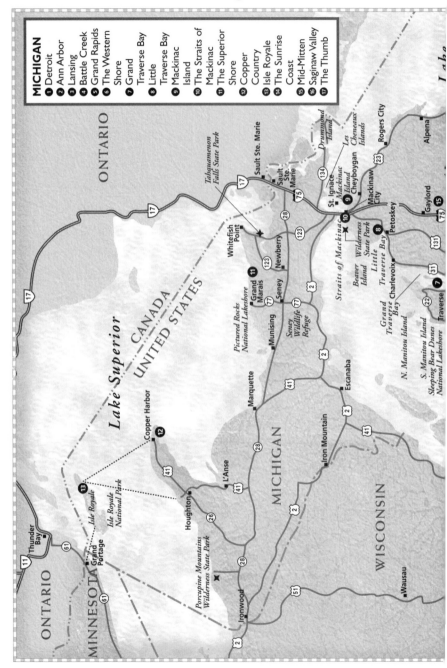

MICHIGAN
1. Detroit
2. Ann Arbor
3. Lansing
4. Battle Creek
5. Grand Rapids
6. The Western Shore
7. Grand Traverse Bay
8. Little Traverse Bay
9. Mackinac Island
10. The Straits of Mackinac
11. The Superior Shore
12. Copper Country
13. Isle Royale
14. The Sunrise Coast
15. Mid-Mitten
16. Saginaw Valley
17. The Thumb

You have permission to photocopy this map.

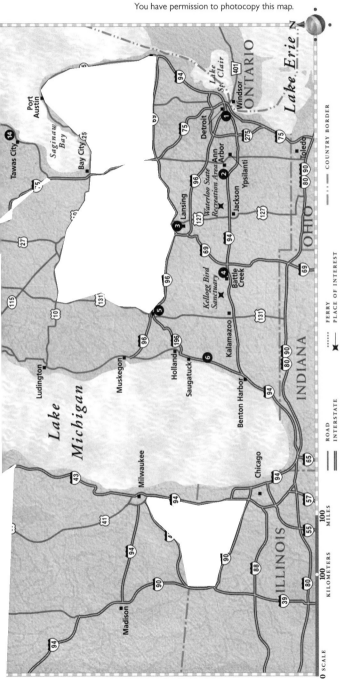

Lake Erie

Lake St Clair

Windsor

ONTARIO

401

Port Austin

Saginaw Bay

Bay City 25

Tawas City 14

75

Detroit

75

Ann Arbor

1

275

75

Waterloo State Recreation Area

2

Ypsilanti

Jackson

96

Lansing

96

80 90

Toledo

3

127

69

127

94

OHIO

69

27

Kellogg Bird Sanctuary

Battle Creek

4

96

115

Ludington

10

131

131

Kalamazoo

US 131

5

Muskegon

96

196

Holland

Saugatuck

6

Benton Harbor

80 90

INDIANA

Lake Michigan

94

43

41

Milwaukee

94

65

94

55

57

Chicago

94

Madison

90

90

88

80

ILLINOIS

39

94

SCALE

0

100 MILES

100 KILOMETERS

N

ROAD
INTERSTATE

FERRY
PLACE OF INTEREST

COUNTRY BORDER

SPECIAL INTEREST TOURS

With *Michigan Travel•Smart* you can plan a trip of any length—a one-day excursion, a getaway weekend, or a three-week vacation—around any special interest. To get you started, the following pages contain six Special Interest Tours geared toward a variety of interests. For more information, refer to the chapters listed—chapter names are bolded, and chapter numbers appear inside black bullets. You can follow a suggested tour in its entirety or shorten, lengthen, or combine parts of each, depending on your starting and ending points.

Discuss alternative routes and schedules with your travel companions—it's a great way to have fun, even before you leave home. And remember: Don't hesitate to change your itinerary once you're on the road. Careful study and planning ahead of time will help you make informed decisions as you go, but spontaneity is the extra ingredient that will make your trip memorable.

BEST OF MICHIGAN TOUR

- **Detroit** (Detroit Institute of Arts, Charles H. Wright Museum of African American History, Greenfield Village and the Henry Ford Museum, Belle Isle Park)
- **Lansing** (State Capitol, Michigan Library and Historical Center, Michigan State University campus and museums)
- **The Western Shore** (Saugatuck art colony, Holland flower displays and museums, Muskegon Museum of Art, Michigan's Adventure Amusement Park)
- **Grand Traverse Bay** (Sleeping Bear Dunes National Lakeshore, scenic drive along Old Mission Peninsula, wineries)
- **Mackinac Island** (carriage tours, historic Fort Mackinac, the Grand Hotel)
- **The Superior Shore** (Michigan Iron Industry Museum, Pictured Rocks National Lakeshore, Seney National Wildlife Refuge, Tahquamenon Falls State Park, Shipwreck Historical Museum, Soo Locks Boat Tours)
- **Copper Country** (Porcupine Mountains Wilderness State Park, Delaware Copper Mine tour, Fort Wilkins State Park)

Time needed: Two weeks

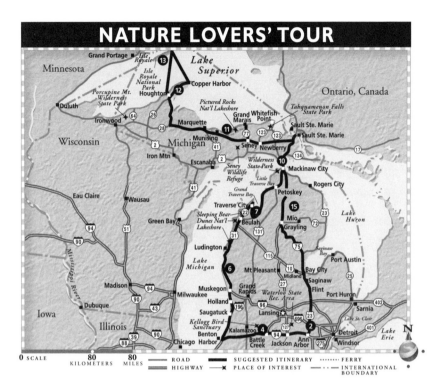

NATURE LOVERS' TOUR

This tour will lead you to Michigan's greatest natural splendors, with plenty of opportunities to view flora and fauna.

- ❷ **Ann Arbor** (hiking, bird-watching at Waterloo Recreation Area)
- ❹ **Battle Creek** (hiking, bird-watching at Kellogg Bird Sanctuary)
- ❻ **The Western Shore**
- ❼ **Grand Traverse Bay** (Sleeping Bear Dunes National Lakeshore)
- ❿ **The Straits of Mackinac** (hiking at Wilderness State Park, wildlife viewing at Seney National Wildlife Refuge)
- ⓫ **The Superior Shore** (Pictured Rocks NationaLakeshore, Tahquamenon Falls State Park)
- ⓬ **Copper Country** (Porcupine Mountains Wilderness State Park)
- ⓭ **Isle Royale**
- ⓯ **Mid-Mitten**

Time needed: Two weeks

ARTS AND CULTURE TOUR

Although many of Michigan's cultural institutions are concentrated in the south-eastern lower peninsula, you'll be rewarded if you look farther afield.

❶ **Detroit** (Detroit Institute of Arts, Museum of African American History, Henry Ford Museum, Greenfield Village, Detroit Symphony Orchestra Hall, Fisher Theater)
❷ **Ann Arbor** (U-M museums, Ann Arbor Street Art Fairs)
❸ **Lansing** (Michigan State University museums, Michigan Library and Historical Center)
❺ **Grand Rapids** (Gerald R. Ford Museum, Grand Rapids Art Museum)
❻ **The Western Shore** (Saugatuck art colony, Muskegon Museum of Art)
❼ **Grand Traverse Bay** (Gwen Frostic Studio near Benzonia, Interlochen Arts Academy, galleries in Traverse City)
⓰ **Saginaw Valley** (Marshall Fredericks Sculpture Gallery at Saginaw Valley State University)

Time needed: 8 to 10 days

FAMILY FUN TOUR

Michigan is a great place for family vacations. State parks, resort areas, theme parks, museums, and historical attractions dot both peninsulas.

❶ **Detroit** (Detroit Zoo, Detroit Science Center, Henry Ford Museum, Greenfield Village, Belle Isle)
❻ **The Western Shore** (sand dunes, Muskegon theme park)
❼ **Grand Traverse Bay** (Sleeping Bear Dunes National Lakeshore)
❽ **Little Traverse Bay**
❾ **Mackinac Island** (carriage tours, Fort Mackinac)
❿ **The Straits of Mackinac** (Beaver Island, Young State Park, Fort Michilimackinac in Mackinaw City)
⓯ **Mid-Mitten** (Hartwick Pines State Park)

Time needed: 9 to 12 days

ISLAND-HOPPING TOUR

With so much water all around the state, it's no wonder that islands are also plentiful in Michigan.

- ❶ **Detroit** (museums, zoo, and picnicking on Belle Isle)
- ❽ **Little Traverse Bay** (Charlevoix and Beaver Island)
- ❿ **The Straits of Mackinac** (Mackinac Island, Les Cheneaux Islands, Drummond Island)
- ⑬ **Isle Royale** (national park wilderness)

Time needed: Two weeks

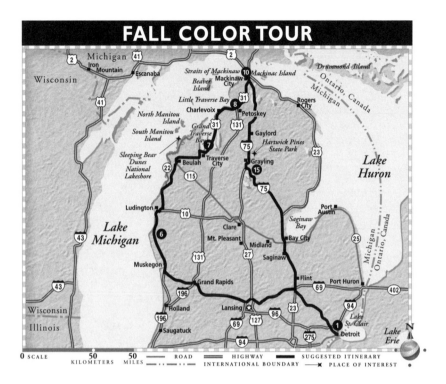

FALL COLOR TOUR

The fall color tour is a Michigan tradition. Note that colors peak early in the northern parts of the state.

- **❶ Detroit**
- **❻ The Western Shore**
- **❼ Grand Traverse Bay**
- **❽ Little Traverse Bay**
- **❿ The Straits of Mackinac**
- **⓯ Mid-Mitten**

Time needed: 2 to 7 days

CALENDAR OF EVENTS

January
North American International Auto Show, Detroit
Ann Arbor Folk Festival, Ann Arbor
Manistee County Winterfest, Manistee
Tip-Up Town (ice-fishing festival), Houghton Lake

February
Michigan Technological University Winter Carnival, Houghton
Snow's Maple Syrup Festival, Mason
Winter Carnival, Ann Arbor

March
U.P. Snowboarding Championships, Marquette
Sport, Fishing, and Travel Show, Grand Rapids
Nordic Invitational Ski Race, Newberry

April
Vermontville Maple Syrup Festival, Vermontville
Michigan Orchid Show, Bridgeman
National Trout Festival, Kalkaska
Perch Festival, Caseville

May
Tulip Festival, Holland
West Michigan Hot Air Balloon Rally, Wayland
National Morel Mushroom Festival, Boyne City
Old Mission Peninsula Blossom Days, Traverse City
World's Largest Pasty Bake, St. Ignace

June
Cereal Festival/World's Largest Breakfast Table, Battle Creek
Gold Cup Powerboat Races, Detroit
Annual Polka Festival, Newberry
International Freedom Festival (includes North America's largest fireworks display), Detroit and Windsor, Ontario

July
National Cherry Festival, Traverse City
Ann Arbor Art Fair, Ann Arbor
Port Huron-Mackinac Boat Race, Port Huron and Mackinac Island

August
Concours D' Elegance (classic autos), Rochester
Leelanau Peninsula Wine and Food Festival, Northport
Wild Blueberry Festival, Paradise
Michigan State Fair, Detroit
Woodward Avenue Dream Cruise (classic autos), Detroit to Pontiac

September
Capital City Riverfest, Lansing
Montreux-Detroit Jazz Festival, Detroit
Labor Day Blast Car Show, Boyne City

October
Autumn Festival, Ludington
Octoberfest, Whitehall
Pumpkinfest, Montague

November
Christmas Tree Galleria, Caspian
America's Thanksgiving Parade, Detroit
Festival of Trees, Detroit

December
Parade Company Indoor Carnival, Detroit
Dutch Winterfest, Holland
Holiday Parade and Snow Carnival, Pontiac
Annual Christmas Arts and Crafts Show, Grand Haven
Christmas Glow, Chesaning

RESOURCES

Michigan Department of Natural Resources, Parks and Recreation Division, 517/373-1270
Travel Bureau, Michigan Department of Commerce, 800/543-2YES
U.S. Forest Service, Eastern Region, 414/297-3693

Ann Arbor Convention and Visitors Bureau, 313/995-7281
Greater Battle Creek/Calhoun County Visitors and Convention Bureau, 616/962-2240
Bay Area Convention and Visitors Bureau, 517/893-1222
Charlevoix Area Chamber of Commerce, 616/547-2101
Cheboygan Area Chamber of Commerce, 616/627-7183
Flint Area Convention and Visitors Bureau, 810/232-8900
Frankenmuth Convention and Visitors Bureau, 517/652-6106
Gaylord Area Convention and Tourism Bureau, 517/732-6333
Grand Rapids/Kent County Visitors and Convention Bureau, 616/459-8287
Grand Traverse Convention and Visitors Bureau, 800/872-8377
Grayling Area Visitors Council, 517/348-2921
Holland Area Visitors and Convention Bureau, 800/506-1299
Houghton Lake Chamber of Commerce, 517/366-5644
Ishpeming-Negaunee Area Chamber of Commerce, 906/486-4841
Isle Royale National Park, 906/482-0984
Kalamazoo County Convention and Visitors Bureau, 616/381-4003
Keweenaw Tourism Council, 906/482-2388
Greater Lansing Convention and Visitors Bureau, 517/487-6800
Mackinac Island Chamber of Commerce, 906/847-6418
Greater Mackinaw City Chamber of Commerce, 616/436-5574
Marquette County Convention and Visitors Bureau, 906/228-7749
Petoskey/Harbor Springs/Boyne Country Visitors Bureau, 616/348-2755
St. Ignace Area Chamber of Commerce, 906/643-8717
Sault Area Chamber of Commerce and Convention and Visitors Bureau, 906/632-3301
Convention and Visitors Bureau of Thunder Bay Region, 517/354-4181

INDEX

MAP INDEX

You'll Feel like a Local When You Travel with Guides from John Muir Publications

CiTY·SMaRT™ GUIDEBOOKS

Pick one for your favorite city: *Albuquerque, Anchorage, Austin, Calgary, Charlotte, Chicago, Cincinnati, Cleveland, Denver, Indianapolis, Kansas City, Memphis, Milwaukee, Minneapolis/St. Paul, Nashville, Pittsburgh, Portland, Richmond, Salt Lake City, San Antonio, St. Louis, Tampa/St. Petersburg, Tucson*

Guides for kids 6 to 10 years old about what to do, where to go, and how to have fun in: *Atlanta, Austin, Boston, Chicago, Cleveland, Denver, Indianapolis, Kansas City, Miami, Milwaukee, Minneapolis/St. Paul, Nashville, Portland, San Francisco, Seattle, Washington D.C.*

TRAVEL✦SMART®

Trip planners with select recommendations to: *Alaska, American Southwest, Carolinas, Colorado, Deep South, Eastern Canada, Florida Gulf Coast, Hawaii, Illinois/Indiana, Kentucky/Tennessee, Maryland/Delaware, Michigan, Minnesota/Wisconsin, Montana/Wyoming/Idaho, New England, New Mexico, New York State, Northern California, Ohio, Pacific Northwest, Pennsylvania/New Jersey, South Florida and the Keys, Southern California, Texas, Utah, Virginias, Western Canada*

Rick Steves' GUIDES

See *Europe Through the Back Door* and take along guides to: *France, Belgium & the Netherlands; Germany, Austria & Switzerland; Great Britain & Ireland; Italy; Russia & the Baltics; Scandinavia; Spain & Portugal; London; Paris;* or *the Best of Europe*

ADVENTURES IN NATURE

Plan your next adventure in: *Alaska, Belize, Caribbean, Costa Rica, Guatemala, Honduras, Mexico*

JMP travel guides are available at your favorite bookstores. For a FREE catalog or to place a mail order, call: 800-888-7504.

John Muir Publications • P.O. Box 613 • Santa Fe, NM 87504

Cater to Your Interests on Your Next Vacation

The 100 Best Small Art Towns in America
3rd edition
Discover Creative Communities, Fresh Air, and Affordable Living
U.S. $16.95, Canada $24.95

The Big Book of Adventure Travel
2nd edition
Profiles more than 400 great escapes to all corners of the world
U.S. $17.95, Canada $25.50

Cross-Country Ski Vacations
A Guide to the Best Resorts, Lodges, and Groomed Trails in North America
U.S. $15.95, Canada $22.50

Gene Kilgore's Ranch Vacations, 5th edition
The Complete Guide to Guest Resorts, Fly-Fishing, and Cross-Country Skiing Ranches
U.S. $22.95, Canada $35.50

Indian America, 4th edition
A traveler's companion to more than 300 Indian tribes in the United States
U.S. $18.95, Canada $26.75

Saddle Up!
A Guide to Planning the Perfect Horseback Vacation
U.S. $14.95, Canada $20.95

Watch It Made in the U.S.A., 2nd edition
A Visitor's Guide to the Companies That Make Your Favorite Products
U.S. $17.95, Canada $25.50

The World Awaits
A Comprehensive Guide to Extended Backpack Travel
U.S. $16.95, Canada $23.95

**JMP travel guides are available
at your favorite bookstores.
For a FREE catalog or to place a
mail order, call: 800-888-7504.**

John Muir Publications ♦ P.O. Box 613 ♦ Santa Fe, NM 87504

STEPHEN JONES

ABOUT THE AUTHOR

Stephen Jones is a teacher, poet, and journalist. He has spent his entire life in the Great Lakes region and all but the first year and a half in Michigan. He lives in Detroit with his wife, Colette Gilewicz, and their son, Alexander.

Jones holds a bachelor's degree in English and a master's degree in American Studies from Michigan State University. He has more than 22 years experience as an editor and writer. He has worked for the *Ypsilanti Press*, the *Detroit Free Press*, the *Detroit Sunday Journal*, and the Associated Press wire service.

He enjoys camping and hiking, loves the performing arts, and prowls art museums and galleries at every opportunity.